Worldwide Destinations Casebook: The Geography of ̶T̶o̶urism

Worldwide Destinations Casebook: The Geography of Travel and Tourism

Second edition

Brian Boniface
and
Chris Cooper

ELSEVIER

Amsterdam • Boston • Heidelberg • London • New York • Oxford
Paris • San Diego • San Francisco • Sydney • Tokyo
Butterworth-Heinemann is an imprint of Elsevier

Butterworth-Heinemann is an Imprint of Elsevier
Linacre House, Jordan Hill, Oxford OX2 8DP, UK
84 Theobald's Road, London WC1X 8RR, UK
Radarweg 29, PO Box 211, 1000 AE Amsterdam, The Netherlands
30 Corporate Drive, Suite 400, Burlington, MA 01803, USA
525 B Street, Suite 1900, San Diego, CA 92101-4495, USA
360 Park Avenue South, New York, NY 10010-1710, USA

Second edition 2009

Notice

No responsibility is assumed by the publisher for any injury and/or damage to persons
or property as a matter of products liability, negligence or otherwise, or from any use
or operation of any methods, products, instructions or ideas contained in the material
herein. Because of rapid advances in the medical sciences, in particular, independent
verification of diagnoses and drug dosages should be made

British Library Cataloguing in Publication Data
A catalogue record for this book is available from the British Library

Library of Congress Cataloging-in-Publication Data
A catalog record for this book is available from the Library of Congress

For information on all Butterworth-Heinemann publications
visit our web site at elsevierdirect.com

ISBN: 978-1-85617-538-8

Printed and bound in Slovenia
09 10   10 9 8 7 6 5 4 3 2 1

Working together to grow
libraries in developing countries

www.elsevier.com | www.bookaid.org | www.sabre.org

ELSEVIER   BOOK AID
International   Sabre Foundation

Casebook Contents

Part 3 Cases Illustrating Regional Travel and Tourism Geography

List of Figures

List of Tables

Preface

This book of case studies is designed to be used in conjunction with its companion text –*World Wide Destinations: The Geography of Travel and Tourism*. However, the book can be used as a stand-alone resource for the teaching and learning of tourism destinations across the world.

This is the second edition of the casebook and has been considerably expanded as a learning resource for students and teachers. We have attempted to achieve a balance of case studies not only across each world region, but also across the key themes of travel and tourism geography including markets, resources and industry sectors. We have also updated the book to take account of emerging issues such as climate change.

Nonetheless, we have retained many of the ingredients of the previous successful edition. In particular we have retained our introduction outlining how to get the most from the case study approach and have provided a comprehensive set of sources at the end of the book. Each case has been written to a flexible template which has allowed us to draw out the key features of the destination or the issue at hand. Every 1 of the 38 cases has clear objectives, themes and reflections, as well as a comprehensive set of relevant teaching and learning resources drawn from the literature and the Internet. We make no apology for this comprehensive approach, as we feel it is needed more than ever before in a subject area dominated by increasing specialisation, and our book therefore complements the more detailed treatment of tourism found in the host of textbooks, reports and academic papers that deal with specific themes or destinations.

Supplemented with a good atlas, the book provides a framework for understanding most aspects of travel and tourism. Geography can make a unique contribution to the study, not only of tourism but also of those man-made and natural events around the world that make the news headlines. One example of this is Tilly, the British girl who was able to warn other holidaymakers on a beach in Thailand of the impending disaster on Boxing Day, 2003, because she had learned about tsunamis at school as part of her geography course. The study of geography provides insights as well as information on people and places.

As before, family, friends and colleagues have supported us in writing this edition. Maria Boniface helped with the research, while Amy and Robyn Cooper compiled the list of destination websites and assisted Chris with research for the cases. We acknowledge the technical help given by Elke, Sarah and other members of staff at Poole Central Library. Our students, including those on distance learning courses from many countries around the world, have provided invaluable feedback and information on current trends in tourism.

Brian Boniface and Chris Cooper,
Poole and Nottingham,
September 2008.

PART 1

Introduction

How to Use this Book

INTRODUCTION

This book provides you with a variety of case studies based upon the geography of travel and tourism. The book is designed and structured to be used as a companion volume with the core text – *Worldwide Destinations: the Geography of Travel and Tourism* (fifth edition). However, as the case studies cover destinations, key issues in the geography of travel and tourism and contemporary points of debate, you can also use this book on its own. In this chapter, we outline the benefits and uses of case studies and provide some hints and tips on how you can get the most out of the case study approach.

TOURISM IN CONTEXT

DEMAND

RESOURCES

CLIMATE

TRANSPORT

FUTURES

THE CASE STUDY APPROACH

Case studies are an important element in the teaching and learning of the geography of travel and tourism. In particular, they enhance and enliven the subject area by examining stimulating issues in real-life situations, illustrating the key elements of tourism destinations and effectively bringing the real world into the classroom – without the need for extensive international travel (Swarbrooke and Horner, 2004). Social sciences make extensive use of the case study approach; indeed much of what we know about the world is drawn from case studies; Darwin's 1836 voyage to the Galápagos Islands is an example, where the observations he made during one short visit gave rise to the idea of evolution.

The case study approach has sparked debate in the research literature, particularly focussing around the ability of researchers to generalise more widely from single cases. However, we find that a valuable use of cases is as a teaching tool to highlight key issues and relationships in the body of knowledge of tourism. We believe that case studies play a key role in teaching learning strategies for the geography of travel and tourism for three important reasons:

1. One of the problems of teaching the geography of travel and tourism is that in lesson/lecture presentation, the various elements of the body of knowledge have to be separated out – the economic, social and environmental impacts of tourism for example are treated individually, yet in real life they are all linked. Case studies allow us to demonstrate these important linkages and relationships and to see 'the big picture'. Case studies work especially well for destinations at the local scale by drawing together the many different elements of tourism and the relevant stakeholders as they focus on one particular place.

2. As well as encouraging integration of tourism material, case studies also allow that material to be linked to other subject areas – for example, finance or human resources. Effectively cases can act as a 'capstone' to teaching and learning programmes by drawing all the elements of a programme together for either teaching and learning, or for the purpose of assessment. Indeed, case studies are ideally suited to creative forms of assessment on tourism programmes.

3. Using case studies as a form of assessment gets around the more arid and theoretical ways of assessing students' understanding of the geography of travel and tourism – for example, cases lend themselves to 'open book' tests. Their role in assessment schemes needs careful thought however. It is important that cases fit into the progression of assessment for a programme and that care is given to the nature of assessment (Cooper *et al.*, 1996). There are two key uses for cases in assessment. The first is where they are used to *deepen understanding* of a particular issue, these are sometimes known as 'intrinsic cases'. On the other hand they can be used to *integrate material* across a range of subjects – such as the major elements of the body of knowledge of tourism at a particular destination.

However they are approached, cases bring a range of benefits to the classroom and by encouraging active learning they allow students to gain valuable experience in:

• Problem solving and decision making.
• Focusing on key issues within a clearly defined situation.

- Teamwork.
- Roles and role play.
- Working to deadlines for say, reports or presentations.
- The development or honing of critical thinking skills.
- Presentation skills.
- Recognising that there is no one 'correct' answer to a problem.
- Judging the relevance of different types of evidence and techniques.

Whilst case studies do much to bring the real world into the classroom, they do differ from reality in a number of ways. For example, the student is provided with the facts and the background to the problem and then asked to come up with a solution. In real life the problem often emerges first, and the facts and relevant background information then have to be sought out in an attempt to address the issue. Similarly, in many cases the student is provided with more information than would be available in reality. One way around this is to design a case where students have to purchase extra information to a budget. Finally, from a teaching and learning point of view the success of the case is very dependent on the communications skills of the teacher, the dynamics of the student group and the interaction between the two.

Hints and tips on how to get the most out of case studies

Case studies are complex and cannot be solved quickly or simply; so do not rush into a solution. When working on the cases in this book try to use the following guidelines (Seperich *et al.*, 1996; Swarbrooke and Horner, 2004):

- **Read the case carefully**, making brief notes as you do so. You may need to read the case more than once to ensure that you fully understand the issues. Try to identify the key issues – to help you in this task we have provided a key issues section in each case study.
- **Be prepared for the first session** – case studies are often made available to you or your group before the session when the case will be introduced and discussed. Make good use of the extra time to arrive prepared. In this first session, the teacher will brief you on the task that you are expected to complete. It is important that this is clearly stated and that you understand exactly what you are being asked to do. Make sure that you fully know the assessment guidelines – for say, a report or presentation.
- **Discuss the case with your group**, and if possible arrange a meeting before class to 'warm up' on the issues. Identify any barriers and problems that may prevent you recommending particular solutions. In many of the cases in this book political realities act in this way. This also means avoiding the easy option solutions such as 'fire the president', 'demolish the hotel' or 'do more research'.
- **Think about all the relevant and realistic alternatives**. For example, at a congested natural attraction or 'beauty spot' is it best to EITHER spread the load of tourists away from the attraction OR make the site more robust and manage it in such a way to increase its *capacity* to take more visitors?
- **Select the best alternative** by evaluating each option against the situation outlined in the case.

TOURISM IN CONTEXT

DEMAND

RESOURCES

CLIMATE

TRANSPORT

FUTURES

- **Develop and implement a planned solution**. Often when students present a solution to a problem they miss the all-important element of how to implement it. For example, you may recommend that a town designs a community tourism plan, but unless it can be put into practice within reasonable financial or other constraints the plan will simply be shelved and be a waste of effort.
- **Be prepared to present your ideas either in a report or as a presentation**. No matter how good your understanding of the case and your ideas, if they are poorly communicated you will fail to convince other people. You may also have to defend your ideas to the rest of the class, as their solutions may well be different to yours. Often, students will be assessed on the case as if they were a consultant or senior manager in an organisation or at a destination. This is good discipline as it forces you not to simply repeat the case in a presentation or report, but to show that you can think creatively and 'add value' – after all that is why consultants are paid a fee. Think about the following checklist when you are finalising your presentation or report:
  1. Do you fully understand the facts and the issues of the case?
  2. Is your presentation or report correctly structured with a logical flow?
  3. Is your solution consistent with the situation of the case?
  4. Is your analysis of the situation comprehensive, taking into account all possible circumstances?
  5. Have you been able to use material, ideas and concepts from other parts of your course to assist you with this case?
  6. Have you made the most of the information provided to you in the case?
- **Closure** In the final session, the teacher will bring the case to a close, summarising the main points and the groups' responses.

THE CASES

This book presents a range of case studies covering a wide variety of destinations, key issues in the geography of travel and tourism and contemporary points of debate, each designed to support courses in the geography of travel and tourism. We have chosen cases which are based on real-life situations and each case

- Has been carefully chosen to highlight key contemporary issues.
- Has been carefully planned and designed.
- Incorporates two of more elements of the body of knowledge of the geography of travel and tourism.
- Illustrates the general principles which emerge from the case study.
- Has clear learning outcomes.

In order to assist you in getting the most out of the book, each case study has been structured to include:

- Key learning outcomes.
- Key issues of the case.
- The main body of the case.
- Reflections to draw the case to a close.

- Case discussion points/assignments.
- Key sources to support your work on the case.

THE STRUCTURE OF THE BOOK

The book has been organised to mirror the structure of the core text – *Worldwide Destinations: The Geography of Travel and Tourism*, and we hope that this also reflects the way that the subject is taught.

Part 2 of the book presents cases that illustrate the basic elements of the geography of travel and tourism. This section has 12 cases drawn from the elements of tourism demand, tourism resources, climate, transport for tourism and tourism futures.

Part 3 of the book presents case studies drawn from Europe, the Middle East and Africa, Asia and the Pacific and the Americas. Some of these focus on particular issues while others give an in-depth view of a particular destination.

In Part 4, we have provided a compendium of resources that can be used to obtain further support material for all of the cases in the book. This is not meant to be comprehensive; as you proceed with your research you will become aware of many sources of information that may not appear to be directly related to tourism, but which are needed to get the 'big picture'. Finally, as geographers we should not overlook the valuable information provided by maps and a good atlas!

REFERENCES

Cooper, C., Shepherd, R. and Westlake, J. (1996) *Educating the Educators in Tourism: A Manual of Tourism and Hospitality Education*. World Tourism Organisation, Madrid.

Seperich, G. M., Woolverton, M. J., Beierlein, J. G. and Hahn, D. E. (eds) (1996) *Cases in Agribusiness Management*. Gorsuch Scarisbrick Publishers, Scottsdale, AZ.

Swarbrooke, J. and Horner, S. (2004) *International Cases in Tourism Management*. Elsevier Butterworth Heinemann, Oxford.

TOURISM IN CONTEXT

DEMAND

RESOURCES

CLIMATE

TRANSPORT

FUTURES

PART 2

Cases Illustrating the Elements of the Geography of Travel and Tourism

Tourism – "The activities of persons travelling to and staying in places outside their usual environment for not more than one consecutive year for leisure, business and other purposes".

Mobilities: Concepts and Definitions of Travel, Tourism and Migration

INTRODUCTION

This case introduces the complex task of defining tourism, in terms of both who a tourist is, and also how we can define the tourism sector. Whilst these tasks may seem straightforward, in fact they have proved difficult and, only in recent years, have definitions been agreed at an international level. On completion of this case you will:

1. Be able to distinguish between the terms leisure, recreation and tourism and relate them to a recreation activity spectrum.
2. Have a clear understanding of the various technical terms involved in defining and measuring tourism.
3. Be aware of the issues involved in defining a tourist.
4. Be aware of the fact that there are different types of mobilities representing travellers as well as tourists.
5. Understand the approaches to defining the tourism sector.

TOURISM IN CONTEXT

DEMAND

RESOURCES

CLIMATE

TRANSPORT

FUTURES

KEY ISSUES

The five key issues in this case study are:

1. Tourism is complex and can be thought of as not only a leisure activity but also a business activity, besides representing a form of temporary mobility.
2. Tourism, leisure, travel and recreation are all related in our lives, and it is the distance travelled that helps to explain their differences.
3. Because of the many different technical terms, such as tourist, traveller and excursionist, we must be very clear in our understanding of these terms.
4. Defining both the tourist and the tourism sector is a complex task, as so many different variables, such as length of stay, are involved.
5. Only in recent years have definitions of tourism and the tourism sector been agreed at an international level. Until then, definitions varied internationally, making standardisation of statistics difficult.

LEISURE, RECREATION AND TOURISM

What exactly is meant by the terms leisure, recreation and tourism and how are they related? **Leisure** is often seen as a measure of time and usually means the time left over after work, sleep and personal and household chores have been completed (Figure 1.1). In other words, leisure time is free time for individuals to spend as they please. This does, however, raise the issue about whether all free time is leisure. A good example of this dilemma is whether the unemployed feel that their free time is in fact 'enforced' leisure, or whether volunteers at a sporting event see their activity as 'serious leisure'. This has led to the view that leisure is as much an attitude of mind as a measure of time, and that an element of 'choice' has to be involved. Of course, these relationships have changed over time – the Industrial Revolution, for example, brought about a sharp contrast between the workplace and the leisure environment, whereas in pre-industrial societies, the pace of life is attuned less to 'clock time' and more to the rhythm of the seasons.

Recreation normally refers to the variety of activities undertaken during leisure time (Figure 1.1). Basically, recreation refreshes a person's strength and spirit and can include activities as diverse as watching television to holidaying abroad. We can make a useful distinction between physical recreation including sport, and activities that involve the arts, culture and entertainment. We can be active participants, or passive spectators and recipients.

If we accept that leisure is a measure of time and that recreation embraces the activities undertaken during that time, then **tourism** is simply one type of recreation activity. It is, however, more difficult to disentangle the meanings of the terms recreation and tourism in practice. Perhaps the most helpful way to think about the difference is to envisage a spectrum with, at one end, recreation based either at home or close to home and, at the opposite end, recreational travel where some

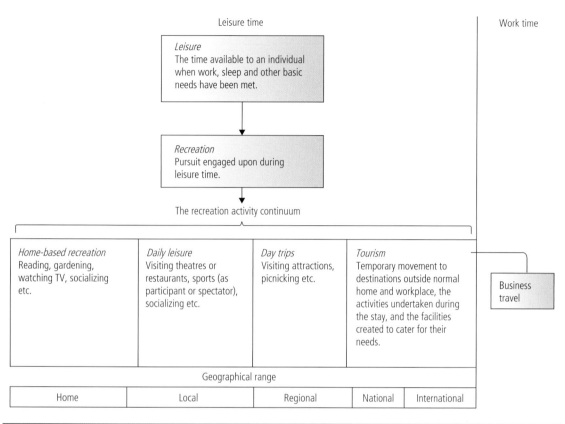

FIGURE 1.1   Leisure, recreation and tourism

TOURISM IN CONTEXT

DEMAND

RESOURCES

CLIMATE

TRANSPORT

FUTURES

distance is involved and overnight accommodation may be needed. This is based on the time required for the activity and the distance travelled, and it places tourism firmly at one extreme of the *recreational activity spectrum* (Figure 1.1). The idea of the spectrum is helpful as, for example, it allows us to consider the role of same-day visitors or excursionists. These travellers are increasingly a consideration in the geography of tourism – they visit for less than 24 hours and do not stay overnight. In other words, they utilise all tourism facilities except accommodation, and put pressure on the host community and the environment.

Clearly, tourism is a distinctive form of recreation and demands separate consideration. In particular, from the geographical point of view, tourism is just one form of mobility that is temporary and also voluntary, and in defining tourism, it is therefore important to distinguish it from other types of travel. There is, however, a need to locate tourism within the broader spectrum of mobilities which include commuters travelling daily between home and workplace, shoppers, excursionists, second home owners and migrants. This is because, since definitions of tourism were attempted, society has become more mobile, facilitated by developments in transport technology, strong economies and information technology. This dramatic increase in mobility has facilitated modern tourism but has also blurred the distinction between home, workplace and recreational environments.

TOURISM IN CONTEXT

DEMAND

RESOURCES

CLIMATE

TRANSPORT

FUTURES

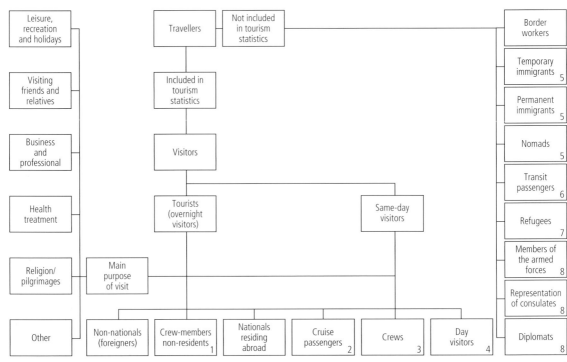

1. Foreign air or ship crews docked or in lay over and who use the accommodation establishments of the country visited

2. Persons who arrive in a country abroad cruise ships (as defined by the International Maritime Organization, 1965) and who spend the night aboard ship even when disembarking for one or more day visits.

3. Crews who are not residents of the country visited and who stay in the country for the day.

4. Visitors who arrive and leave the same day for; leisure, recreation and holidays; visiting friends and relatives; business and professional; health treatment; religion/pilgrimages and other tourism purposes, including transit day visitors en route to or from their destination countries.

5. As defined by the United Nations in the Recommendations on Statistics of International Migration, 1980.

6. Who do not leave the transit area of the airport or the port, including transfer between airports and ports.

7. As defined by the United Nations High Commissioner for Refugees, 1967.

8. When they travel from their country of origin to the duty station and vice versa (including household servants and dependants accompanying or joining them).

FIGURE 1.2 Classification of travellers
Source: World Tourism Organization

This makes the drawing up of definitions of tourism problematic, simply because certain mobile groups have to be excluded from tourism statistics. Figure 1.2 shows the various classifications of travellers who are both included in and excluded from official tourism statistics, but we need to look more closely at the following categories:

- **Travellers** The term 'traveller' has a very wide definition here and includes 'nomads' – people constantly on the move – who as hunters and herders have origins pre-dating civilisation itself. In all periods of history, some travellers have been motivated by *wanderlust* or curiosity, in contrast to the great majority whose journeys are regarded as essential, such as merchants, missionaries, diplomats, soldiers and sailors. Visitors to remote parts of the world often see themselves as 'travellers' or even 'explorers', rather than as tourists, and their journeys as 'expeditions' rather than tours. They would argue that tourism nowadays has become altogether too commercialised, comfortable and predictable, and that real travel should involve an element of hardship and improvisation, as in the past. The fact remains that from an official viewpoint, these self-styled travellers still count as tourists.

- **Migrants**   Migration is clearly different from tourism in terms of purpose and length of stay, and migrants are excluded from tourist statistics. Migration can be defined as travel with a commitment to live and work in another country, or another region (internal migration). The world's largest migration is in fact within China, involving the movement of many millions of rural villagers from the interior to the cities of the east coast. People leaving their home country or region are emigrants, whereas on arrival in their place of adoption they become immigrants. At an international level, they require special documentation to legally enter, reside and work in that country. Emigrants provide a great deal of business for some airlines and shipping companies, and they may require specialised freight forwarding and resettlement services. International migration is subject to more restrictions in the new millennium than during the nineteenth and early twentieth centuries; for example, Australia, the USA and the European Union place strict controls on immigration. Moreover, with travel so much easier than in the past, most migration is short term, with the objective of seeking employment for a few years rather than with the intention of making a permanent home in another country. The *gastarbeiter* (guest workers) of Germany and Austria are one example of such short-term migrants. Smaller numbers of expatriates from countries like Britain are working as highly paid professionals in areas such as the oil-rich Gulf states. These people generate a considerable demand for tourism in their country of temporary residence, as do UN and NATO personnel stationed for peacekeeping in some of the world's 'trouble spots'.

  The mass movement of people, mainly from the Third World to the developed countries, evident since the early 1990s, is part of the process of *globalisation*. National economies are increasingly interconnected, and since capital can now move freely from one country to another, some argue that labour should also be able to do so. One of the consequences of an ageing population in the developed world is a shortage of manpower, especially in the hotel and catering industries, and immigration clearly fulfils a need, at least in the short term. Emigrants are motivated to seek a better life than is possible in their homeland. However, in much of Africa, climate change is also a factor, forcing people to move through its impact on agriculture and food supplies.

- **Refugees**   Although economic pressures are the motivation for most migrants, refugees are forced by war or political oppression to find sanctuary in another country. Since the 1950s, the numbers of refugees have remained persistently high at around 15–20 million, although their origins and destinations change as new 'trouble spots' appear on the world scene. The protection of refugees is one of the responsibilities of the United Nations, which seeks to persuade member states to be more generous in extending the *right of asylum* to those fleeing from persecution. The 1951 Geneva Convention on Refugees was drafted

TOURISM IN CONTEXT

DEMAND

RESOURCES

CLIMATE

TRANSPORT

FUTURES

TOURISM IN CONTEXT

DEMAND

RESOURCES

CLIMATE

TRANSPORT

FUTURES

primarily to deal with the situation in Europe following the Second World War, whereas the 1976 New York Protocol could apply to a wide variety of groups and individuals claiming to be at risk from persecution for their political views, ethnicity, religious beliefs or sexual orientation. It is estimated that 90 per cent of refugees are from Third World countries, but contrary to popular belief in the West, the great majority of refugee flows are to neighbouring countries that lack the resources to deal with the problem.

In reality, the distinction between these categories of traveller is difficult, as visitors often evade visa restrictions by, for example, staying on to work illegally after a period of study. The distinction between illegal economic migrants and genuine refugees, whose circumstances prevent them from obtaining documentation, is also subject to controversy. Because of these complex issues, international debate as to the definition of tourism still continues, and there are many different interpretations.

DEFINING TOURISTS AND THE TOURISM SECTOR

Why should we be so concerned with definitions? In fact there are a number of reasons:

- Until we can define tourism or the tourism sector, we cannot measure it. This means that other, more straightforward economic sectors, such as the oil industry, will be able to claim how important they are to the government whilst tourism fails to make its case.
- Until we can define tourism and the tourism sector, we will not be able to pass legislation that applies to either the individual traveller or the businesses in the sector.
- We need to define tourism or the tourism sector for our own sense of professionalism. Until we are able to solve the conundrum of 'what is tourism' we can never truly call ourselves tourism professionals.

There are two key approaches to definitions:

Firstly, we can define tourism from the **demand side**, that is, the person who is the tourist. This approach is well developed, and the United Nations Statistical Commission now accepts the following definition of tourism:

The activities of persons travelling to and staying in places outside their usual environment for not more than one consecutive year for leisure, business and other purposes

This definition raises a number of issues:

- What is a person's *usual environment*?
- The inclusion of 'business' and 'other' *purposes of visit* demands that we conceive of tourism more widely than simply as a recreation pursuit.
- Certain types of traveller are excluded from the definition. We saw earlier that tourism itself is only one part of the spectrum of travel, which ranges from daily

travel to work or for shopping to migration, where the traveller intends to take up permanent or long-term residence in another area.

Secondly, we can define the tourism sector from a **supply-side** point of view. Here the difficulty lies in disentangling tourism businesses and jobs from the rest of the economy. After 20 years of debate, the accepted approach is the 'Tourism Satellite Account' (TSA) adopted by the United Nations in 2000. The TSA measures the demand for goods and services generated by visitors to a destination. It allows tourism to be compared with other economic sectors, by calculating its contribution to investment, consumption, employment, the gross domestic product (GDP) and taxation.

REFLECTIONS ON THE CASE

Whilst definitions and terms may seem very 'dry', they are essential for the measurement and clear understanding of tourism. This case has shown how leisure, recreation and tourism are linked in a spectrum of activity, and we can also think of different types of mobility or travel that do not count as tourism but which are important in our lives. Fortunately, international agreement has now been reached on definitions of both the tourist and the tourism sector and this will go a long way to recognise tourism as an important contributor to economies in the world.

DISCUSSION POINTS

1. Make a list of all of your trips away from home in the last month and classify them on the recreation activity spectrum. Thinking about the last month, estimate roughly how much of your time was truly spent 'at leisure'. Compare notes with your classmates and explain the differences.
2. A tourist attraction in your local area has asked you to design a visitor survey. What questions would you ask to be able to classify the visitors into local residents, day excursionists and tourists?
3. Thinking about your own town, or a town nearby, make a list of all of the elements of the tourism sector, not forgetting to include catering and local government services. Against each category estimate the percentage of activity that derives from tourism and the percentage of activity that relates to other sources.
4. Using the UNWTO website, draft a briefing note for your local tourist board on the use and benefits of tourism satellite accounts.
5. Draft a checklist of the characteristics of the following types of mobility – migration, commuting, shopping, day excursion, leisure tourism, business tourism, second home owners.

TOURISM IN CONTEXT

DEMAND

RESOURCES

CLIMATE

TRANSPORT

FUTURES

KEY SOURCES

Gilbert, D. (1990) Conceptual issues in the meaning of tourism, in C. Cooper (ed.), *Progress in Tourism, Recreation and Hospitality Management*. Chapter 1, Belhaven Press, London, pp. 4–27.

Hall, C. M. (2005) *Tourism: Rethinking the Social Science of Mobility*. Prentice-Hall, Harlow.

Hall, C. M. and Page, S. (2002) *The Geography of Tourism and Recreation*. Routledge, London.

UN World Tourism Organization (1995) *Concepts, Definitions and Classifications for Tourism Statistics*. UNWTO, Madrid.

UN World Tourism Organization (2001) *Basic Concepts of the Tourism Satellite Account (TSA)*. UNWTO, Madrid.

UN World Tourism Organization and UNSTAT (1994) *Recommendations on Tourism Statistics*. UNWTO, Madrid.

Urry, J. (2000) *Sociology Beyond Societies. Mobilities for the Twenty First Century*. Routledge, London.

Williams, S. (1998) *Tourism Geography*. Routledge, London.

TOURISM IN CONTEXT

DEMAND

RESOURCES

CLIMATE

TRANSPORT

FUTURES

Sign showing tsunami evacuation instructions at the beach on Koh Lipe, Thailand.
© istockphoto.com/George Clerk

Crisis and Risk Management in Tourism

INTRODUCTION

Since 2001 the tourism sector has been affected by a series of 'shocks' including 9/11, the Bali bombings, the bombings in Madrid and London, health crises and the Asian tsunami. This case shows how the sector has come to terms with the inevitability of such 'wild card' events and the process of crisis management that has been developed. On completing the case you will:

1. Recognise that crises can be either man-made, natural or a combination of both.
2. Understand the severity of the impact of major crises on the tourism sector.
3. Be aware of the process of crisis management and the stages of planning following a crisis.
4. Be familiar with the tourism sector's response to bird flu.
5. Evaluate the response to health crises that can disrupt international tourism.

TOURISM IN
CONTEXT

DEMAND

RESOURCES

CLIMATE

TRANSPORT

FUTURES

KEY ISSUES

There are five key issues in this case:

1. Crises are now seen as an inevitable part of doing business in tourism – the 'new normal', but this fact means that the tourism sector must plan to anticipate crises and manage them better when they occur.
2. There have been a series of shocks to the tourism sector since 2001, including 9/11. It is these shocks that have prompted the tourism sector to engage in crisis management.
3. The impact of the major crises that have occurred since 2001 have been severe, driving airlines into bankruptcy and affecting tourism flows around the world.
4. Crisis and risk management has been embraced by the tourism sector as it struggles to come to terms with these events. This planning approach is now a disciplined one with a series of stages and guidelines for anticipating and dealing with crises.
5. Not all crises are a result of terrorist acts, but crisis management provides a framework to deal with different types of crisis such as avian influenza (bird flu) or natural disasters such as the Asian tsunami.

TOURISM AND CRISIS

Tourism is potentially at risk from natural and man-made disasters, particularly in developing countries that can ill afford the loss of foreign exchange, and where the rescue services and infrastructure are inadequate to cope. The vulnerability of the tourism sector has been highlighted since 2001 through several major events. The first of these was the terrorist attack on the Twin Towers of the World Trade Center in New York on 11 September 2001, followed by the war in Afghanistan, the Bali bombings, the bombing of an Israeli-owned hotel in Mombasa, the SARS (severe acute respiratory syndrome) epidemic in 2003, the Iraq War, bombings of train systems in Madrid and London and the Asian Boxing Day tsunami in 2004. It was 9/11 that had the most impact, simply because it was so unexpected and affected international tourism so dramatically. This crisis forced a number of airlines into bankruptcy and reduced the profitability of tourism businesses worldwide. Travellers deferred their trips, initially through fear of further attacks, and later by anxiety that their jobs might be at risk in the subsequent downturn of the global economy.

The 9/11 incident triggered a number of significant effects on tourism:

- Firstly, there was an immediate response on behalf of governments and international agencies to put together rescue packages for the tourism industry.
- Secondly, there was a call for better market intelligence in all sectors of tourism.
- Thirdly, the term 'crisis and risk management' entered the vocabulary of tourism.
- Fourthly, security measures and immigration procedures were tightened.

You should be aware of the many other crises and natural disasters that have a more localised effect, such as the following:

- Man-made crises, such as fires, riots, prolonged strikes, kidnappings, air crashes and other transport disasters, business failures, oil spillages destroying beaches and ecosystems.
- Natural disasters, such as earthquakes and volcanic eruptions, floods, hurricanes and tsunamis.
- Crises that are partly man-made and partly due to natural causes, such as outbreaks of disease following the destruction of basic infrastructure, widespread power blackouts disrupting transport and other public services, and most forest fires.

CRISIS AND RISK MANAGEMENT PLANNING

Crisis and risk management recognises that we must be prepared for crises and lays down a response pattern to such events. A risk management plan allows a destination or organisation to prepare for and manage a crisis and so reduce its potential impacts. Such impacts can be severe, not simply in terms of loss of life or damage to property, but also in negative media coverage.

The Pacific Asia Travel Association (PATA) defines a crisis as 'any situation that has the potential to affect long-term confidence in an organisation or a product, or which may interfere with the ability to continue operating normally' (PATA, 2003, p. 2).

Crisis and risk management plans are now in place for many destinations. International agencies such as the UN World Tourism Organisation (UNWTO), United Nations Conference on Trade and Development (UNCTAD) and PATA have published guidelines for the sector on the development of such plans. The essence of risk management is to assess what can go wrong at a destination or in an organisation, to determine the most significant risks and implement strategies to deal with those risks. However, once a crisis occurs, then a crisis management plan is put into action. This typically demands strong leadership from within the organisation and often the formation of a crisis management team. The template for a crisis management plan normally contains the following elements – sometimes known as 'the four Rs of crisis management':

1. **Reduction** The initial identification of potential crises and risks, and also the strengths and weaknesses of the destination or organisation, in order to reduce the impact of a crisis.
2. **Readiness** The development of a plan and continual assessment of response tactics and strategies.
3. **Response** If a crisis occurs, this takes effect in the immediate aftermath of the event. It involves an operational response focused on damage limitation, and a communications response focusing on reassurance.
4. **Recovery** In the event of a crisis, a useful gauge of the effectiveness of the plan is the speed with which the organisation re-assumes normal operations and business returns to pre-crisis levels. It is interesting that business in the tourist sector has returned to normality more quickly after each successive crisis following 9/11.

It is interesting to observe the way that the response of the tourism sector to these crises has matured since 9/11. In the first two years post-9/11 the response tended to be ad hoc, as agencies got to grips with the new operating environment. This then evolved into the development of information systems to speed responsiveness. Finally, the response has become more structured and sophisticated, utilising web-based portals containing outreach tools for industry and government, resources and media packs. The response of the sector to the threat of avian flu outlined below is an example of this recent approach.

THE RESPONSE TO HEALTH CRISES

The connection between foreign travel and the spread of infectious disease has been recognised for centuries with the imposition of quarantine restrictions on travellers arriving at a country's ports. These originated in medieval Venice, where ships had to wait for 40 days (*quaranta giorni* in Italian) before passengers and crew were permitted to land, in order to protect the city from bubonic plague. The outbreak of SARS was a reminder of how rapidly disease can spread in the age of jet travel. The authorities were able to contain the epidemic, helped by the co-ordinating role of the World Health Organization (WHO), while the wearing of surgical masks by people flying to and from Asian countries also proved fairly effective in limiting the spread of infection. In theory bio-terrorists might get hold of the smallpox virus, which is much more readily transmitted through the air than other diseases. Of more everyday concern to customs officers are the illegal imports of plant and animal materials by travellers – such as 'bushmeat' from West Africa – that can contaminate a country's agricultural products.

RESPONSE TO THE POTENTIAL THREAT FROM AVIAN FLU

Avian flu became a serious global concern in the middle of the first decade of the new millennium. Effectively, there was a fear that the avian form of influenza could transmute into a virulent form that could be transmitted to humans. The response of the tourism sector to avian flu demonstrates two key differences from previous crises:

1. The disease was predicted and preparations can therefore be made in advance.
2. The tourism sector has gone through a steep learning curve in dealing with crises since 2001 and the response to avian flu has been effective and sophisticated.

The response to the potential avian flu threat has been co-ordinated internationally through the United Nations, with WHO and the Food and Agriculture Organization (FAO) working alongside the UNWTO. Under this international structure, governments have put plans in place for the possibility of a pandemic.

The UNWTO is co-ordinating a sophisticated, web-based portal incorporating an emergency planning system. This has been rolled out across the tourism sector and is known as the Tourism Emergency Response Network (TERN). The approach involves engaging the tourism sector through information, capacity building and co-ordinating activities, with the goal of supporting tourism stakeholders in developing strategies and tools to prepare for, and respond in an effective and efficient fashion to an avian flu pandemic. This will include ensuring that all stakeholders respond wisely and in a co-ordinated and complementary fashion; this means preventing the spread of unnecessary panic among consumers, but at the same time sharing information. According to the UNWTO website, specific actions include:

- Establishment of a UNWTO Risk Management Committee, with the aim of directly involving tourism administrations in the preparedness and response system.
- Designation of an Avian Flu Response Coordinator to ensure that internal and external action is totally aligned with the goals and activities of the UN.
- A UNWTO Avian Flu Support Team to help support countries affected by avian influenza.
- Publication of guidelines for tourism destinations on how to prepare for and respond to avian flu. This extends the UNWTO Crisis Management Guidelines.
- Tools to support tourism integration into national plans and help industry preparedness and response planning. The main focus will be to encourage tourism destinations to engage fully in national plans so as to better assist tourists and the tourism sector.
- An intensified web-based communication system – to synthesise the rapidly changing situation and focus on its tourism-related aspects and impacts. This will include a daily bulletin to support the dissemination of information from UN, national, industry and other relevant sources.
- An avian flu simulation exercise taking place in Asia.

REFLECTIONS ON THE CASE

Crises are now seen as an inevitable part of the business of tourism. The tourism sector therefore recognises the need for effective crisis and risk management at both destination and company levels and its response has evolved into a sophisticated approach. This is an important step forward, ensuring that the sector is better prepared for future disasters and hopefully more capable of reducing their impact.

DISCUSSION POINTS

1. Draft a report to the mayor of Phuket outlining how consumer behaviour might be affected in the long term by the Asian 2004 Boxing Day tsunami.

TOURISM IN CONTEXT

DEMAND

RESOURCES

CLIMATE

TRANSPORT

FUTURES

2. Draw up a classification of the major crises which can affect tourism and against each draft a brief paragraph explaining how crisis management might help to reduce their impact.
3. Take a recent crisis that has affected the tourism industry and, using the Internet and media sources, plot a timeline of how the major events affecting tourism unfolded following the crisis. Compare notes with others in the class – is there a common pattern to the timeline?
4. Take a tourism destination that you know well and draft a report to the manager of a resort outlining 'the four Rs' of crisis management and how that resort might use 'the four Rs' to plan for a future crisis.
5. Why do you think it took an event of such magnitude as 9/11 to prompt the tourism sector to take crisis management seriously?

KEY SOURCES

Bierman, D. (2002) *Restoring Tourism Destinations in Crisis: A Strategic Marketing Approach*. CABI, Wallingford.

Keller, P. (2003) *Crisis Management in the Tourism Industry*. Elsevier Butterworth-Heinemann, Oxford.

Miller, R. (2005) Estimating the impact of crisis events on the travel and tourism industry. *The Tourism Society Journal* (125), 16–17.

Pacific Asia Travel Association (2003) *Crisis: It Won't Happen to Us!* PATA, Bangkok.

Pizam, A. and Mansfield, Y. (1996) *Tourism, Crime and International Security Issues*. Wiley, Chichester.

Tate, P. (2002) The impact of 9/11: Caribbean, London and NYC case studies. *Travel and Tourism Analyst*, 5 (October), 1–25.

UN World Tourism Organization (1996) *Tourist Safety and Security: Practical Measures for Destinations*. UNWTO, Madrid.

UN World Tourism Organization (1998) *Handbook on Natural Disaster Reduction in Tourist Areas*. UNWTO, Madrid.

UN World Tourism Organization Emergency web site: http://www.ternalert.org/emergencies/.

Wilks, J. and Page, S. (2003) *Managing Tourist Health and Safety in the New Millennium*. Elsevier Butterworth-Heinemann, Oxford.

Withers, R. (2002) Managing the impact of natural and man-made disasters on tourism. *Tourism*, 28–30.

Paris adapts to 'new' tourism with rent-bikes, which can be hired, self-service with a credit-card.
© istockphoto.com/Marco Maccarini

CASE 3

Understanding the 'New Tourist'

INTRODUCTION

This case study analyses the driving factors behind the 'new tourist' phenomenon, dissects their characteristics and looks at the implications of this change in consumer behaviour. On completion of this case you will:

1. Recognise the significance of the changing consumer behaviour of tourists.
2. Understand the underlying causes of the changed consumer behaviour.
3. Be able to explain the key features of the 'new tourist'.
4. Be aware of the implications of the 'new tourist' for destinations.
5. Be aware of the implications of the 'new tourist' for tourism marketing.

TOURISM IN CONTEXT

DEMAND

RESOURCES

CLIMATE

TRANSPORT

FUTURES

KEY ISSUES

1. There are five issues in this case: With a maturing tourism market, consumer behaviour has changed. With increased travel experience consumers have learnt how to get the best from technology and the travel sectors; they are discerning in their choice of destination and increasingly they are demanding that the environment and communities in the destinations are given due concern.
2. There are a number of driving factors influencing the new tourist, these are interlinked and have resulted in the changed consumer behaviour outlined in the case study.
3. The new tourists have a variety of key characteristics that set them apart from the tourist of earlier decades. In particular they are flexible and they demonstrate different values, emphasising sustainability.
4. The new tourist has implications for how destinations and products are developed as they are involved in the co-creation of their product, in particular in terms of a greater emphasis on activity and sustainable tourism and away from passive, mass tourism.
5. The new tourist has to be approached differently by tourism marketing organisations, researchers and enterprises. They are familiar with information technology and understand the workings of the travel sector.

THE DRIVERS OF CONSUMER CHANGE

The tourism market has matured in the last 30 years and one of the key features of this maturity has been the changing consumer behaviour of the tourist. In recent years, a large number of tourists have become frequent travellers, both internationally and domestically. Increased travel has made them experienced, discerning and increasingly caring of the destinations that they visit. Poon (1993), for example argues that the standardised mass tourism of the 1960s and 1970s is being superseded by a new tourism revolution. This represents a sea change in the nature of tourism demand that has implications not only for the planning and management of tourism destinations, but also for the way that the tourism sector operates. A range of key influences can be identified which have encouraged the growth of this *new tourist*:

- Trip frequency (both leisure and business), and therefore travel experience, has increased.
- New destinations, particularly long-haul, are within reach of the mass market.
- The selling of travel has become technologically driven, allowing individual access to computer reservation systems and the Internet, whilst travel blogs and the posting of travel reviews on the Internet have empowered tourists.
- The media and pressure groups (such as Tourism Concern) have taken a real interest in the responsible consumption and development of tourism, raising the profile of sustainability and placing issues such as the environment, climate change and concern for host populations centre stage. The UNWTO's Global Code of Ethics for Tourism has set a new standard here and a number of tourism companies now have their own codes of practice for responsible travel.

- Deregulation in the tourism sector has allowed the individual consumer access to efficient direct reservation systems and Internet booking sites – particularly those offering, for example 'last-minute' air fares and hotel room availability. This allows the tourists to 'co-create' their product with the sector.
- Concentration in the industry has meant that one group of companies can offer a complete range of travel options.
- Emergence of the knowledge-based society creates a demand for authentic and well-interpreted experiences, as the passive beach holiday becomes less popular in certain market segments.
- Changing demographics in many key tourist-generating regions with ageing populations, smaller household sizes and higher discretionary incomes all combine to change lifestyles and the nature of tourism needs.

CHARACTERISTICS AND BEHAVIOUR OF THE NEW TOURIST

These drivers of change have created a new breed of tourist who:

- Are critical and discerning – they have travelled frequently and know what they want. They seek quality, good service and value for money as they are *empowered* by their experiences elsewhere. They also know their rights and will complain if the experience is not as expected or advertised. In this respect, their experience allows them to make comparisons with other destinations and products, and to post them on the Internet for other travellers to see. Sites such as Mytripadvisor.com have pioneered this approach. They therefore often adopt a *high-satisfaction/low-loyalty* travel pattern of purchasing behaviour.
- Have considerable consumer and technology skills, for example in manipulating their trip to take advantage of last-minute bargains. They are prepared to be flexible in travel arrangements – for example they will travel at short notice or even spontaneously.
- Are motivated by *wanderlust* – they travel out of curiosity and cultural reasons rather than for *sunlust*. This means that tourism destinations and products must build in an element of interpretation, education and seeing the 'real' place. They will seek out activity and adventure vacations and involvement in the destination – they no longer wish to relax on a beach for 14 days. They are also motivated to search for the authentic and the natural experience at the destination.
- Have values which encourage the *ethical consumption* of tourism, and they will choose destinations and companies on this basis. Their values are oriented to the environment and reflect a changing lifestyle which has concerns for the planet. Here the rising awareness of the impact of tourism on climate change has led to many tourists 'offsetting' their carbon emissions by paying for tree planting or low energy light bulbs in the developing world.

THE IMPLICATIONS OF THE NEW TOURIST

Poon sees the new tourist as the driving force of change behind the new tourism revolution as the sector metamorphoses from the rigid, packaged tourism of the

31

TOURISM IN CONTEXT

DEMAND

RESOURCES

CLIMATE

TRANSPORT

FUTURES

1960s and 1970s to a new flexible form of tourism. This revolution in tourism demand has implications for both destinations and the tourism sector itself.

- **Destinations** will need to recognise that these *critical consumers* seek quality, sound environmental and sustainable practices, ease of access to reservation systems, good web sites and authentic, well-managed experiences. Destinations too, will need to demonstrate that they are moving in the direction of becoming carbon neutral. As Poon (1994) states, 'travellers are increasingly prepared to shun over-commercialised and polluted resorts' (p. 91).
- **The tourism sector** will need to rethink its marketing strategies and provide tailor-made, customised vacations which demonstrate an understanding of the motivations and needs of the new tourist – in other words, the way that the new tourist thinks, feels and behaves. This will involve sophisticated approaches to the *segmentation* of the tourism market as well as development of customer databases and relationship marketing where customer loyalty is encouraged. In addition, the new tourist renders traditional market research techniques of classifying individuals obsolete, for example by age or occupation, or by categories such as leisure, business and visiting friends and relatives. Instead, more sophisticated (and expensive) techniques are needed to expose underlying values and motivations. These techniques will depend upon deep and meaningful market research, often taking a qualitative rather than a quantitative approach.

REFLECTIONS ON THE CASE

This case has shown how much consumer behaviour in tourism has changed over recent decades. With more frequent travel, consumers are now experienced and know what they want. Their preferences for travel are changing to 'co-creating' more active, experience-oriented products. The real lesson here is the need for both the tourism sector and tourism destinations to understand this sea change in the market place and develop appropriate destinations and products.

DISCUSSION POINTS

1. The Brown family are the classic breed of new tourist – draft an itinerary for them to tour Spain. Show how this itinerary might differ from one made for a typical family in the 1960s.
2. Using the Internet, identify up to three companies that you feel are providing products for the 'new tourist'. Establish the key elements of the product – features, price, distribution channels and target markets. Summarise your findings in a product/market fit table with one column listing the characteristics of the new tourist (the market) and the other the features of the products which meet these characteristics.

3. Select a tourism destination that you know well. Draft a report to the destination manager suggesting how it might be repositioned to appeal to the 'new tourist'.
4. Using travel brochures or the Internet, find four examples of codes of conduct set out by tourism companies for the 'consumption of tourism' or 'responsible tourism/travel codes of behaviour'. Compare these with the WTO's Global Code of Ethics for Tourism (available on the WTO web site). How does the private sector approach differ from the WTO?
5. Choose a particular type of tourism trip. Using the Internet, investigate how you can calculate your carbon emissions and offset them for the trip.

KEY SOURCES

Cooper, C. and Hall, C. M. (2007) *Contemporary Tourism*. Elsevier Butterworth Heinemann, Oxford.

Poon, A. (1993) *Tourism, Technology and Competitive Strategies*. CAB, Wallingford.

Poon, A. (1994) The new tourism revolution. *Tourism Management*, 15 (2), 91–92.

Swarbrooke, J. and Horner, S. (1999) *Consumer Behaviour in Tourism*. Butterworth Heinemann, Oxford.

World Tourism Organization (2001) *Tourism 2020 Vision – Global Forecast and Profiles of Market Segments*. WTO, Madrid.

TOURISM IN CONTEXT

DEMAND

RESOURCES

CLIMATE

TRANSPORT

FUTURES

Busy airport arrivals and departures.
© istockphoto.com/Christoph Ermel

Analysing the World Pattern of International Tourism Flows

INTRODUCTION

This case study is designed to illustrate and explain the patterns of international tourism demand in both time and space. On completion of the case you will:

1. Be aware of the historical growth of international tourism demand.
2. Be able to reflect on the role of crises, natural disasters and terrorism in affecting tourism demand.
3. Understand how tourism demand varies across world regions.
4. Explain why some countries are major generators of international tourism and some are leading destinations.
5. Be able to explain the underlying causes of these patterns.

TOURISM IN CONTEXT

DEMAND

RESOURCES

CLIMATE

TRANSPORT

FUTURES

KEY ISSUES

The five key issues in this case study are:

1. Compared to domestic tourism, international tourism trends are relatively well documented because measurement is standardised across the world and more straightforward than domestic tourism measurement.
2. The growth of international tourism since 1950 has been phenomenal, driven by social, technological and economic factors.
3. In recent years, 'shocks' to the tourism system such as '9/11' and 'wild card' events such as the 2004 Asian tsunami have set back these rates of growth.
4. The determinants of demand, allied to the characteristics of the mosaic of tourism destinations around the world, combine to produce global rhythms and patterns of tourism.
5. Understanding these global patterns of international tourism demand is essential for the successful marketing and development of tourism destinations.

WHY INTERNATIONAL FLOWS?

This case is confined to *international* tourism flows and receipts, as the collection and estimation of statistics of international tourism is more accurate than that for *domestic* tourism. The collection and aggregation of statistics into five world regions by the UN World Tourism Organization (UNWTO) necessarily means that their regions, whilst failing to conform to geographical logic, are used throughout this case study.

THE HISTORICAL TREND AT THE WORLD SCALE

The end of the Second World War represented the beginning of a remarkable period of growth for international tourism, with an annual average growth rate approaching 7 per cent for the second half of the twentieth century (Table 4.1). Until the early years of the twenty-first century, international tourism was remarkably resilient to factors that might have been expected to depress growth – recession, oil crises, wars and terrorism. However, in 2001 9/11 represented the first 'shock' to the tourism system and demand fell as a result. However, as the decade progressed, tourism volumes recovered exceeding 800 million arrivals in 2005.

- **The 1950s** In 1950, international tourist arrivals stood at 25.3 million. Growth of international tourism was sluggish as the world recovered from the Second World War. However, the adoption of the jet engine in the closing years of the decade provided an important technological enabling factor for international travel.

TABLE 4.1 International tourism arrivals: the historical trend

Year	International tourism arrivals (millions)	International tourism receipts (US$ millions)
1950	25.3	2 100
1960	69.3	6 867
1970	159.7	17 900
1980	284.8	102 372
1985	321.2	116 158
1990	454.8	255 000
1995	567.0	372 000
2000	696.8	477 000
2001	692.6	463 600
2005	806.0	680 000
Forecast for 2020	1560.0	N/A

- **The 1960s** By 1960, arrivals had reached 69.3 million. The decade of the sixties saw demand for international tourism realised by:
  - *demand-side factors* – large numbers of those living in the developed world had the desire, time and income to travel; and
  - *supply-side factors* – the response by the tourism industry to develop the 'standardised' approach of inclusive tours offered at a competitive price.

Business travel also emerged as an important sector of the market.

- **The 1970s** In 1970, international arrivals had risen to 159.7 million. Growth slowed due to the oil crisis in 1974 and economic recession at the end of the decade. However, recession demonstrates the 'ratchet' effect of tourism demand with an increasing rate of growth in times of prosperity, and at times of recession, demand remains fairly constant, as consumers are reluctant to forego travel.
- **The 1980s** By 1980, international arrivals had reached 284.8 million and growth rates began to slow as the market moved towards maturity. The mid-1980s were a period of substantial travel with European destinations experiencing record years. However, in 1986 the Chernobyl incident, the Libyan bombing and the fall in the US dollar saw a shift in demand away from Europe and North Africa. The late-1980s saw a return to the normal pattern of tourism flows, and accelerating growth, only to be disrupted by the Gulf War.
- **The 1990s** In 1990 international arrivals stood at 454.8 million. The decade opened with the Gulf War that severely depressed international travel and had a long-term impact upon tourism enterprises such as airlines. Over the decade,

TOURISM IN CONTEXT

DEMAND

RESOURCES

CLIMATE

TRANSPORT

FUTURES

growth of arrivals was strong and a shift in patterns of demand was evident with the opening up of the former Eastern Bloc, and the expansion of tourism in the Pacific Rim countries. In the closing years of the decade, the Asian currency crisis depressed intra-regional travel in Asia, though inbound travel was boosted as prices fell.

- **The new millennium** Tourism grew substantially in 2000 to reach almost 700 million international arrivals. This growth continued in 2001 until the 'shock of 9/11' which depressed travel significantly in the final quarter of the year and resulted in the first recorded annual decrease in international arrivals since 1982. Further shocks to the tourism system then ensued with the war in Afghanistan, bombings in Bali, the outbreak of SARS, the Iraq War, terrorist bombings in Madrid and London and the 2004 Boxing Day Asian tsunami. It is the climate of uncertainty created by these events that had the greatest impact on international travel. Nonetheless the pattern appears to be that tourism recovers more quickly after each crisis and that confidence in international travel had returned by the middle of the decade.

It is difficult to generalise about the pattern of international tourism flows as individual countries display marked differences and contrasts. Similarly, each destination receives a distinctive mix of tourist origins and modes of transport. On a world basis it is estimated that:

- 55 per cent of international arrivals are by surface transport.
- 45 per cent are by air.
- 16 per cent of international arrivals are for business purposes.
- 50 per cent are for pleasure.

However, it is also true that the impact of 9/11 completely changed the international tourism market as symbols of tourism – aircraft – were used as weapons. The impact was such that major international airlines were bankrupted, many destinations and companies saw their markets devastated and consumer confidence in travel was severely tested. As the most significant 'shock' to the tourism system, the effects of 9/11 are important and can be summarised as:

1. A worldwide decrease in international arrivals of 0.6 per cent in 2001 – somewhat less than initially feared.
2. Regionally, the Americas were the hardest hit (−6 per cent international arrivals), followed by the Middle East (−2.5 per cent).
3. Some destinations with Moslem populations suffered, whilst others, such as Australia were perceived as safe havens.
4. Destinations that were hit the hardest were those dependent on the North American market and those dependent on the long-haul market. Also preferences changed and consumers sought out 'greener' destinations.
5. In many countries, demand switched from international travel to domestic, partly as a result of the reduced availability of airline seats, but also because domestic travel, often by surface transport was perceived as safer.
6. Governments and international agencies put into place 'crisis recovery strategies' including support for the tourism sector, subsidies for airlines and marketing campaigns.

THE CHANGING REGIONAL PICTURE

Determinants of tourism demand include both lifestyle factors such as income and mobility as well as life cycle factors such as a person's age or family circumstances. These determinants when allied to the characteristics of the mosaic of tourism destinations around the world, combine to produce global rhythms and patterns of tourism. International tourism arrivals and departures are concentrated into relatively few countries, mainly in Europe and North America. This produces an unbalanced picture that favours developed Western economies and disadvantages the developing world, which is left to compete for the long-haul market – and this accounts for a minor share of the total market. For both generators and destinations of international tourism, as more countries have entered the market, the dominance of the leading players has been gradually reduced.

GENERATORS

The major tourism-generating countries are those in the *high mass-consumption stage* of economic development, although as countries reach the *drive to maturity stage* they become significant generating markets. For any particular destination country, a typical list of the top generating markets would contain neighbouring states together with at least one from a list containing Germany, the UK, Japan, and the USA. However, it is clear that by 2030 if not earlier, both China and India will become major generating countries. In part, the pattern of generating countries is explained by two conflicting trends:

- The importance, though declining, of short-haul travel to neighbouring countries which represents up to 40 per cent of total international trips.
- A substantial growth in long-haul travel. This is due to both consumer demand for new, more exotic destinations and the response from the travel industry to package long-haul destinations. Aircraft technology and management can now deliver these at a price and length of journey acceptable to the consumer. This may however, be tempered by demand responses to climate change.

DESTINATIONS

The post-war period has been marked by the rapid emergence of the East Asia and the Pacific region (EAP) as an international tourism destination, largely at the expense of the Americas and Europe (Table 4.2).

EAST ASIA AND THE PACIFIC

In 1950 the EAP region (which also includes South Asia), had a share of less than 1 per cent of international tourism; by 2010 this share is forecast to exceed 20 per cent. The key to the region's success is due to:

- A number of rapidly developing countries with large populations.
- Well-managed airlines based in the region and emergent budget airlines.

TOURISM IN CONTEXT

DEMAND

RESOURCES

CLIMATE

TRANSPORT

FUTURES

TABLE 4.2 International tourism arrivals: the changing regional picture: percentage share of international arrivals by UNWTO region

Region	1950 (%)	1960 (%)	1970 (%)	1980 (%)	1990 (%)	2000 (%)	2005 (%)	Forecast for 2010 (%)
Europe	66.5	72.5	70.5	68.4	63.5	57.8	54.8	50.2
Americas	29.6	24.1	23.0	18.9	18.8	18.4	16.6	18.6
East Asia and Pacific (EAP) (including South Asia)	1.0	1.3	3.6	7.8	12.1	16.6	19.3	22.1
Africa	2.1	1.1	1.5	2.5	3.4	3.9	4.6	4.4
Middle East	0.9	1.0	1.4	2.4	2.1	3.3	4.8	3.5

- An exotic culture (at least as perceived by the West).
- World class natural attractions.
- Good quality tourism infrastructure such as airports.
- Dynamic societies with positive, welcoming attitudes to tourism, including newly emergent destinations such as China and Vietnam.
- Favourable exchange rates.
- Competitively priced inclusive tours.
- High quality accommodation products and cuisine.

Europe's traditional pre-eminence in international tourism has been eroded since the 1960s. While Europe still has the largest volume of international arrivals, growth has been at a slower rate than regions such as the EAP. The trend of new destination regions taking market share from Europe is clear and will continue. Nonetheless, Europe still dominates world tourism flows simply because it contains:

- Many of the world's leading generating countries.
- A number of relatively small but adjacent countries generating considerable volumes of cross-border travel.
- A mature travel and transport industry.
- Natural and cultural attractions of world calibre.
- Many themed attractions such as Disneyland Paris.
- Attractive capital cities.
- Emerging destinations such as the former Eastern Bloc countries.
- A variety of tourism products from beach to winter sports holidays.
- A mature tourism infrastructure, including the Channel Tunnel and other transport developments.
- Highly trained personnel.

- A pan-European currency – the *euro*.
- An integrated industrial base which is important for business tourism.

Elsewhere in the world, the **Americas** account for a significant share of international tourism activity, with an increasing volume of inbound travel to supplement the huge domestic market, but this masks major differences between the USA and Canada on the one hand and the economically much less prosperous Latin American countries on the other. The North American domestic market has benefited from the fall in outbound travel resulting from the fear of terrorism. In **Africa**, due to the prevailing political instability and poor infrastructure, tourism growth is relatively slow. The majority of arrivals are in North Africa, but the newly emergent and 'politically acceptable' South Africa is shifting the emphasis of tourism. In the **Middle East**, the stop-go nature of the peace process inevitably has an impact on tourism demand and supply.

REFLECTION ON THE CASE

This case shows that the world picture of international tourism demand is not random. It follows predictable patterns that are related to the different mix of tourism destinations around the world and to the social and economic characteristics of generating countries. However, the various 'shocks' to the tourism system are rewriting these rules and patterns of demand are changing, changes which may also accelerate due to responses to climate change. It is important to understand the global picture of international tourism demand because they determine tourism flows and the fortunes of all tourism destinations.

DISCUSSION POINTS

1. This case is dependent on accurate statistics of international tourism demand. Make a checklist of ways to measure international tourism demand – which is the most accurate? How is international tourism demand measured in your country?
2. Plot the growth of international tourism demand since 1950 on a graph, supplementing the data in this case with that from the UNWTO website. Explain why the growth rate was more rapid in the first 25 years and slower in later years.
3. On the graph pinpoint dates when growth was checked – identify the events that caused these checks. Choose one event and explain its effect on tourism in your own country.

TOURISM IN CONTEXT

DEMAND

RESOURCES

CLIMATE

TRANSPORT

FUTURES

TOURISM IN CONTEXT

DEMAND

RESOURCES

CLIMATE

TRANSPORT

FUTURES

4. Identify the 'top ten' tourist generators and the ten leading tourism destinations in the world. This is available from the UNWTO website or their publications. Explain why the leading generators tend to be from developed Western economies. How is the pattern of destinations changing and why?

5. Taking your own country as the example, compile a statistical report on tourism demand (including domestic tourism if the information is available). Write a brief report explaining the patterns you have found and comparing them to the world patterns of demand.

A curious Galápagos Sea Lion (Zalophus californianus wollebaeki) considers backpacks left by tourists. Galápagos Islands, Ecuador.

The Galápagos Islands: Balancing Resource Conservation and Tourism Development

INTRODUCTION

This case is focused upon the unique wildlife of the Galápagos Islands as a tourism resource. The case raises important issues about how unique natural resources should be conserved and managed for tourism, with the associated conflicts over management priorities. On completion of this case you should:

1. Understand the significance of the Galápagos Islands as a natural tourism resource.
2. Be aware of the impact of visitors upon wildlife.
3. Recognise the variety of approaches to conserving wildlife resources.
4. Understand the fact that unique tourism resources are the focus of a wide range of interest groups.
5. Recognise that political and economic realities intervene in the management of tourism resources.

KEY ISSUES

The five key issues in this case are:

1. The fact that the tourism appeal of the Galápagos Islands is firmly based on its unique wildlife attractions, which are vulnerable to increasing numbers of visitors.
2. Visitor impacts upon both the wildlife and the community have been significant.
3. The management of the islands' wildlife resources has been implemented through the designation of national park status as well as international recognition as a World Heritage Site and Biosphere Reserve.
4. Visitor management is achieved through the use of qualified guides, strict regulations on visitor activity, cruise itineraries and the zoning of the national park, as well as using price and permits as a means of restricting the numbers of visitors.
5. There is a range of stakeholders involved in the management of the Galápagos as a tourism resource, but there is considerable disagreement between them over priorities for the islands.

THE GALÁPAGOS ISLANDS

The Galápagos Islands lie in the Pacific Ocean about 1000 kilometres west of Guayaquil on the South American mainland (see Figure 5.1). The unique wildlife of the Galápagos is a world-class attraction and a non-reproducible resource, which has been given international recognition as a World Heritage Site and Biosphere Reserve. Most of the animals have no fear of man, as there are no natural predators. Although the islands are situated on the Equator, penguins and sea lions flourish alongside species more closely associated with the tropics, as this is the meeting place of four ocean currents. The best-known animals are the marine iguanas and giant tortoise, of which there are 14 distinct species on the different islands. This provided the inspiration for Darwin's theory of evolution by natural selection, and the islands' scientific value has long been recognised. Until recently the Galápagos were protected by their remoteness, and the human impact was relatively slight. Since the 1970s, the growing popularity of eco-tourism has focused public interest on the islands, providing support for conservation but posing a greater threat to the fragile ecosystems than the occasional havoc wreaked by pirates and whalers in the past. The widespread perception that the islands are a 'tropical Eden' is far from the reality. The climate is dry and since the islands are volcanic, the scenery is for the most part barren and rugged. The plants and animals are well adapted to the conditions, including the periodic heavy rains and warmer temperatures resulting from the periodic weather event known as El Niño, but their survival is affected by a number of serious problems due to human interference with the environment. Introduced plant and animal species may soon outnumber those native to the islands, despite the attempts to impose a quarantine system.

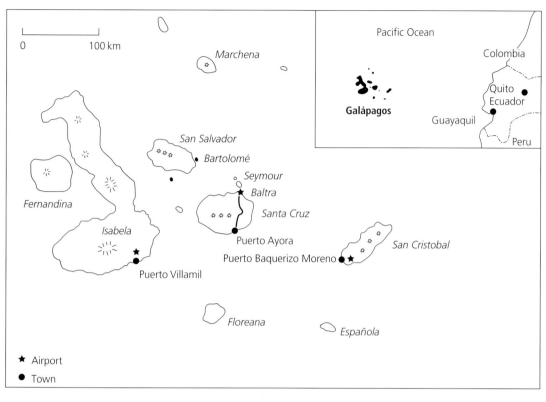

FIGURE 5.1 The Galápagos Islands

MANAGING THE RESOURCE

NATIONAL PARK DESIGNATION

In Europe and North America conservationists and even representatives of the travel industry are seriously considering the introduction of 'no-go areas' for tourists as a solution to the damage caused by tourism to fragile physical and cultural resources. In the Galápagos this has been the policy for many years. As early as 1959, when the number of visitors was less than 1000 a year, the Ecuadorian government designated 97 per cent of the archipelago, excluding only those areas already settled, as a National Park. In 1968 the Charles Darwin Foundation, an international non-profit organisation, was established to protect the islands' ecosystems in co-operation with the Galápagos National Park Service (GNPS), a government agency. Organised tourism began in the late 1960s and in 1974 a master plan for the national park set a limit of 12 000 visitors a year, later expanded to 40 000 for economic reasons, with a maximum visitor stay of six days. By 2007, the park had a new strategic plan.

TOURISM IN CONTEXT

DEMAND

RESOURCES

CLIMATE

TRANSPORT

FUTURES

ZONING

The National Park is divided into five zones to give varying degrees of protection and balance the needs of tourists against the primary objective of conservation, as follows:

- Special use zone – adjoining the areas already colonised – for the use of local residents under strict controls.
- Intensive use zone – this includes the most visited sites where a maximum of four or five groups of up to 20 visitors are allowed to disembark daily.
- Extensive use zone – includes the less interesting sites where a maximum of 12 visitors are allowed to disembark daily.
- Primitive use zone – where access is prohibited without special permit.
- Primitive scientific zone – where access is for scientific research only.

VISITOR MANAGEMENT

Tourism is controlled in the interest of conservation, through:

- The National Park certified guide programme.
- Strict regulations to prevent any contamination and disturbance to the wildlife.
- The paperwork necessary for tour vessels to leave port.

Access is also controlled by price; it costs almost as much for foreign tourists to reach the Galápagos by air or cruise ship from the mainland of Ecuador as it does to fly from Europe to Quito or Guayaquil. Foreign visitors to the National Park have to pay a substantial entrance fee. The majority of tourists find accommodation on the cruise ships and yachts that tour the islands. Tourists are restricted to some 54 visitor sites designated by the GNPS; these are reached from the ship by *pangas* (inflatable craft with an outboard motor) – and usually involve a 'wet landing' through the surf rather than a 'dry' landing at a jetty. At each visitor site a rough waymarked trail provides the sole access to the wildlife, unusual plants and volcanic landforms of the Galápagos. Tourists are always accompanied by a naturalist-guide licensed by the GNPS with a maximum of 20 visitors per guide. Itineraries for tourists on cruise ships visiting a large number of sites, or on day excursions based at island hotels, are arranged well in advance by the tour operator. Those arriving in chartered yachts and other small vessels are allowed some flexibility in organising their own itineraries subject to a maximum number of sites per boat.

VISITOR IMPACTS

Eco-tourism in the Galápagos was worth an estimated US$160 million to Ecuador in 2004. In fact tourism is one of the few commercial uses of the islands' limited resource base – various attempts at agricultural development in the past have met with failure, due mainly to problems of water supply. Most foreign visitors are high-income, middle-aged Europeans and North Americans. The value to the national

TOURISM IN CONTEXT

DEMAND

RESOURCES

CLIMATE

TRANSPORT

FUTURES

economy is even greater if we consider that most of these tourists spend three days in mainland Ecuador, principally in the cities of Quito and Guayaquil, as part of their holiday. Conservationists are concerned that this controlled 'educational tourism' could grow to become conventional tourism. At present visitors to the pristine beach at Gardner Bay on Española Island – one of the most popular sites – are outnumbered by sea lions. There are no clearly defined limits on the annual number of visitors, and the planned limit of 40 000 has long been exceeded and in 2005 approached 150 000. The number of tour vessels has not increased since the mid-1990s, but tour companies are now tending to use larger, more luxurious ships than before, with some accommodating 100 tourists. More controversial are the occasional visits of large cruise ships to the islands, as it is difficult to impose quarantine regulations on passengers. There is some evidence that the environmental capacity has already been reached in the most visited areas, with disturbance to nesting birds and path erosion.

From the viewpoint of the islanders there is little to attract conventional tourists. Most tourists spend only a few hours ashore in Puerto Ayora, the largest community, and Puerto Baquerizo Moreno, the administrative capital. Only a small proportion of the visitor-spend actually benefits the local economy, as most tourist requirements have to be imported from the mainland and eco-tourism creates relatively few jobs. Recreational activities are limited to scuba diving and snorkelling that are supervised by GNPS guides, and sport fishing, which is not compatible with marine conservation. Further growth in these and land-based activities such as horse riding will generate a demand for more facilities. At present the three port communities offer little more than basic amenities, a few 'cybercafés', and small hotels of varying standard. Puerto Ayora, with 15 000 inhabitants – half the population of the islands – has the most potential for development as a resort. So far proposals for intensive development here and elsewhere have been resisted, and the only resort hotel offering luxury accommodation is located in the interior of Santa Cruz Island.

Ecuadorians and foreign visitors evaluate the island's resources in different ways. Domestic tourists, for example, are much more likely to buy black coral souvenirs from local traders, which is illegal. Tourism has resulted in an influx of workers from the mainland, helped by subsidised domestic airfares. They are attracted by the prospect of short-term financial gain and a climate which is free of tropical diseases. Population growth is putting pressure on scarce resources such as water, foodstuffs and building materials, and increases the risk of oil spillage from the supply ships. All of which further tips the balance against the survival of the islands' wildlife.

It is now generally acknowledged that the islands have reached some kind of crisis point in terms of conservation, and in 2007 they were placed on the list of 'World Heritage Sites in Danger'. President Correa declared the Galápagos 'at risk' and a national priority for Ecuador, and an action plan was put into effect. A new governor was appointed to implement stricter immigration measures, and quarantine systems have been planned in Quito and Guayaquil. There are also plans to develop renewable sources of energy to make the islanders more self-sufficient.

THE STAKEHOLDERS

Conservation is also vital for the surrounding seas, and tourism has to share use of this resource with the important fishing industry; this includes both small-scale

TOURISM IN
CONTEXT

DEMAND

RESOURCES

CLIMATE

TRANSPORT

FUTURES

local operators and large, well-equipped ships based on the mainland and supplying international markets. In 1986 the government established the Galápagos Marine Resources Reserve, reputedly the world's largest, covering an area of over 130 000 square kilometres. In 1995 a concerted effort was made to ban commercial fishing, especially of sea cucumbers which are valued in the Far East as an aphrodisiac. In protest, islanders threatened the staff of the GNPS and the Charles Darwin Research Station, causing deliberate damage to wildlife habitats. Similar incidents have occurred in other national parks where local communities feel excluded – the Coto Doñana in Spain is another example. In the case of the Galápagos the government has taken on board the principle of local involvement. The 'Special Law for the Galápagos' passed by the Ecuadorian Congress in 1998, recognises the importance of sustainable development. Its main points are:

- Greater co-operation between the organisations concerned with conservation and tourism development. (The various stakeholders are shown in Figure 5.2.)
- Promotion of locally based nature tourism.
- Greater control over tourism development by INGALA, the regional planning agency, which will require environmental impact statements from developers.
- Stabilisation of population growth by making it more difficult to obtain rights of residence in the islands.
- Allocation of 40 per cent of the visitor entrance fee to the GNPS for conservation.
- Protection of native island species to be achieved through prevention by stricter quarantine regulations and inspection against plant and animal imports and damage limitation by eradication of introduced species.

The Galápagos Islands are a unique natural resource ©istockphoto.com/Alexander Deursen

It remains to be seen how effective the Special Law will be in practice. Like other developing countries, Ecuador takes pride in its heritage, but has limited financial resources to set aside for conservation when there are more pressing economic and social problems. It may also be difficult to find experienced professional workers to enforce the regulations in the face of opposition from local politicians, an inefficient bureaucracy, and the multinational corporations. It is clear that there are many interests in the conservation of the islands of which tourism is an important, but not the only, stakeholder. Nevertheless, schemes to train young islanders in conservation and catering are cause for optimism for the future of the Galápagos.

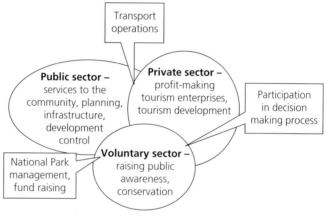

The **public sector** includes:
• The government of Ecuador and its agencies:

> Ecuadorian Institute for Forestry and Natural Areas (INEFAN)
> National Fisheries Directorate
> Ministerio del Ambiente (Ministry of the Environment)
> the Ecuadorian Navy
> Marine Reserve Commission
> National Tourist Corporation (CETUR)
> the Galápagos National Park Service
> Instituto Nacional Galápagos (INGALA)

• Provincial Council of Galápagos
• The municipios (local authorities)

The **private sector** includes:
• The National Association of Tourist Enterprises in Galápagos (ASEGAL)
• Shipping services
• Yacht charter
• The fishing industry

The **voluntary sector** includes:
• The Charles Darwin Foundation (CDF)
• The International Galápagos Tour Operators Association (IGTOA)
• The Galápagos Conservation Trust in the UK and similar organisations in different countries affiliated to the CDF

FIGURE 5.2   Stakeholders in Galápagos tourism

TOURISM IN CONTEXT

DEMAND

RESOURCES

CLIMATE

TRANSPORT

FUTURES

TOURISM IN CONTEXT

DEMAND

RESOURCES

CLIMATE

TRANSPORT

FUTURES

REFLECTIONS ON THE CASE

The Galápagos Islands are a unique tourism resource, but this case highlights the difficulties of conserving and managing such a resource in the face of multiple priorities from a range of different stakeholders. In particular, we can see the different effectiveness of the various measures used to limit visitor impacts. The Galápagos are an excellent example of political and economic realities intervening in attempts to sustain the islands' wildlife resources.

DISCUSSION POINTS

1. Using the Internet and travel brochures, put together a full tour itinerary for a visit to the Galápagos for a tourist based in New York. Include all stop-overs and transfers and provide a detailed itinerary for the visit to the islands themselves.
2. Draft a list of ways to manage visitors in national parks. Which of these do you feel is effective – and which measures are being used in the Galápagos Islands to prevent any contamination and disturbance to the wildlife?
3. Thinking of the various stakeholders involved in the Galápagos, devise a chart that shows each stakeholder and their major interests in the tourism sector. Where do the potential conflicts lie?
4. Devise a list of the positive and negative effects of tourism upon wildlife generally – how many of these effects would you expect to find in the Galápagos?
5. The Galápagos are home to a community of islanders, who are often overlooked in media reports on the islands. In class have a debate about the pros and cons of tourism and assign key roles to members of the class. These roles might include the local mayor, business people, other representatives of the local community and GNPS staff.

ACKNOWLEDGEMENT

We appreciate the help given by the Galápagos Conservation Trust in researching this case study.

KEY SOURCES

Crowley, P. (1999) *The Galapagos: Tourism at the Crossroads*. Tourism Concern, London.
Hall, C. M. and McArthur, S. (1998) *Integrated Heritage Management*. The Stationery Office, London.

Jackson, M. (1997) *Galapagos: A Natural History*. University of Calgary Press, Calgary.

Mac Farland, C. and Cifuentes, M. (1995) Case Study: Ecuador, in V. Dompka (ed.) *Human Population, Biodiversity and Protected Areas: Science and Policy Issues*. American Association for the Advancement of Science, Washington.

McWilliam, F. (1995) Unnatural Selection. *Geographical*, 67 (2), 20.

WEBSITES

www.galapagosonline.com.

www.igtoa.org.

TOURISM IN CONTEXT

DEMAND

RESOURCES

CLIMATE

TRANSPORT

FUTURES

Santiago de Compostela Cathedral is situated in Santiago de Compostela, Galicia, Spain. The cathedral is the reputed burial-place of Saint James the Great, one of the apostles of Jesus Christ and is the destination of the Way of St. James.

The Way of St James: The Pilgrimage as a Cultural Resource

INTRODUCTION

Give me my scallop shell of quiet
My staff of faith to walk upon
My scrip of joy, immortal diet
My bottle of salvation
My gown of glory, hope's true gauge,
And thus I'll take my pilgrimage.

In this poem the great Elizabethan adventurer Sir Walter Raleigh, awaiting execution in the Tower of London, uses the pilgrimage to Santiago as a metaphor for the journey through life. Indeed for many travellers today, the Camino de Santiago (the Way of St James) is both a spiritual quest and a physical test of endurance.

Faith tourism – travel with a religious motivation – accounts for between 2 and 5 per cent of world tourism (Russell, 1999). Demand has been fuelled by rising incomes, improvements in transport and people's need to find a purpose in travel that is not materialistic. This case introduces one of the world's most important examples of Christian pilgrimage – the Camino or route to the shrine of St James at Santiago de Compostela in north-west Spain – and examines its role in the development of cultural tourism. On completion of this case you will:

1. Appreciate the role of the pilgrimage in the history of travel and tourism in Europe.

2. Understand the differences between the mindset of medieval pilgrims and the motivations of modern travellers on the Camino.
3. Recognise that this is a case where the journey is more important than the destination.
4. Be aware of the significance of Santiago de Compostela as a destination and the other cultural attractions en route.

KEY ISSUES

There are four key issues in this case:

1. The pilgrimage has played a crucial role in the historical development of tourism.
2. The pilgrimage to Santiago is pre-eminent among Christian pilgrimages.
3. The sites along the Camino and other pilgrim routes are significant cultural attractions.
4. The revival of the pilgrimage has assisted in the development of Galicia, formerly one of the poorest regions of Spain.

HISTORICAL BACKGROUND TO THE PILGRIMAGE

Santiago de Compostela, the shrine of St James, is located in the region of Galicia, some 30 kilometres from the Atlantic coast of Spain. Despite its peripheral location, this became the most important centre of Christian pilgrimage in medieval Europe, second only to Rome. According to tradition, James, one of the twelve apostles, was the first Christian missionary to Spain. On his return to Palestine he was martyred and his body taken to Galicia, where it lay undiscovered for the next eight centuries. Both the time and the place are significant. In Roman times this area already had religious significance as the end of the known world, where people gathered to watch the sun disappear into the Atlantic at Fisterra (Finisterre). Moreover, in the ninth century Christendom was under threat from the Muslim Moors who then controlled all of the Iberian Peninsula, except for the area north of the Cantabrian mountains. The miraculous discovery of the tomb of St James provided the Christians with a rallying point, and the peaceful apostle was transformed into Santiago Matamoros (St James the Moor-slayer) to invigorate the Christian reconquest of Spain, which was finally completed in 1492. In the following century the Spanish were to found a number of cities named after Santiago as part of their conquest and evangelisation of the Americas.

In the Middle Ages Santiago de Compostela was linked to most parts of western Europe by a network of pilgrim routes. A cult of St James developed, for example, at Reading Abbey in England, at Vadstena in Sweden and at Aachen in Germany, the city of Charlemagne, who was associated with the legend of the tomb's discovery. The many subsidiary pilgrim routes crossing Europe came to focus on four assembly points in France, which also had religious significance – Paris, Vézelay, Le Puy and Arles (see Figure 6.1). The throngs of pilgrims then pushed towards Spain, crossing the Pyrenees at Roncesvalles and Somport. At Puente la Reina in Navarra two major pilgrim routes converged, to form the Camino Francés (French Route), or 'route of the stars', following the line of the Milky Way westward to Santiago. The Camino linked a number of places of religious significance, such as the cathedral cities of Burgos and León, and some important monasteries. Gradually an infrastructure of bridges, hostels and inns, hospices for the sick, markets, churches and wayside crosses developed to cater for the vast numbers undertaking the pilgrimage. There was even a travel guide for the route, but as this was written in Latin it would have been understood by relatively few pilgrims.

The pilgrimage was especially popular in the British Isles and Scandinavia. The sea routes to Galicia were important here. For English pilgrims the four-day voyage to the ports of La Coruña and Ribadeo was preferred to the much longer and possibly dangerous overland routes through France. Even so, the Bay of Biscay had a reputation for storminess, and it was said in the fifteenth century that 'men may leave all games, that sail to St James'. Pilgrim ships from Bristol and the Channel ports usually travelled in convoy as a protection against pirates. Pilgrims were not allowed to take money out of the country beyond what was needed for the journey, and gave an undertaking not to disclose state secrets.

Then as now, the pilgrimage was characterised by sometimes contradictory motivations that were not always religious or spiritual. This is implied by one of the characters in Chaucer's *Canterbury Tales*, a much-travelled widow known as the Wife of Bath. She had visited Rome, 'St James in Galice' (Santiago), the shrine of St Mary at Boulogne, seen the relics of the Magi at Cologne and had made three pilgrimages to Jerusalem. We should recognise that the mindset and world view of medieval pilgrims was fundamentally different from today's tourists. They believed in the universality of the Catholic Church, the authenticity of holy relics and the journey to a shrine as a way to salvation. Pilgrimage was seen as an act of atonement for past sins, as an act of grace bringing the believer into closer contact with the saints and as an act of thanksgiving. Yet for many it was also an adventure, an opportunity to escape from the narrow routines of medieval life. Pilgrims came from all classes of society, and generally travelled in large groups, for protection, and to mitigate the hardships of the road with music and storytelling.

From the sixteenth century onwards the flow of pilgrims to Santiago de Compostela dwindled to a trickle. In the Protestant countries of northern Europe the demand for this type of travel virtually disappeared, until pilgrimages were revived in a different form in the late twentieth century.

CHARACTERISTICS OF THE MODERN PILGRIMAGE

The revival of the pilgrimage in recent times is due to a number of factors. One of these is the growing disillusionment with materialism and secularism, and the personal need for self-fulfilment taking a spiritual direction to give meaning to life. People are now more aware of the pilgrimage to Santiago through the influence of writers such as Paulo Coelho.

TOURISM IN CONTEXT

DEMAND

RESOURCES

CLIMATE

TRANSPORT

FUTURES

TOURISM IN CONTEXT

DEMAND

RESOURCES

CLIMATE

TRANSPORT

FUTURES

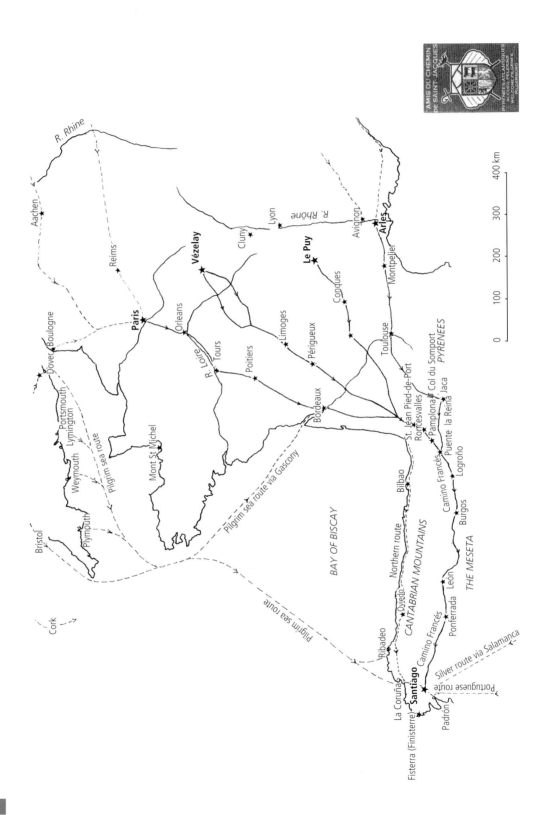

FIGURE 6.1 The Pilgrim Routes to Santiago.

The revitalisation of the pilgrim routes to Santiago has been recognised at a number of levels:

- At the international level the Council of Europe has sought to develop a series of cultural itineraries or themed routes rich in historical associations that are representative of European culture as a whole. Göethe claimed that the medieval pilgrim routes to Santiago were crucial in the making of a European identity, and they were the first cultural itinerary to be designated in 1987. In France the pilgrim routes have been incorporated in the system of *grands randonées* (long-distance waymarked trails). In Spain the route of the Camino is signposted by a motif featuring the scallop shell of St James and lines representing the roads of Europe leading to Santiago de Compostela, which moreover was made European capital of culture for the year 2000.
- In Spain the cult of St James was revived after the civil war by the regime of General Franco and the Catholic Church as a symbol of national unity. The route itself was promoted in 1993, as part of a concerted effort by the Spanish government to diversify the tourism product away from the Mediterranean coast. The modern Camino provides a focus for heritage tourism in the four northern regions of Galicia, Castile and León, La Rioja and Navarra.
- At regional level the effect of the revival of the pilgrimage has been most marked in Galicia. The Xunta (regional council) has made a considerable investment in hostel-type accommodation along the Camino. The Xunta has also designated seven other pilgrim routes. These include an extension of the Camino to Fisterra, an 'English route' from the port of Ribadeo, and a northern route via Bilbao following the coast of the Bay of Biscay. This is a more scenic alternative to the Camino Francés, which crosses large expanses of the Meseta. The historic city of Santiago has been regenerated, and a number of art and music festivals celebrate the region's cultural heritage. Galicia has been one of the main beneficiaries of EU regional funding, particularly those directed towards rural tourism initiatives and job creation.
- At local level a number of community-based action groups have established tourism enterprises in villages along the Camino. This has helped to stem the out-migration which for so long has been a feature of Galicia, one of the poorest and least developed regions of Spain.

The modern Camino is clearly demarcated, with sections reserved solely for walkers, cyclists and horse riders. Some of the towns along its route, especially Pamplona, Burgos and León, do act as nodal tourist attractions, but *recreational business districts* – areas given over to tourism – have not developed on any scale. In contrast, Santiago has become one of the major tourist centres of Spain. Its historic core has been designated a World Heritage Site by UNESCO, with heritage attractions that include:

- The cathedral which contains the tomb of St James. The Portico de la Gloria, the main entrance to the cathedral, is a superb example of Romanesque architecture, while its main column bears the imprint of millions of hands as witness to the power of religious faith.
- The Hostal de los Reyes Católicos, originally a fifteenth century pilgrim hostel, which is now a *parador* (state-owned hotel) offering first class accommodation.

TOURISM IN CONTEXT

DEMAND

RESOURCES

CLIMATE

TRANSPORT

FUTURES

TOURISM IN
CONTEXT

DEMAND

RESOURCES

CLIMATE

TRANSPORT

FUTURES

A large student population ensures that Santiago is a city with a thriving entertainment scene. Nevertheless, tourists stay on average less than two days, as attention tends to focus on the route and its attractions rather than the destination.

The surviving elements of the medieval infrastructure of the Camino, including many Romanesque churches and the ruined castle of the Knights Templar at Ponferrada, now function as secondary attractions. For most of today's tourists travelling by car or coach, the Camino is only part of the itinerary, due to the many diversions which lie a short distance off-route. These include the historic city of Oviedo, the monastery at Santo Domingo de Silos, the ultra-modern Guggenheim Museum in Bilbao and the wineries of La Rioja.

There has been a steady growth in arrivals in Santiago since the 1980s, but with a pronounced peaking in demand during Holy Years, when the festival of St James (July 25) falls on a Sunday. These occur at 5, 6 and 11-year intervals, when plenary indulgencies are granted to pilgrims. For the 1999 and 2004 Holy Years, 5.1 and 6.5 million tourist arrivals were recorded. In 2004 over half of these visitors stayed in hotels, a quarter in hostels and similar accommodation and 15 per cent in campsites. The majority of visitors are Spanish, and foreign pilgrims, as defined by the cathedral authorities in Santiago, account for less than 2 per cent of the total.

Travellers on the Camino who regard themselves as pilgrims come from all over the world and include many from Brazil and Japan. Spain, France, Germany and Italy are the main European countries represented. Although the British only account for 1 per cent of the pilgrims, English is increasingly the common language, while the greeting 'Buen camino' is universally understood. These modern pilgrims are from a variety of religious and social backgrounds, with a predominance in the 40 plus age groups. Most prefer to stay in *refugios*, hostels providing basic accommodation, which are manned by volunteers called *hospitaleros*. Many pilgrims tend to disparage those travelling by car who stay in hotels.

The distinction between pilgrim and conventional tourist is not always clear. The cathedral authorities in Santiago issue a certificate known as a *Compostela* to those who have completed the pilgrimage in the approved manner. To qualify, travellers must produce a route book which has been duly stamped at the refugios, hostels and churches along the Camino; this proves that they have walked at least 100 kilometres (65 miles) of the 850-kilometre route between Santiago and St Jean-Pied-de-Port on the French side of the Pyrenees. For cyclists and horse riders the equivalent distance is 200 kilometres. This is good for the environment, but green credentials are no guarantee that the motivation for the trip is religious, although it may be spiritual in a wider sense. Many pilgrims are non-Catholics, and some may even be regarded as New Age followers rather than Christians. This is implied by the growth in popularity of the route to Fisterra. Here pilgrims burn their clothing on the beach at sunset to begin a new life, evoking a pre-Christian ritual. According to some hospitaleros, the hostels are used by many young travellers as a place to socialise, and the pilgrimage treated as a rite of passage, while groups of cyclists may be more concerned with competition than contemplation.

People may undertake the pilgrimage at a time of crisis in their lives, and for some it is a life-changing experience. Many modern pilgrims believe that hiking alone, spending frugally, and suffering the hardships of the road is essential to achieve spiritual well-being, rather like the 'burn' in physical exercise. This ascetic, puritanical attitude would have been viewed with incomprehension by most of Chaucer's contemporaries, who rode to Canterbury whenever possible, rather than trudging there on foot.

REFLECTIONS ON THE CASE

The pilgrimage to Santiago shows that religion as a motivation for travel is growing in our secular, materialistic world. Many of today's pilgrims, unlike their medieval predecessors, subscribe to a variety of beliefs other than Roman Catholicism. Some may begin the journey as secular tourists and finish as devout Christians. The pilgrimage differs from other types of tourism in terms of motivation, the means of travel, and the type of accommodation used. The physical legacy of the medieval pilgrimage is mainly represented today by large numbers of churches and some of Spain's most interesting historic towns.

DISCUSSION POINTS

1. Compare Santiago with other Roman Catholic shrines such as Lourdes and Fátima. What are the differences as well as the similarities between these pilgrimages?
2. Compare the pilgrimage to Santiago with the Muslim *haj* to Mecca, or to journeys with a religious motivation to Buddhist and Hindu holy places in Japan, China and India. You should include the type of accommodation and the methods of transport used by these pilgrims.
3. Debate in class whether visits to the homes of former celebrities can legitimately be regarded as another form of pilgrimage for a secular age.
4. Imagine that you are a volunteer at one of the pilgrim hostels on the Camino. How would you explain the significance of the pilgrimage to a group of typical young Londoners, without any religious affiliation, who are cycling the route to raise money for charity?
5. Investigate the reasons for the decline in the pilgrimage to Santiago between the sixteenth and early twentieth centuries. In your opinion, what could cause a decline in its present popularity?

KEY SOURCES

Graham, B. and Murray, M. (1997) The spiritual and the profane: the pilgrimage to Santiago de Compostela. *Ecumene*, 4, 389–409.

TOURISM IN CONTEXT

DEMAND

RESOURCES

CLIMATE

TRANSPORT

FUTURES

Lamb, T. (2005) The Road to Santiago. *Geographical*, January, 94–98.

Murray, M. and Graham, B. (1997) Exploring the dialectics of route-based tourism: the Camino de Santiago. *Tourism Management*, 18, 513–524.

Russell, P. (1999) Religious travel in the new millennium. *Travel and Tourism Analyst*, 5, 35–68.

Santos, X. M. (2002) Pilgrimage and tourism at Santiago de Compostela. *Tourism Recreation Research*, 27 (2), 41–50.

Starkie, W. (1957) *The road to Santiago*. John Murray, London.

Timothy, D. and Olsen, D. (eds) (2006) *Tourism, Religion and Spiritual Journeys*. Routledge, London.

WEBSITES

caminosantiago.com
www.xacobeo.es
www.csj.org.uk

Downtown Los Angeles bathed in smog.
© istockphoto.com/Daniel Stein

The Impact of Climate Change on Tourism

INTRODUCTION

Climate change is one of the most significant events facing mankind and has taken centre stage in the work of international tourism agencies. This case introduces the causes of climate change and looks at its effects upon tourism and tourists. On completion of this case you will:

1. Recognise the significance of climate change for tourism.
2. Understand the key elements of climate change and their causes.
3. Be aware of the consequences of global warming for tourism.
4. Be aware of the consequences of the thinning of the ozone layer for tourism.
5. Recognise the response required by destinations, governments, the tourism sector and tourists themselves to climate change.

TOURISM IN CONTEXT

DEMAND

RESOURCES

CLIMATE

TRANSPORT

FUTURES

KEY ISSUES

The five key issues in this case are:

1. Climate change is already a significant factor in human life and is becoming increasingly important. Climate change effects are generally taken to involve a combination of global warming and the thinning of the ozone layer.
2. Global warming is thought to be caused by the burning of fossil fuels creating a greenhouse effect, which prevents heat escaping from the earth. Its impact on tourism includes the flooding of low-lying resorts as the sea level rises and the need for ski resorts to diversify as the snowline recedes.
3. The thinning of the ozone layer is caused by the emission of gases into the atmosphere by such devices as aerosols and refrigerators. Its effects on tourism include increased exposure to ultraviolet radiation at resorts and severe damage to iconic tourism resources such as the bleaching of coral reefs.
4. Climate change is prompting a change in tourist behaviour, with sunbathing becoming less popular, and tourists becoming aware of their carbon footprint when they travel.
5. There is a need for most destinations to rethink their products in the future.

CLIMATE CHANGE

The various elements of the climate, such as air and sea temperatures, sunshine, wind speed and direction, humidity, and precipitation in the form of rain and snow, all play an important role in determining the best conditions for different types of outdoor recreation. Although artificial snow can be manufactured for indoor ski centres, this is expensive and an imperfect substitute for the real thing – a mountain landscape such as the Alps in winter. We could make similar observations, for example, about artificial surf in leisure centres and artificial reefs for scuba diving. In Mediterranean countries and tropical islands the climate at the present time is one of their main assets, a *pull factor* attracting tourists, whereas the cold winters and cloudy skies characteristic of northern countries such as Britain act as a powerful incentive or *push factor* for outbound tourism. Although average temperatures, etc., are usually considered when we describe the climate of a destination, climate change means that extreme weather events such as heat waves, and hurricanes will become much more frequent in the future.

The impact of climate change upon tourism is potentially very significant and is already being felt in some parts of the world. Whereas in the past, climate changes took place over long periods of time, there is now considerable evidence that the rate of change is accelerating, due to man's interference with the natural environment and this in turn is linked to natural disasters such as Hurricane Katrina. The two key dimensions of climate change can be thought of as:

- Global warming
- Thinning of the ozone layer.

Global warming: the causes

Since the beginning of the twentieth century, average temperatures worldwide have increased by about 0.5 °C and may rise by another 2.0 °C in the twenty-first century. The causes and effects of this *global warming* are as yet not fully understood. Some scientists link the rise in temperature directly to major increases in emissions of carbon dioxide, methane and nitrous oxide into the atmosphere. These in turn have resulted from the burning of fossil fuels such as oil and coal by transport, industry and domestic consumers, or from the widespread forest clearance that is taking place throughout the tropics. It is known that carbon dioxide is largely responsible for the *greenhouse effect* of the atmosphere, which prevents excessive radiation of heat from the earth's surface back into space.

The evidence for climatic change is not one-way and is capable of several interpretations. Some scientists believe that the recent changes are well within the limits of fluctuations that have occurred over the last millennium, as evidenced by the advance and retreat of glaciers in the Alps. They point out that some glaciers have actually advanced in recent times, for example in Norway, Alaska and Patagonia. On the other hand, these exceptions to the rule could be explained as a symptom of global warming, with higher temperatures resulting in increased precipitation in the form of snow. At high latitudes the rise in temperatures since the 1990s has been well above that for the world as a whole, causing a decrease in the extent of pack ice in the Arctic Ocean. With greater expanses of open water, much more solar energy is absorbed, rather than being reflected, resulting in further warming. The release of methane from the thawing permafrost beneath the tundra might have an even more dramatic effect in terms of rapid and irreversible climate change. On the other hand, greatly increased snowfall resulting from higher temperatures in the Arctic could eventually lead to another Ice Age. According to this scenario the flow of the iceberg-laden Labrador Current would strengthen, deflecting the warm Gulf Stream well to the south of its present path across the North Atlantic. It is not difficult to predict areas in northern latitudes experiencing a general deterioration of the climate.

Global warming: the impact on tourism

Climate change affects tourist destinations in the following ways:

- **Ski resorts**   The effects of global warming appear to be most obvious in mountain regions, where glaciers and the snowline have retreated, the permafrost at high altitudes has thawed and the risk of avalanches has increased. Many ski resorts, especially those situated at low altitudes, and in marginal areas such as Scotland and the Australian Alps, are becoming unprofitable as the snow cover becomes less reliable. In response, ski resorts are diversifying into year-round tourism to compensate for poor winter seasons.
- **Rising sea level**   The Antarctic Peninsula and Greenland are good examples of the situation in high latitudes, where the ice caps are melting back rapidly and possibly becoming unstable. Full-scale melting of the polar ice would result in

TOURISM IN CONTEXT

DEMAND

RESOURCES

CLIMATE

TRANSPORT

FUTURES

a rise in sea levels worldwide, spelling disaster for many coastal cities and low-lying island destinations.

- **Coastal resorts** The Mediterranean zone in particular would become hotter and drier, aggravating already serious water shortages in some resort areas. These would be less popular with visitors from northern Europe, who conceivably could bask in subtropical warmth in their own seaside resorts, benefiting from an extended summer season. This means that most tourism destinations have to rethink the products that they will offer in the future and effectively reposition themselves in the market place to cope with the changing climate.

The undesirable side effects of climate change include:

- Invasions of insects, and pathogens spreading disease (such as the West Nile virus that afflicted much of North America following a prolonged drought in 2002).
- Possible ecological disaster for native plants and animals, particularly in mountain areas where habitats become increasingly restricted.
- Prolonged heat waves, especially in cities, with episodes of poor air quality.
- More erratic and unpredictable weather patterns impacting upon tourism operations and planning.
- An altered hydrological cycle impacting on resources such as lakes, wetlands and rivers, causing severe droughts and aggravating water shortages in urban areas.
- Increased and more violent storm activity and consequent coastal erosion.
- Increased algal growth at the coast depleting water quality.
- Bleaching of corals due to a rise in sea temperature, with a severe impact, for example, on the Great Barrier Reef.
- Rises in sea level threatening low-lying destinations such as Bangladesh, the Maldives, and Tuvalu in Micronesia.

THINNING OF THE OZONE LAYER: THE CAUSES

The thinning of the ozone layer was first discovered over Antarctica in winter but is now noticeable year-round, and to a lesser extent over the Arctic. The causes of the thinning are thought to be the emission of chlorofluorocarbons (CFCs) from devices such as air conditioners, refrigerators, freezers and aerosols. Of course, tourism must be a contributory factor here. In the meantime action is being taken by governments, industry and consumers, mainly in the developed countries, to curb the use of CFCs, but it remains to be seen whether a worldwide ban on CFCs can be made effective. A start was made in this respect with the adoption of the First International Protocol for Control of Greenhouse Gases at Kyoto, Japan, in 1996.

THINNING OF THE OZONE LAYER: THE IMPACT ON TOURISM

The ozone layer protects us from excessive ultraviolet (UV) radiation, filtering out the lethal UVC rays and reducing the impact of the harmful UVB rays of the sun.

As so-called *ozone holes* have been identified, certain destinations already pose a health hazard to visitors – for example, parts of the Southern Hemisphere such as Australia, New Zealand, South America and even the cool and cloudy Falkland Islands. (You should note that the thinning of the ozone layer has no effect on air and sea surface temperatures and is unrelated to global warming.) There is little doubt that increased UV radiation is causing a higher incidence of skin cancer and eye cataracts worldwide. Fair-skinned people risk sunburn within 15 minutes of initial exposure, while the use of oils and creams with a high sun-protection factor (SPF) will not prevent long-term damage to the skin. Media interest has affected attitudes to sunbathing, and to beach tourism in the following ways:

- Excessive exposure of the skin may become unfashionable as holidaymakers see the advantages of wearing clothing with a high SPF.
- Destinations that have traditionally relied on beach tourism will need to diversify by offering *beach plus* products and tours.

CLIMATE CHANGE: THE RESPONSE OF THE TOURISM SECTOR

Tourism is responding to climate change in two ways. The first is to attempt to 'mitigate' the effects of climate change by altering behaviour, for example through reducing the carbon footprints of travellers. The second is in terms of 'adaptation' where the sector, particularly destinations, develops strategies to cope with the realities of climate change. We can think of the response of the tourism sector as coming from four main sources:

1. Government and international agencies
2. Tourists
3. The travel and tourism industry
4. Destinations

The international tourism agencies such as the UNWTO and PATA have firmly embraced the climate change agenda. Their role is in terms of educating the tourist and assisting both the industry and government to prepare. The UNWTO, for example held a series of high-level meetings in 2007 to communicate the message that tourism needs to respond urgently to climate change. Governments have also responded by levying 'green' taxes in an attempt to change people's behaviour. Both air and car travel for example is becoming more expensive, due to the taxes imposed on the use of environment-damaging fuel. This in turn is influencing tourists' behaviour. Whilst it is now possible for travellers to 'offset' their carbon footprint emitted by travelling through tree planting schemes, there is evidence that people will stop flying if climate change worsens. Instead travel patterns will change to shorter trips and the use of more environment-friendly transport. In response to these potential changes in demand, the tourism industry is also assisting tourists to offset their carbon emissions and is working with destinations and entrepreneurs to reduce their carbon footprint. Finally, it is the destinations that are feeling the real impact of climate change as noted above. Destinations can introduce both 'technological' adaptation to climate change (such as snow-making machines in ski resorts), and 'business' adaptation through seeking new markets and diversifying their products.

TOURISM IN CONTEXT

DEMAND

RESOURCES

CLIMATE

TRANSPORT

FUTURES

TOURISM IN CONTEXT

DEMAND

RESOURCES

CLIMATE

TRANSPORT

FUTURES

REFLECTIONS ON THE CASE

This case has demonstrated the significance of climate change for tourism, and the fact that weather events will be increasingly erratic and more severe in the future. Effectively, tourism is affected by climate change through changes to its resource base – such as the receding snowline, rising sea level and also the increased strength of the sun as the ozone layer thins. Tourism is beginning to respond to these challenges in a number of ways, including diversifying activities at beach resorts. Nonetheless, as this case foreshadows, future climate change will require a shift in thinking on the part of both the tourism sector and the tourist.

DISCUSSION POINTS

1. Draft a memo to the manager of a beach resort in southern Europe outlining the potential impacts of climate change for the market and the response that should be taken by the resort.
2. A significant amount of tourism investment is at the coast. Using an atlas, locate the destinations that might be at risk from a rise in sea level projected for 2030.
3. As the manager of a low altitude ski resort in the Australian Alps, what measures would you take to counteract the threat posed by global warming and ensure a profitable resort?
4. Research the phenomenon of 'coral bleaching' and write a briefing note to the Australian Minister for the environment on the impact of coral bleaching on tourism to the Great Barrier Reef.

KEY SOURCES

Becken, S. and Hay, J. (2007) *Tourism and Climate Change*. Channelview, Clevedon.

Giles, A. and Perry, A. (1998) The use of a temporal analogue to investigate the possible impact of projected global warming on the UK tourist industry. *Tourism Management*, 19 (1), 75–80.

Hall, C. M. and Higham, J. (2005) *Tourism, Recreation and Climate Change*. Channelview, Clevedon.

Henson, R. (2002) *The Rough Guide to Weather*. Rough Guides, London.

Pearce, E. A. and Smith, C. G. (1990) *The World Weather Guide*. Hutchinson, London.

Serrese, M. C. and Francis, J. A. (2006) The Arctic on the fast track of change. *Weather*, 61 (3), 65–69.

UN World Tourism Organization (2003) *Climate Change and Tourism*. UNWTO, Madrid.

UN World Tourism Organization (2007) *Climate Change and Tourism: Responding to the Global Challenge*. UNWTO, Madrid.

Viner, D. and Agnew, M. (2000) *The Implications of Climate Change on Tourism Markets and Demand*. Climate Research Unit University of East Anglia, Norwich.

Viner, D. (ed.) (2006) Tourism and its interactions with climate change. *Journal of Sustainable Tourism*, 14(4), 317–415.

WEBSITES

The UNWTO website dealing with climate change: www.unwto.org/climate/index.php
Climate.ngm.com
www.ipcc.ch
www.ukcip.org.uk
www.snw.org.uk/tourism

TOURISM IN CONTEXT

DEMAND

RESOURCES

CLIMATE

TRANSPORT

FUTURES

Damaged bridge and storm clouds building in the Florida Keys.
© istockphoto.com/Derek Warr

CASE 8

The Significance of the El Niño Effect for Tourism

INTRODUCTION

This case analyses the impact of one of the most profound weather effects on the globe.

The El Niño effect dominates the weather pattern of the Pacific, creating severe weather events which have major impacts upon not only tourism but also the societies and economies of nations bordering the Pacific. On completion of this case you will:

1. Understand the weather pattern of the El Niño effect.
2. Be aware of the frequency and significance of El Niño.
3. Recognise that the effect can be monitored and predicted.
4. Understand the range of impacts that El Niño has upon tourism.
5. Recognise that these impacts will depend upon the situation of individual destinations.

TOURISM IN
CONTEXT

DEMAND

RESOURCES

CLIMATE

TRANSPORT

FUTURES

KEY ISSUES

There are four key issues in this case:

1. Climate change is one of the most significant events facing mankind. The El Niño effect is a profoundly significant weather pattern that occurs every few years and has major impacts upon tourism. Global warming is forecast to increase the severity of El Niño.
2. The science of the El Niño effect is well understood and the phenomenon is monitored by arrays of sensors in the ocean. This allows the effect to be modelled and predicted.
3. Tourism around the Pacific Rim is greatly influenced by the El Niño effect due to the severe weather events that El Niño generates – this includes heavy rain, storms and rough seas.
4. The preparedness of destinations has a major influence upon the levels of impact that El Niño can have. Even so, developed nations such as Australia have been severely affected by drought and forest fires caused by El Niño.

THE EL NIÑO EFFECT

Periodically the cold Peruvian or Humboldt Current along the west coast of South America is displaced by a warm current flowing from the Equator. This current is known as El Niño (the Christ Child in Spanish) – because it occurs around Christmas, at intervals of three to seven years. El Niño is characterised by a weakening of the trade winds, a reversal of the surface ocean currents, and a surge of abnormally warm water towards the west coast of South America. The El Niño effect is a graphic reminder of the power of ocean currents when coupled with minor shifts in atmospheric circulation. The El Niño effect not only brings heavy rain to the arid coastal belt of Peru and causes destruction of marine life, but it is also responsible for extreme weather conditions that can influence many parts of the world. The El Niño pattern is one of torrential rain in some parts, drought in others, and severe storms and hurricanes.

An El Niño event is sometimes followed by La Niña ('the little girl'), a period of exceptionally cool sea surface temperatures off South America, which causes a reversal of the previous situation. The severity of El Niño episodes in the 1990s increases the probability that the world can expect more extreme fluctuations in weather conditions and this poses serious problems for resort planners, developers and the tourism industry generally. Both El Niño and La Niña refer to large-scale changes in sea surface temperatures across the central and eastern Pacific. In El Niño conditions, the pool of warm water is located in the eastern and central Pacific and expands into the tropics. In La Niña conditions, the warm water contracts to the west. La Niña produces the opposite effect of the weather pattern of El Niño, often leading to colder weather. El Niño reduces the amount of high cloud in the Caribbean and suppresses hurricane formation, whilst La Niña has the opposite effect.

Although the El Niño phenomenon has been recognised for over three centuries, it was not until 1923 that the effect was fully recorded. It was later realised that El Niño was related to a wider climatic phenomenon in the Southern Hemisphere known as the Southern Oscillation, and the two are therefore known by meteorologists as the El Niño Southern Oscillation (ENSO). However, it took the severity of the 1982/83 event to bring it to the world's attention. This prompted the establishment of a system for monitoring sea temperatures using an array of ocean-borne sensors in an attempt to predict future events. The system monitors the Southern Oscillation Index (SOI), which is an influential weather signature used as the basis for weather forecasts on Australian television. It refers to the air pressure difference between Tahiti and Darwin, Australia. The next El Niño pattern occurred in the late 1990s and the fact that monitoring was in place meant that its impact was reduced.

MONITORING THE EL NIÑO EFFECT

The International Research Centre on El Niño (CIIFEN) has been established to monitor the ENSO and its impacts. The main activities of CIIFEN are to:

1. Generate specific forecasts and tailor assistance according to the needs of the user – such as agriculture, water resources and fisheries.
2. Promote the practical use of climate scenarios in the process of decision-making.
3. Strengthen collaboration between the national meteorological services of the countries of the Pacific region.
4. Strengthen relationships with other scientific fields such as health, sociology and economics.

The SOI is a highly predictable climate signal that allows meteorologists to forecast weather patterns with reasonable accuracy. This allows governments to respond to any predicted major variations in weather patterns, when they have the potential to create major social and economic disruption. The CIIFEN is assisting governments to engineer solutions to El Niño weather patterns, including construction regulations for resorts and making accommodation hurricane-proof. However, a destination's ability to respond to the demands of El Niño engineering will depend upon the levels of investment in tourism and its economic capacity.

THE IMPACTS OF EL NIÑO

The impact of El Niño events can be severe with many lives lost, economic sectors such as fishing devastated, and the spread of disease. For tourism, the severe weather events are highly disruptive not only to existing tourism patterns, but also to the construction of new infrastructure and superstructure. The effects of El Niño are not confined to the Pacific coast of South America, as the weather system characterised by the trade winds is generally stable and spans the entire tropical zone and beyond. The collapse of this system has almost a global impact, affecting

TOURISM IN CONTEXT

DEMAND

RESOURCES

CLIMATE

TRANSPORT

FUTURES

TOURISM IN CONTEXT

DEMAND

RESOURCES

CLIMATE

TRANSPORT

FUTURES

areas as far apart as California, southern Africa, Indonesia, Australia and Polynesia with unseasonal floods, droughts and hurricane-force winds. The following are some specific impacts of El Niño on tourism:

- Heavy rainfall and flooding impact upon both California and Florida's tourism industry, particularly as much of the visitor attraction business (such as theme parks and zoos) and sports tourism such as golf is dependent upon good weather.
- Rainfall and heavy seas disrupt whale-watching activities off the Pacific coast of the USA.
- Severe weather events such as heavy seas, low cloud and heavy rainfall impact upon cruising.
- Heavy rain, mudslides and flooding have destroyed archaeological resources in Peru.
- El Niño creates mild winters in the north east of the USA, reducing demand for tourism to Florida and the Caribbean.
- The El Niño effect impacts upon both the diversity and distribution of wildlife resources of the Galápagos Islands. With warmer sea temperatures fish stocks decline and species that feed from the seas are vulnerable. This can have a disastrous effect on the fishing industry of Peru and Ecuador.
- Increases in sea level brought about by El Niño along the Pacific coast of Latin America cause coastal erosion, destroying tourism structures and reducing demand for beach resorts.
- Flooding and mudslides disrupt transportation infrastructure throughout much of Latin America.
- El Niño caused the drought in Australia, which lasted from 2003 to 2007, impacting on domestic tourism.
- The El Niño of 1997/98 was blamed for the intensity of the forest fires and smog conditions that afflicted South-east Asia.
- Heavy rains combined with warmer temperatures encourage the spread of disease such as malaria and dengue fever.
- In the Pacific, corals, which can only tolerate a small range of sea surface temperature, have been affected by bleaching.
- The 1997/98 El Niño event triggered drought and forest fires in parts of Africa, South-east Asia, the Middle East, Australia and parts of Central and South America.
- The El Niño effect creates heavy seas with strong waves for surfing.
- Increased precipitation creates good snow conditions for winter resorts in north-western USA and Canada.

The level of impact of El Niño does depend upon a number of variables. These include the condition of the country's infrastructure, political and socio-economic conditions such as poverty and conflict, levels of media coverage which can reduce tourism to a destination affected by El Niño, and the level of co-ordination amongst government agencies.

The significance of the El Niño effect means that governments need to have an awareness of the importance of weather and climate information for effective disaster response, and this should include an explicit consideration of El Niño in national disaster planning.

TOURISM IN CONTEXT

DEMAND

RESOURCES

CLIMATE

TRANSPORT

FUTURES

REFLECTIONS ON THE CASE

The El Niño effect is a significant weather phenomenon that has major impacts upon tourism. The El Niño effect occurs every few years and there are concerns that it will become more severe with global warming. Whilst the science is understood and the effect can be predicted with reasonable accuracy, destinations vary in their ability to mitigate the effects of El Niño. The impacts of El Niño include disruption to existing tourism operations, such as theme parks and beach resorts, as well as the construction of future resorts and attractions. What this means in effect is that governments will begin to view severe El Niño effects as natural disasters and plan accordingly.

DISCUSSION POINTS

1. Draft a list of the positive and negative impacts of the El Niño and the La Niña effect upon tourism. In class, rank these by significance.
2. Using statistics from the UNWTO draw up a table of the international tourist arrivals to Pacific Rim countries. Rank the countries by their tourist volume and highlight those that are most vulnerable to the El Niño effect.
3. Draft a memo to the statistics office of a Pacific Rim government highlighting the importance of, and reasons for, the publication of the SOI for government agencies and the general public.
4. How should Pacific Rim governments plan for the El Niño effect in their national disaster strategy?
5. How might a theme park proof itself against regular wet weather caused by El Niño?

KEY SOURCES

Becken, S. and Hay, J. (2007) *Tourism and Climate Change*. Channelview, Clevedon.

Hall, C. M. and Higham, J. (2005) *Tourism, Recreation and Climate Change*. Channelview, Clevedon.

Henson, R. (2002) *The Rough Guide to Weather*. Rough Guides, London.

Pearce, E. A. and Smith, C. G. (1990) *The World Weather Guide*. Hutchinson, London.

Soplee, C. (1999) El Ninō/La Niña: nature's vicious cycle. *National Geographic*, 195 (3), 73–95.

UN World Tourism Organization (2003) *Climate Change and Tourism*. UNWTO, Madrid.

UN World Tourism Organization (2007) *Climate Change and Tourism: Responding to the Global Challenge*. UNWTO, Madrid.

TOURISM IN CONTEXT

DEMAND

RESOURCES

CLIMATE

TRANSPORT

FUTURES

WEBSITES

The UNWTO website dealing with climate change:
www.unwto.org/climate/index.php
The World Meteorological Organization web site dealing with El Niño
www.wmo.ch/pages/publications/meteoworld07/_archive/en/apr2005/wmoactivities.htm

The vast majority of travel at the destination takes place by surface transport, predominantly by car.
© istockphoto.com/P_Wei

Managing Transport at the Tourism Destination

INTRODUCTION

With the high profile given to air travel, it is easy to forget that most international tourist journeys as well as domestic trips are undertaken by surface modes of transport. This case study examines the issues relating to motor vehicles at the destination and the various approaches to transport management. On completion of this case study you will:

1. Understand the benefits of motorised travel for the tourist.
2. Be aware of the problems that motorised transport poses at the destination.
3. Recognise the benefits of managing transport at the destination by creating new facilities and separating tourist traffic from local traffic.
4. Recognise the benefits of park and ride schemes where motor vehicles are separated from the visitor attraction.
5. Understand the success criteria for the various approaches to traffic management.

TOURISM IN CONTEXT

DEMAND

RESOURCES

CLIMATE

TRANSPORT

FUTURES

KEY ISSUES

The five key issues in this case are:

1. Motorised transport is the dominant mode of travel to both domestic and international destinations, as most tourist trips are over short distances.
2. This form of transport causes a range of problems at tourism destinations including safety, intrusion and congestion.
3. By separating out tourist traffic through such management solutions as scenic drives and tourist routes, the trip becomes a valued travel experience in its own right and the transport problems are reduced.
4. By persuading tourists to separate from their vehicles and visit the destination using another form of transport (such as park and ride schemes), the impact on environmentally sensitive areas is reduced.
5. Each of these management approaches is appropriate in particular circumstances and each is associated with a variety of issues and success criteria.

MOTORISED TRANSPORT AT THE DESTINATION

The vast majority of travel at the destination takes place by surface transport, predominantly by car but with coaches/buses playing a significant role. This immediately creates a number of issues and problems for tourism destinations:

- **Safety** The car is more dangerous than other modes of transport, causing an average of a quarter of a million deaths and seven million serious injuries worldwide every year, with young children featuring prominently among the victims. Clearly, unrestricted use of the car is not conducive to safe and secure holiday destinations or attractions.
- **Speed** Holiday driving is on average 10 per cent slower than normal driving and visitors are often uncertain of their route.
- **Facilities** Cars need facilities such as car parks that are often visually intrusive. In coastal resorts, a busy highway along the seafront acts as a barrier separating the tourist accommodation, retailing and other activities from the beach.
- **Visual intrusion** Cars parked en masse are brightly coloured and reflect light, often creating an eyesore adjacent to a natural or historic attraction, or within a resort or historic town.
- **Congestion** Cars cause traffic congestion on the approach routes and at the destination itself.
- **Environmental impact** Cars are a source of pollution in destination areas with their noise and exhaust fumes.

Yet, the reasons that cars are used at the destination are compelling:

- They allow door-to-door flexibility, providing much more privacy than any form of public transport and the freedom to travel at will.

- They are perceived as an inexpensive form of travel, especially for family groups, because running costs and vehicle depreciation are not seen as part of the cost of individual trips.
- They allow unparalleled viewing.
- They can comfortably contain luggage, pets, and recreational equipment as well as people (including the elderly or the handicapped who otherwise may not have access to tourism destinations).
- They can be used to tow caravans, trailer tents or boats.
- They act as a secure base for the tour – whilst picnicking, or enjoying an attraction.

MANAGEMENT SOLUTIONS AT THE DESTINATION

Despite these advantages of the car for the visitor, the impact of the car has become severe at many tourism destinations. As a result transport management measures are now being adopted to solve these problems and balance the needs of local community traffic with those of visitors. Implementation of these measures can be difficult, as motorists are often resistant to restrictions. We seem able to accept restrictions on motoring for business or everyday domestic travel, but are rather less willing to comply when we are 'at leisure'. Even so, our increasing desire for a quality experience at destinations will inevitably lead to the demand that leisure traffic is also 'managed'.

There are two key management approaches:

1. SEPARATE VISITORS FROM THEIR CARS

PARK AND RIDE SCHEMES

These involve the provision of an alternative form of transport for the visitor. Normally, the visitors are invited to park their car and to travel to the attraction by bus, or some other form of transport. Park and ride schemes need a number of conditions to be successful:

- A road configuration that prevents 'short circuiting the system'.
- Local resident and business community support – often such schemes are seen as an infringement of residents' freedom and businesses worry that trade will be lost.
- Effective and visible marketing, publicity, signposting and information.
- Visitors who are prepared to sacrifice their own freedom to travel at will for an enhanced experience at the destination.
- A landscaped yet secure parking area, adjoining weatherproof waiting areas/bus stops.
- A regular shuttle service to the attraction – a key benefit of park and ride schemes is that the numbers of visitors arriving at the attraction can be monitored and controlled.

Park and ride schemes are well suited to destinations such as historic towns and villages where the streets are narrow and access is difficult; natural attractions where the presence of traffic is intrusive; and family-based attractions or

TOURISM IN CONTEXT

DEMAND

RESOURCES

CLIMATE

TRANSPORT

FUTURES

destinations where children's safety needs to be given special consideration. Park and ride is a flexible management option, as it can be used only at peak times if necessary – weekends and busy holiday periods, for example.

PROVISION OF ALTERNATIVE FORMS OF TRANSPORT

The imaginative provision of alternative forms of transport also acts as an effective management tool at the destination to separate visitors from their cars, for example:

- Circular sight-seeing city bus and boat tours with regular 'hop-on-hop-off' stops at key tourist 'sights' as in London and New York, many historic cities and also rural areas such as the UK's Peak District National Park.
- Public transport that meets the needs of the user, as for example at Hadrian's Wall, a heritage attraction of Roman origin in the north of England. Here a bus service calls at key points along the Wall to save visitors from having to make repeat journeys back to their cars.

- Journey planner software to make the public transport system 'legible' at tourist destinations.
- Novelty forms of transport such as cable cars, horse-drawn trams, recreational road trains or steamboats. Monorails are used in some theme parks and exhibition sites but tend to be too intrusive and costly for most attractions.

2. SEPARATE VISITOR TRAFFIC FROM LOCAL TRAFFIC

SCENIC DRIVES

The creation and development of scenic drives allows the separation of touring traffic from local traffic. Given that tourists drive more slowly and are seeking to enjoy the drive, rather than simply to get from A to B as quickly as possible, it is logical to create special linear attractions for the holidaymaker touring by car. These are known as scenic drives and are designed primarily to provide a distinctive driving experience for pleasure travel. They allow the destination manager to control the numbers of vehicles entering the drive and environmental impact can be reduced, as visitors tend to stay within their vehicles.

Scenic drives are often provided with a range of facilities and features:

- Interpretation and information for the visitor
- Frequent stopping places for views, picnics and barbecues
- Landscaped and purpose-designed driving experiences to maximise the impact of the scenery
- Motels, shops and cafes.

Scenic drives are found mainly in North America – the Blue Ridge Parkway is a good example; snaking through Virginia and North Carolina, it is often used in car advertisements. They are much less common in Europe and other parts of the world.

REFLECTIONS ON THE CASE

There is no doubt that motorised transport is the preferred mode of transport to destinations by tourists, simply because of the benefits that it delivers. However, as this case shows, motor vehicles pose a range of management issues for destinations, not least those of safety, intrusion and congestion. This means that if the quality of the experience at the destination is to be maintained, then tourists will have to accept management restrictions on their driving freedom. With imagination on our part, this can be turned into an opportunity to create attractive scenic drives and linear attractions, as well as great travel experiences when the car is left behind.

DISCUSSION POINTS

1. From your own experience make a checklist of the advantages and disadvantages of the car as a form of tourist transport.
2. Devise a class debate on the trade-off *between* (i) the freedom to drive anywhere and thus perhaps spoil some tourism experiences *versus* (ii) the need for our freedom to be curtailed in order to create better experiences at the destination, and perhaps also improve the quality of life for people in the places we visit.
3. In your local area select a transport scheme that has been implemented at a tourism destination or attraction. Assess the benefits and costs of the scheme from a tourism point of view.

TOURISM IN CONTEXT

DEMAND

RESOURCES

CLIMATE

TRANSPORT

FUTURES

TOURISM IN
CONTEXT

DEMAND

RESOURCES

CLIMATE

TRANSPORT

FUTURES

4. A number of park and ride schemes have failed due to objections from local residents. State the case for the advantages or the disadvantages of park and ride schemes for local residents at a destination.
5. Take a popular destination or attraction in your region. Analyse the traffic issues at that destination and draft a report recommending the most appropriate solutions.

KEY SOURCES

Breakell, B. (1999) Moorbus – on the right road. *Countryside Recreation*, 7 (2), 11–14.

Breakell, B. (2006) Activity tourism – developing cycle tourism in the North York Moors and Coast. *Countryside Recreation*, 14 (2), 14–16.

Olwen, E. *et al.* (1999) The Northern Snowdonia Study – an innovative approach to sustainable tourism development. *Countryside Recreation*, 7 (2), 6–10.

Saunders, K. (2003) Linking National Trust Properties to the National Cycle Network. *Countryside Recreation*, 11 (1), 2–5.

WEBSITE

www.sustrans.org

An aeroplane's wing in flight.
© istockphoto.com/Ryan Lane

Low-Cost Carriers: Revolution or Evolution?

INTRODUCTION

Low-cost carriers (LCCs) are one of the most significant developments in air transport in recent years. With their innovative business model they have reduced both the fares and levels of service on routes. At the same time, they have increased the number of people who have access to air travel and greatly increased the range of airports available for holiday travel. Yet the jury is out as to whether LCCs are a true revolutionary concept or simply an evolutionary development in air transport. On completion of this case you will:

1. Understand the history of LCCs.
2. Be aware of the significance of LCCs in transforming patterns of tourism.
3. Recognise the characteristics of the ILCC business model.
4. Understand the difference between LCCs and full service airlines (FSAs).
5. Be aware of a range of issues surrounding the LCC concept.

TOURISM IN CONTEXT

DEMAND

RESOURCES

CLIMATE

TRANSPORT

FUTURES

KEY ISSUES

There are four key issues in this case:

1. Low-cost carriers have emerged alongside deregulation of air space across the world. Deregulation has freed up routes and the fares that can be charged, paving the way for the LCC concept. As a result, the evolution of LCCs reflects the pace of deregulation of airspace across the world.
2. The low-cost carrier concept is dependent upon offering very low fares and a minimal customer service. This is based upon a very different business model compared to FSAs: a business model that depends on significantly paring back operating costs and highly efficient operation and utilisation of aircraft.
3. Despite, their success, LCCs have been criticised on environmental grounds as they have encouraged more people to fly and are responsible for significant growth in the air transport sector.
4. The success of LCCs, and the innovations in doing business have led many FSAs to adopt similar operating models. This has led to a blurring of the distinction between the two types of carrier.

LOW-COST CARRIERS

As air travel continues to expand across the world, there is no doubt that LCCs have fuelled this growth by creating a more competitive environment for air travel. LCCs have been one of the most significant developments in air travel in this century and have completely changed the way that people travel and make choices,

EasyJet is one of Europe's two leading low cost carriers. ©istockphoto.com/Paul Trendell

not just in terms of carriers, but in terms of the mode of transport and where they travel from. Indeed LCCs have transformed the language of airlines as the traditional distinction between scheduled and charter airlines has in effect disappeared, and LCCs have risen to take their place. The British Airports Authority estimates that LCCs flew less than 8 million passengers in 1998 compared to 59 million in 2005 and that in Europe alone the two leading LCCs – EasyJet and Ryanair – account for around one third of capacity. In the future there will be more LCCs on long haul routes and variants on the model are emerging such as 'business only' carriers operating a 'less frills' rather than a 'no frills' service.

THE LOW-COST CARRIER CONCEPT

Low-cost carriers are airlines that work to a business model of low fares and few extra services for the passenger. They are sometimes known as 'no frills' or discount airlines. The concept developed in response to the deregulation of airlines, firstly in the USA in 1971; in Europe in the 1990s; and then in the rest of the world. LCCs have a business model that delivers much lower operating costs and a different debt structure to FSAs (Table 10.1). This is because FSAs trade on their convenience and levels of service to passengers, both of which imply higher operating costs. A range of innovations characterise the LCC business model:

- Paperless ticketing.
- Internet-based bookings.

TABLE 10.1 Comparison of strategies of LCCs and traditional carriers

	FSAs	LCCs
Business model	Global strategy and high cost	Niche strategy and low cost
Network	Hub band spoke Global alliance	Point-to-point Regional airports
Fleet	Different types of aircraft Moderate aircraft utilisation	One type of aircraft High aircraft utilisation
Product	Full service Branding supports full service concept Complex fare structure	Self-service Branding emphasises price Simple fare structure
Sales policy/distribution	Sales departments Global distribution system	Direct sales Internet based
Operations	Traditional check in procedures Multiple classes In-flight service	e-ticketing and self-service check in One class In-flight extras available for purchase

Source: Based on Duval (2007) and Keller (2000)

Sidebar: TOURISM IN CONTEXT · DEMAND · RESOURCES · CLIMATE · TRANSPORT · FUTURES

TOURISM IN CONTEXT

DEMAND

RESOURCES

CLIMATE

TRANSPORT

FUTURES

- Minimising staffing levels and encouraging the multi-skilling of staff, so they can take on a variety of roles in the organisation.
- Using only one type of aircraft to reduce training costs.
- One class for passengers.
- No frequent flier service.
- Earning income from services that are provided free on FSAs – such as catering, headphones and pillows.
- Flights to regional airports that charge lower landing fees and often have spare capacity. This reduces congestion at the busier airports.
- Flying point-to-point without the need to set up a feeder network for their airports.
- Operating a yield management system by selling seats at different prices according to supply and demand. On any one flight there may be many different fares, allowing loss-leading (and headline-grabbing) fares to be charged.

This business model allows LCCs to charge significantly lower prices than the FSAs. In turn, this increases load factors and allows LCCs to make a profit on smaller operating margins. As a result, LCCs pose a significant threat to the FSAs on many routes. In Australia for example, the LCC (Virgin Blue) competes head-to-head with the FSA (Qantas) on intercity routes – such as Sydney/Melbourne – and has significantly lowered fares on these busy routes. In response Qantas has launched its own LCC-Jetstar, but as with other scheduled carriers there is a danger that the LCC takes sales from the FSA. The FSAs have responded in other ways to the threat of the LCCs. They are adopting the low-cost sales model by using the Internet for ticketing, increasingly using paperless tickets and self-check in booths, as well as operating their own yield management systems.

ISSUES ASSOCIATED WITH LOW-COST CARRIERS

Whilst at first sight, LCCs appear to be a very good addition to the airline industry, particularly for the passenger, a range of issues and controversies are associated with LCCs:

- Their business model leaves LCCs vulnerable to significant changes in their operating costs, particularly in terms of fuel prices.
- There are concerns that the growth of LCCs means that they end up by competing with each other on routes. In response they need to differentiate themselves by adding extra services – such as business class seats, reserved seating and catering, in effect reverting to the full service model. Other airlines, such as Ryanair have responded by aggressive cost cutting (e.g. eliminating window blinds and reclining seats) in an attempt to compete on price.
- LCCs tend to quote the fare exclusive of airport fees and other taxes and costs. This has been criticised as misleading.
- A major issue is the fact that the low fares charged by LCCs have allowed many more passengers to fly when otherwise they would have used surface modes of transport. This supports jobs both in the air and on the ground and by opening up travel horizons, enhances the quality of life of consumers. It also is changing

the face of tourism as the old-fashioned charter airlines cannot compete with the LCC model and tourists are encouraged to 'unbundle' their packages with DIY trips using LCCs. LCCs have therefore had a significant impact on the pattern of tourism.

- With flights growing at the rate of 5 per cent per year globally, aircraft are the fastest growing source of carbon emissions. Some therefore argue that the LCC revolution has come at a high environmental cost, not only in terms of emissions, but also noise pollution.

- The perceived environmental pollution caused by aircraft may mean that the deregulation of the skies which has facilitated the development of LCCs will change to a higher degree of regulation through environmental controls. Options here include regulation of emissions through a carbon-trading scheme for LCCs, reduction of carbon emissions through carbon offsetting, and technological solutions such as cleaner engines and the use of bio-fuel. It must however also be remembered that LCCs tend to fly with full aircraft, and as their aircraft tend to be newer, quiet and fuel efficient, the environmental costs are reduced to some extent.

- LCCs take advantage of regional airports where costs are lower and this has increased the number of destinations available. For example, it has made it easier for the British to make frequent trips to their second homes in rural France, and to take advantage of cheap city breaks in a number of East European countries. However, this opens up tourism in regions that are not always prepared in the early years of the LCC service. This can lead to unregulated accommodation development, often of low quality, and poor destination management on the part of ill-prepared local authorities.

In summary, the Civil Aviation Authority (2006) argues that whilst the media thinks of LCCs as a revolution in travel, in fact they may simply be an evolution. There has been no technological breakthrough; rather the revolution is in terms of the business approach. Equally, FSAs are now adopting many of the business ideas of the LCCs and so we are seeing a 'convergence' of what were two very different types of carriers.

REFLECTIONS ON THE CASE

There is no doubt that LCCs have been one of the most significant developments in air transport in this century and they have had a major impact upon tourism demand and patterns of travel. Their innovative business model is now being adopted by FSAs, blurring the distinction between various types of carrier. This case has shown however, that LCCs have created a range of issues, not least their environmental impacts and consequences. It remains to be seen how sustainable the concept is in an era of high fuel prices, and also how the concept will evolve as LCCs begin to offer variants on the model, such as business airlines and long haul routes.

TOURISM IN CONTEXT

DEMAND

RESOURCES

CLIMATE

TRANSPORT

FUTURES

TOURISM IN
CONTEXT

DEMAND

RESOURCES

CLIMATE

TRANSPORT

FUTURES

DISCUSSION POINTS

1. In class, debate the 'evolution' or 'revolution' point about LCCs.
2. Choose a destination or resort of your choice that is served by a LCC. What has been the impact of the LCC service on the market for the destination and has the destination itself changed as a result of the LCC service?
3. Draw up a table listing the positive and negative sides of the environmental debate surrounding LCCs.
4. Taking a region of your choice, investigate how LCCs have changed the travel choices of tourists in that region.
5. Draw up a list of the key elements of the business model of LCCs. Rank the list in order of significance and annotate the table with the elements of the business model that have been adopted by FSAs.

KEY SOURCES

British Airports Authority (2006) *Issue Brief Low-Cost Airlines*. BAA, London.

Civil Aviation Authority (2006) *No Frills Carriers: Revolution or Evolution*. CAA, London.

De Groote, P. (2005) *The Success Story of Low-Cost Carriers in a Changing Air world*. GaWC Research Bulletin 174.

Doganis, R. (2001) *The Airline Business in the 21st Century*. Routledge, London.

Duval, D. T. (2007) *Tourism and Transport. Models, Networks and Flows*. Channelview, Clevedon.

Gross, S. and Schroeder, A. (2007) *Handbook of Low Cost Airlines – Strategies, Business Processes and Market Environment*. Kluwer, Berlin.

Keller, P. (2002) Introduction, in *Air Transport and Tourism*, Vol. 44. AIEST, St. Gallen, pp. 13–23.

WEBSITES

http://www.virgin-express.com/
http://www.easyjet.com/en/book/index.asp
http://europa.eu.int/comm/environment/climat/aviation_en.htm
http://www.dft.gov.uk/stellent/groups/dft_aviation/documents/page/dft_aviation_031516.pdf
http://www.ryanair.com/site/EN/
www.southwest.com/about_swa/airborne.html

Launch of the Space Shuttle Atlantis (STS-122)
© istockphoto.com/Serdar Uckun

Space: The Final Tourism Frontier?

INTRODUCTION

This case study analyses the future activity of space tourism by referring to Leiper's (1979) tourism system and the tourist area life cycle. On completion of the case you will:

1. Be aware of the history of space tourism as an idea.
2. Understand the barriers to space tourism.
3. Be aware of the various stages of the life cycle of space tourism.
4. Be able to identify the various components of the space tourism system.
5. Have an awareness of the future of space tourism.

TOURISM IN CONTEXT

DEMAND

RESOURCES

CLIMATE

TRANSPORT

FUTURES

KEY ISSUES

There are five key issues in this case:

1. Space tourism has long been the goal of many individuals and corporations, but the practicalities of sending tourists into space are difficult.
2. Space tourism can mean many different things, including Earth-based space tourism attractions as well as actually travelling into space.
3. The barriers to space tourism are significant and include both the cost and the safety aspects of space travel.
4. There is no doubt that space tourism will become a reality in the future when technological and cost barriers have been reduced.
5. The future of space tourism is assured with not only low orbit activity but also visits to the Moon and possibly Mars.

SPACE TOURISM

We can define space tourism as:

> The taking of short pleasure trips in low earth orbit by members of the public
> (Collins and Ashford, 1998).

'Space' begins at an altitude of 100 kilometres, where air density ceases to have any effect on the movement of aircraft and the stars are always visible in the black sky. On a sub-orbital flight to just above this altitude in *near space* you would experience a few minutes of weightlessness before your craft re-entered the atmosphere at 'Mach 5' (five times the speed of sound).

Space travel emerged from the realms of science fiction with the unmanned Russian Sputnik launch in 1957, followed by the first cosmonaut flight in 1961 and the success of NASA's Apollo missions in landing 12 American astronauts on the Moon between 1969 and 1972. However the 'space race' was inspired by the Cold War rivalry between the two superpowers, and the momentum for further exploration was not maintained. Popular interest in space travel also received a severe setback in 1986 with the *Challenger* disaster, in which Christa McAuliffe, a school teacher, died along with the crew of the space shuttle. The space race – this time for tourism – was boosted after 1996 by the 'X prize' – a US$10 million award by an American foundation to the first entrepreneur to build a craft that can carry three passengers into space, return them safely and make another voyage within two weeks. This was achieved in 2004 with the prototype *SpaceShipOne*, but the first space tourist, the Californian multi-millionaire Dennis Tito, actually appeared on the scene in May 2001, as a paying passenger (to the tune of US$20 million) on a Russian mission to the International Space Station. There is now the very real possibility of space tourism subsidising the costs of space exploration. In 2004, the US House of Representatives passed the first bill to regulate commercial space flights. According to the Space Tourism Society, we are seeing an emerging type of tourism that not only includes sub-orbital and orbital voyages in near space, but also related activities here on Earth, such as simulated space experiences (e.g. Disney's ride SPACE, simulating a mission to Mars), and tours of space research centres. The goal of the Space Tourism Society is:

> To conduct the research, build public desire, and acquire the financial and political power to make space tourism available to as many people as possible as soon as possible.

But if space tourism has attracted so much attention – and is technically feasible – why has it taken so long to be realised? We can identify a number of key reasons for this:

- **Cost and investment** Space tourism is prohibitively expensive, because of the high cost of launches and the fact that space vehicles are not yet truly 're-usable'. Powering a spacecraft requires vast amounts of heavy fuel. To date, space programmes have relied on ballistic missile technology to launch or service satellites and space stations. This is both costly and wasteful, as the launch rockets are destroyed each time they are used, while NASA's space shuttles have to jettison their fuel tanks during each launch. The development of rocket-propelled *spaceplanes* as re-usable launch vehicles (RLVs) would greatly reduce costs, with a turnaround of a few days between landing and re-launch. Even so they would need significant demand to make them profitable. This is where the private sector would provide the marketing expertise, with access to venture capital for investment in spaceplane development. However, entrepreneurs would also need the co-operation of government space agencies, who generally have shown little interest in space tourism.
- **Health and safety issues** Between 1961 and 2007 only 460 people had visited space, and all of these were handpicked, with a standard of health and fitness far above the average. Incidents such as the *Columbia* shuttle disaster in 2002 mean that safety will continue to be a real issue for space tourism, in terms of consumer perceptions, and the willingness of insurance companies to become involved. Spaceplanes would be a much lower risk than the existing shuttles; these have had a fatal accident rate 10 000 times higher than commercial airliners (Ashford, 2003, p. 89). Health issues in space also act as a constraint, as does the noise associated with the launch. Space exploration results in a number of changes to the human body due to zero gravity such as a loss in bone density. Astronauts adapt quickly to weightlessness, but exposure to solar and cosmic radiation is a more insidious problem. None of these would constitute a health risk to tourists, as distinct from crew members, on a sub-orbital flight lasting a few hours, but the situation might well be different for those staying at a 'space hotel' or undertaking longer orbital flights, let alone interplanetary voyages in deep space.

THE LIFE CYCLE OF SPACE TOURISM

We can broadly envisage the life cycle of space tourism as four phases of development:

- **Pioneer phase** Here the price per trip ranges from US$100 000 to US$20 million, but even so the market is currently estimated to be 10 000 a year in the

TOURISM IN CONTEXT

RESOURCES

CLIMATE

TRANSPORT

FUTURES

USA alone, and many of these prospective travellers have already paid thousands of dollars as a deposit for their first adventure in space. Elaborate facilities will not be required or developed in this phase, and wealthy tourists ride in spare seats on existing space missions, so that accommodation would be spartan rather than 'de luxe'.

- **Exclusive phase** By now the price has fallen to US$10 000–US$100 000 per trip, attracting a wider market. The trips will be available on a regular basis, with greater levels of comfort and attention to issues such as the quality of the experience. Facilities will be more extensive and accommodation could be in clusters of pre-fabricated modules.
- **Mature phase** The price has fallen to US$2000–US$10 000, with significant growth in the market, fuelled by competition between the various suppliers. Facilities would be available on a large scale with accommodation constructed in orbit for hundreds of guests.
- **Mass market phase** This phase is reached when sub-orbital space trips become the equivalent of the air inclusive tour of the late twentieth century, with tens of millions of passengers every year. We can then expect segmentation of the market to cater for different interest groups.

THE COMPONENTS OF A MATURE SPACE TOURISM SYSTEM

Using Leiper's tourism system, we can analyse space tourism in terms of the generating region, the destination region and the transit zone.

THE GENERATING REGION FOR SPACE TOURISM

The actual volume of demand for space tourism will depend upon price, the length of stay in space, and the associated facilities. Also, medical advances, such as drugs to combat motion sickness, would make the flight more appealing. On Earth, demand will be stimulated by the development of spaceports in locations as diverse as Singapore, the United Arab Emirates, New Mexico and Kazakhstan, and space tourism centres – such as Florida's 'Space Coast' – where prospective tourists can experience simulated space flights. We can expect an increasing number of developing countries, now in the forefront of space research, such as Brazil, China and India, to join the USA, the EU and Japan as the leading generators of space tourism. In the generating region, there are currently two leading suppliers of space tourism. Spaceadventures was the first to enter the market providing a range of exclusive experiences. Virgingalactic was a later entry to the market basing its product on the development of commercial space-vessels launched from New Mexico.

THE DESTINATION REGION FOR SPACE TOURISM

Accommodation may be expected to grow from orbiting hotels for a few hundred guests, to orbiting resort-theme parks with accommodation for thousands of guests. On offer is the experience of a lifetime, including:

- Viewing 'Spaceship Earth' or the 'Blue Planet', with a constantly changing panorama.
- Astronomy – viewing the stars with a clarity not experienced anywhere on Earth.
- Recreation activities designed to make use of micro-gravity, such as swimming, diving, gymnastics, new forms of dance, unassisted human flight and new types of ball games.
- Weddings and honeymoons – expected to develop into one of the strongest market segments.
- Space walks 'on the outside' (wearing a pressure suit).
- Simulated exotic worlds using hydroponics to grow low-gravity plants, possibly as an experiment in '*terraforming*' – with the eventual aim of making Mars habitable for life on Earth.

THE TRANSIT ZONE

By the mature phase of space tourism, transportation will involve *shuttle ferries* to take passengers to their orbiting hotel/resort, as well as cargo vehicles for launching the accommodation modules. By this stage, the ferries will operate like airlines with substantial numbers of craft. The flight experience will be designed to provide moderate acceleration during boost and re-entry, and the ferries would have the capability to operate from conventional airports.

MARS: THE NEXT FRONTIER?

According to the UNWTO, tourism in near space (defined as anywhere closer than the Moon) should be almost commonplace by 2020. Travel in outer space on the other hand will probably not be feasible for at least another generation. A spaceship would take nine months to reach Mars, plus a stay of at least a year on the 'red planet', waiting for orbital alignment with the Earth, before the return voyage could take place. Nevertheless, there will inevitably be a demand for voyages beyond low orbit from the adventurous, 'elite' type of tourist, and this will provide the impetus for a technological breakthrough in space travel. Robot 'landers' will provide a great deal of information about Mars – its immense volcanoes and other landscape features, some Earth-like, others completely alien – but only a human visitor can communicate the *experience* of actually being there.

REFLECTIONS ON THE CASE

Space tourism has long been the dream of many, but the significant technological, cost and safety barriers have meant that currently it is a reality for only a handful of millionaires. However, as this case shows, by taking a longer look into the future and applying the life-cycle concept, space tourism will be a reality at some point in the future once these barriers have been overcome.

TOURISM IN CONTEXT

DEMAND

RESOURCES

CLIMATE

TRANSPORT

FUTURES

TOURISM IN CONTEXT

DEMAND

RESOURCES

CLIMATE

TRANSPORT

FUTURES

DISCUSSION POINTS

1. Draft a timeline of the events associated with the history of space travel using the Internet and other sources. Extrapolate events on the timeline into the future using the life-cycle concept.
2. Draw up a brochure for a short, low orbit space tourism product. Focus your product *either* on the whole experience from Earth to space and back; *or* on the space experience element of the product at the destination.
3. Visit the websites of the two providers of space tourism (www.spaceadventures.com and www.virginglactic.com). Compare the positioning of the products of the two companies.
4. Draw up a market segmentation for space tourists in the mature stage of the space tourism life cycle.
5. Debate in class the UNWTO's assertion that space tourism will be commonplace by 2020.

KEY SOURCES

Ashford, D. (2003) *Spaceflight Revolution*. Imperial College Press, London.

Collins, P. and Ashford, D. (1998) Space tourism. *Ada Astronautica*, 17 (4), 421–431.

Crouch, G. (2001) The market for space tourism: early indications. *Journal of Travel Research*, 40 (2), 213–219.

Leiper, N. (1979) The framework of tourism. *Annals of Tourism Research*, 6 (4), 390–407.

Monbiot, G. (2000) Space tourism: burning up the planet. *Contours*, 10 (3), 17–18.

Newberry, B. (1997) The ultimate room with a view. *Geographical*, 69 (10), 9–14.

Smith, V. L. (2000) Space tourism: the 21st century "Frontier". *Tourism Recreation Research*, 25 (3), 5–15.

WEBSITES

www.spacetourismsociety.org
www.xprize.org
www.spaceadventures.com
www.virgingalactic.com

Stunning Rice Terrace Landscape in highlands near Sapa attracts tourists to Vietnam, one of the world's poorest countries.
© istockphoto.com/Ashley Whitworth

Tourism as Agent of Poverty Alleviation

INTRODUCTION

Poverty has become one of the world's major challenges. This case study outlines recent attempts to use tourism as one means of alleviating poverty. On completion of the case you will:

1. Understand the definition of poverty.
2. Recognise the benefits that tourism can bring to alleviating poverty.
3. Understand the various strategies that can be used by tourism to alleviate poverty.
4. Be aware of some of the difficulties in implementing these strategies.
5. Be aware of some of the scepticism surrounding the use of tourism as an agent of poverty alleviation.

TOURISM IN CONTEXT

DEMAND

RESOURCES

CLIMATE

TRANSPORT

FUTURES

KEY ISSUES

There are five key issues in this case:

1. Poverty can be defined in a number of different ways, but international agencies recognise that, however defined, it is important to address poverty.
2. The nature of tourism as an activity means that it lends itself well to being used as an agent of poverty alleviation. It is for example labour intensive and requires little in the way of skills;
3. There is a variety of strategies that can be adopted for pro-poor tourism (PPT). These include boosting local employment, incomes, lifestyle and involvement.
4. A number of issues affect the success of PPT strategies including identifying beneficiaries and the distribution of benefits, ownership of the activity and the area's access to tourism resources.
5. There are a number of significant barriers to the successful adoption of PPT.

POVERTY

Poverty has become one of the world's major challenges and defeating it is the first of the UN's Millennium Development Goals – to 'eradicate extreme poverty and hunger'. The World Bank's definition of poverty is anyone living on less than one US dollar per day. We are clearly not talking here about *relative poverty* as experienced by many people in the West, meaning insufficient income to afford a holiday or consumer goods, but the inability to meet more basic needs. However, poverty is much more than just an economic condition; other ways of thinking about the problem include issues of living conditions, access to resources and intangibles such as pride and self esteem. One of the conclusions of the World Summit on Sustainable Development held in Johannesburg in 2002 was the recognition that tourism could make a real contribution to poverty reduction. Yet surprisingly, the role of tourism in poverty alleviation is a recent initiative. In the past, economic, regional and environmental issues dominated thinking on tourism development. However, the Johannesburg agenda is emerging as a central issue for tourism in the future – the role of tourism development as a means of reducing world poverty.

PRO-POOR TOURISM

Sometimes called PPT, this new agenda has been enthusiastically embraced by the developing world and international agencies (including the UNWTO, UNCTAD and the World Bank). The UNWTO for example has developed a programme 'sustainable tourism – eliminating poverty' (ST-EP).

PPT is an approach, not a product or a type of tourism – a good definition is 'tourism that results in increased net benefits for poor people'. The critical issue

TABLE 12.1	Relative importance of tourism compared to exports of goods in 2000			
	OECD countries	**European union**	**Developing countries**	**Least developed countries (LDCs)**
Tourism receipts as percentage of export earnings	8.0	7.5	8.5	11.3

is 'how can tourism reduce poverty at the local level, and therefore what policies, strategies and plans can be put into place to enhance poverty alleviation?' As yet there is little real experience of operating PPT – or evaluating its success – and the answers to these questions represent a steep learning curve for aid agencies and destinations alike.

Tourism has many advantages as a sector for pro-poor development:

- Tourism is produced where it is consumed – the tourist has to visit the destination allowing opportunities for economic gain.
- Tourism is labour intensive and employs a high percentage of women.
- Tourism is naturally attracted to remote, peripheral areas where other economic options are limited.
- Tourism is one of the few development opportunities for the poor.
- Tourism is significant and growing in the developing and least-developed countries (LDCs), such as most of the 12 countries that are home to 80 per cent of the world's poorest people (see Table 12.1). These include China, Vietnam, Laos, Cambodia, Myanmar and a number of Pacific islands. (On the other hand many of the LDCs in Africa have failed to develop a significant tourism sector so far.)

STRATEGIES FOR PPT

We can classify pro-poor strategies into three types:

- Delivering economic benefits such as:
  - Creating jobs allowing a measure of security in household income.
  - Providing opportunities for small businesses both directly and indirectly supplying tourists with goods such as handicrafts and food.
  - Development of local co-operatives.
  - Increasing the economic benefits for the whole community – by renting communal land for camping, for example.
- Delivering improved living conditions:
  - Training and education, reducing environmental impacts of tourism, reducing competition for natural resources, and improved access to services such as schooling, health care, communications and infrastructure improvements.
- Delivering participation and involvement benefits:
  - Changing the policy and planning framework to allow participation by local communities, increasing participation in decision-making and developing partnerships with the private sector.

TOURISM IN CONTEXT

RESOURCES

CLIMATE

TRANSPORT

FUTURES

TOURISM IN
CONTEXT

DEMAND

RESOURCES

CLIMATE

TRANSPORT

FUTURES

Delivery of PPT will depend upon both the destination itself, as poverty varies by location, and the types of strategic objectives taken from the above list:

- Destination-based strategies work well for poverty alleviation in particular groups, encouraging economic linkages between say, tourism businesses and local farmers to reduce leakage through imports, boosting partnerships, developing local enterprises and increasing community pride.
- National policy-based strategies are preferred for objectives such as changing systems of land tenure, improving planning procedures, training and education and infrastructure development.

Successful implementation of these strategies will depend upon some key principles recognising:

1. The imperative of local ownership and control.
2. That tourism is a system demanding access to transport, accommodation and the wider range of support services and products.
3. That the principles of PPT are the same everywhere, but that their implementation will vary according to the type of tourism product from say, small scale eco-tourism to mass tourism.
4. The need to develop partnerships with the private sector on an equitable footing;
5. The reality that not all the poor will benefit equally.
6. The focus must be on delivering benefits, not just cutting costs.

However, there are barriers to the implementation of PPT strategies. These include:

- A perception by aid agencies that tourism is for the wealthy.
- Significant economic leakages out of the local community to buy imported goods for tourist consumption, thus reducing the net benefits of tourism.
- Lack of education, training and understanding about PPT.
- Lack of investment and low interest loans to allow local tourism enterprises to get under way.
- Lack of infrastructure and basic services in very poor areas.

But despite these barriers, the idea of PPT is gaining momentum and should be central to the agenda of tourism development in the future.

REFLECTIONS ON THE CASE

There is no doubt that poverty is one of the world's major challenges. Recent international initiatives have shown that tourism can play an important role in alleviating poverty. This is known as PPT and well-tried strategies now exist to use tourism in this way. However, despite the optimism surrounding the idea of PPT, there are a number of barriers that will have to be overcome, if tourism is to become an effective agent of poverty reduction.

DISCUSSION POINTS

1. Using the Internet and other media sources, identify a tourism project that is designed to alleviate poverty. Identify the type of pro-poor strategy that is being used and draft a list of possible issues that may affect the success of the project.
2. Design a brochure for a tourism experience that contains a significant pro-poor element. Think carefully about how you should transmit the benefits of the tour. Web sites from organisations such as OXFAM may help here.
3. Draft a code of conduct for a tour operator to give to their clients visiting poverty-stricken countries. The code should identify appropriate forms of behaviour and strategies for ensuring that the tourists' expenditure and activity benefits the poorer people in the community.
4. Utilising United Nations sources identify the countries with the most severe poverty problems on a world map. From your knowledge of tourism generating and destination countries in the world (the UNWTO web site will help here), how much hope is there that the two maps may one day look similar?
5. Draft a report to the sceptical head of a large charity justifying why you feel tourism could play a role in the charity's key objective of reducing poverty in Africa.

KEY SOURCES

Ashley, C., Boyd, C. and Goodwin, H. (2000) Pro-poor tourism: putting poverty at the heart of the tourism agenda. *Natural Resource Perspectives*, 51 (March), 1–12.

UN World Tourism Organization (2002) *Sustainable Tourism-Eliminating Poverty*. UNWTO, Madrid.

UN World Tourism Organization (2004) *Tourism and Poverty Alleviation: Recommendations for Action*. UNWTO, Madrid.

UN World Tourism Organization (2006) *Poverty Alleviation though Tourism: A Compendium of Good Practices*. UNWTO, Madrid.

WEBSITES

http://www.adb.org/Documents/Policies/Poverty_Reducation/default.asp
http://www.propoortourism.org.uk
http://www.worldbank.org/poverty
http://www.world-tourism.org

TOURISM IN CONTEXT

DEMAND

RESOURCES

CLIMATE

TRANSPORT

FUTURES

PART 3

Cases Illustrating Regional Travel and Tourism Geography

Flags in front of the European Parliament building in Brussels.
© istockphoto.com/Franky De Meyer

European Policy and Tourism

INTRODUCTION

The European Union (EU) is one of the few regions in the world to have attempted to devise a policy for tourism which is truly international in its scope. This case study traces the history of the policy and examines the issues surrounding tourism in Europe. On completion of the case you will:

1. Be aware of the role and importance of tourism in the EU.
2. Understand the background to the formation of the European Community.
3. Understand the role of various European institutions managing tourism in the EU.
4. Be aware of the tourism policy initiatives in the EU.
5. Recognise the influence of other areas of EU policy in tourism matters.

TOURISM IN CONTEXT

DEMAND

RESOURCES

CLIMATE

TRANSPORT

FUTURES

KEY ISSUES

There are five key issues in this case:

1. Europe remains the world's most significant tourism region.
2. The EU is a union of sovereign states and is unusual in having a tourism policy that covers all states.
3. Tourism has few statutory rights under the EU constitution.
4. Most issues that affect tourism are dealt with by other areas of policy such as transport or regional development.
5. Tourism has a chequered history regarding policies in the EU.

TOURISM IN EUROPE

Europe is a region of immense economic, social and cultural diversity. In part this diversity explains why Europe continues to be a crucible of conflict, with two world wars in the twentieth century, which ended with a civil war in the Balkan region. Europe is also under economic pressures from both North America and the newly industrialising countries of South East Asia. Here, Europe's failure to perform as a region is brought into clear focus when shares of international tourism are examined:

- In 1960 Europe accounted for 72 per cent of international tourism arrivals.
- By 2005 this share had fallen to 55 per cent.
- By 2010 the share is forecast to be 50 per cent.

Nonetheless, Europe continues to dominate world tourism. This is despite the fact that Europe accounts for less than 10 per cent of the world's population and an even smaller share of its total land area. In 2005 it received over 440 million of the world's 806 million international tourist arrivals, and accounted for over 50 per cent of the world's receipts from international tourism. The strong economies in the region account for most of the world's top tourist generating countries, dominating the outbound flow of international travel, and are also estimated to generate massive demand for domestic trips.

Europe is pre-eminent in the world's tourism system for the following reasons:

- Most of the region's economies are in the high mass-consumption stage, or in the drive to maturity. The population, though ageing, is in general affluent, mobile and has a high propensity to travel.
- Europe consists of a rich mosaic of languages, cultural resources and tourist attractions of world calibre.
- The adoption of the single European currency, the euro, in many European countries in 2002 has facilitated tourism.

- Europe comprises many relatively small countries in close proximity, encouraging a high volume of short international trips.
- The region's climatic differences are significant, leading since the 1950s to a considerable flow of sun-seeking tourists from northern Europe to the south.
- Europe's tourism infrastructure is mature and of a high standard.
- The tourism sector throughout most of the region is highly developed, and standards of service – though not the best in the world – are good.
- Most European governments have well-funded, competent tourist authorities with marketing and development powers.

BACKGROUND TO THE POLICY

The impetus for a united Europe emerged from the devastation of the Second World War. The idea of a customs union for coal and steel dates back to 1951 and led to the European Coal and Steel Community (ECSC). The ECSC was successful and as more countries joined it broadened to other sectors of the economy. This led to the signing of the Treaty of Rome in 1957 as the basis of all European legislation; however, tourism was not included as a policy area in the original Treaty. The Treaty of Rome founded the European Economic Community which became the present EU and in the ensuing decades the number of members grew from the original 6 signatories to 15 in 1994. By the mid-1980s impetus for a Single European Market led to the Single European Act that aimed to abolish the following barriers to movement in Europe by the end of 1992:

1. Physical barriers.
2. Technical barriers.
3. Fiscal barriers.

The Single European Market operates within a framework of European organisations and decision-taking bodies, each of which has a role in tourism:

- **The European Commission** Based in Brussels, the Commission was created to implement the Treaty of Rome and is effectively the 'civil service' of Europe. Its remit is to provide the *European* dimension by initiating, implementing and policing EU legislation. It is made up of a series of departments or Directorates. Tourism is in the Enterprise Directorate.
- **The European Parliament** The Parliament is based in Brussels and Strasbourg. It is an elected body and debates and amends European legislation. The Parliament has traditionally been supportive of tourism initiatives at Community level.
- **The Council of Ministers** The Council makes decisions about European legislation, once it has been initiated by the Commission and debated by Parliament. The Council acts as a counterbalance to the unifying role of the Commission by representing the *national* interest of member countries. Statements by the Council relating to tourism have triggered significant policy initiatives.
- **The European Court of Justice** The European Court is based in The Hague with the remit to interpret the Treaty of Rome and make judgements. The Court would make judgements over any dispute concerning tourism policy or related policy as it impacts upon tourism.

- **European Investment Bank (EIB)**   The EIB provides long-term loans and supports regional development in the EU. Tourism projects benefit from regional development schemes.
- **Committee of the Regions**   The Committee comprises representatives of regions and cities across the EU, and is an increasingly important forum for tourism initiatives.
- **The Economic and Social Committee**   This advisory committee is focussed on social and employment issues – both critical areas for tourism.

In the early years of the twenty-first century the impetus for a united Europe has spread to countries of the former Eastern bloc and those on the fringes of Europe such as Malta, Turkey and Cyprus. There is evidence that entry of these countries may re-focus the distribution of regional funds away from the original members of the EU.

THE IMPLICATIONS OF EUROPEAN POLICIES FOR TOURISM

The legislation and initiatives that have created the Single European Market have had a number of implications for tourism. These can be considered in terms of:

1. Tourism policy – which is a minor element of the Community's business and budget.
2. Other policy areas – such as transport and regional development – which have considerable influence and budgets.

TOURISM POLICY IN THE EUROPEAN UNION

The fact that Europe has a supra-national tourism policy that relates to all member states is unusual if we compare it to other geographical regions of the world. It reflects the importance of tourism in the EU, estimated to directly generate over 8 million jobs and account for at least 5 per cent of gross domestic product. However, the tourism policy for Europe is relatively recent and has undergone a number of changes over time; indeed it has been criticised as being piecemeal and ad hoc. Equally, the policy has had much less impact upon the tourism sector than some of the other policies we later outline in this case. This is partly because, at European level, there is no legal authority to act in the tourism field, and the view has been that the 'subsidiarity' principle operates – that is, tourism is a matter for member states and not for Europe as a whole.

Significant events in the development of a tourism policy for Europe include:

- **1980**   Establishment of a *Tourism Commissioner*.
- **1982**   *Initial Guidelines on a Community Policy for Tourism* stressing: the need for freedom of movement; the importance of social tourism; improving working conditions in the tourism sector; the problem of seasonality; regional development; and the importance of cultural tourism.

- **1984** European Court judgement that the EU could intervene in tourism matters under the principle of free movement of persons, services and capital. The Council of Ministers emphasised the need for tourism to be given greater consideration in the Community.
- **1986** *Community Action in the Field of Tourism* was published, setting out the Commission's objectives in tourism as: freedom of movement; addressing temporal and spatial imbalances; providing information and protection for tourists; improving working conditions; and improving tourism statistics. This document firmly established tourism as an element of Community policy and saw an increase in the tourism budget.
- **1988** Proposal for the *European Year of Tourism* to be held in order to stress preparations for the 1992 initiative; this would promote tourism generally, but with an emphasis on different cultures and lifestyles, and a more even distribution of tourism, both seasonally and by region.
- **1989** *Directorate General XXIII (DG XX111)* of the Commission was established to implement the European Year of Tourism. Also the Council of Ministers made a statement on the direction that tourism should take in the Community, emphasising the following:
  - The subsidiarity rule for tourism.
  - Co-operation between member states on tourism strategy.
  - A Community tourism policy benefiting the individual traveller and tourism enterprises.
  - The need for a better distribution of tourism.
  - The need to invest in human resources in tourism.
  - The setting up of a statistical action plan for tourism.
  - The need to co-ordinate Community policies in terms of infrastructure for tourism.
- **1990** *European Year of Tourism* – not an unqualified success.
- **1991** *The Community Action Plan to Assist Tourism* was published based on the Council of Ministers' statement in 1989. The plan ran from 1993 to 1995 aiming to: improve tourism statistics; stagger holidays; encourage co-operation between members; consumer protection; cultural tourism; tourism and the environment; rural tourism; social tourism; youth training; and promotion of Europe as a destination.
- **1995** A Green Paper was published on *The Role of the Union in the Field of Tourism*. This advisory document laid out four options for future EC involvement in tourism ranging from effectively doing nothing and leaving tourism to member states (option 1), to a full treatment of tourism at Community level (option 4).
- **1996** *The First Multiannual Programme to Assist European Tourism* – *Philoxenia* (Greek word meaning 'hospitality towards visitors') was proposed by the Commission as a new programme to ensure continuity of action in tourism. This also addressed issues such as the impact of tourism, competitiveness and quality.
- **1997** The European Parliament voted for option 4 in the 1995 Green Paper, effectively creating a new tourism role for the European Commission working together with member states. This implies that the Treaty of Rome would need to be revised to include a 'tourism competence'. This year also saw the publication of the first in a series of European Commission reports on employment in tourism – *Employment in Tourism – Guidelines for Action*.

TOURISM IN CONTEXT

DEMAND

RESOURCES

CLIMATE

TRANSPORT

FUTURES

TOURISM IN CONTEXT

DEMAND

RESOURCES

CLIMATE

TRANSPORT

FUTURES

- **1999** was a significant year for tourism in the EU. Firstly it saw the introduction of the 'euro' as the EU's currency with major implications for tourism. Secondly, for the first time, the Council of Ministers failed to support tourism and rejected Philoxenia – the European programme to assist tourism. As a result the policy focus shifted towards tourism as an employment generator with the publication of the European Commission's document *Enhancing Tourism's Potential for Employment*.
- **2001** Establishment of DG XX111 working groups to examine the future of tourism in Europe. These informed the Commission's policy paper on *Working Together for the Future of European Tourism*. This document stressed the need for partnerships and co-operation in the tourism sector and for the sustainability and competitiveness of European tourism.
- **2002** Adoption of Council of Minister's decision to support *Working Together for the Future of European Tourism*, the closer monitoring of the impact of EU policy on tourism, and examination of the promotion of Europe as a destination.
- **2005** Moves began to renew the EU's tourism policy to respond to contemporary challenges including an ageing society, competitiveness and sustainability.
- **2006** Publication of the policy document *Renewed EU Tourism Policy: Towards a Stronger Partnership for European Tourism*. The main aim of this policy is to improve the competitiveness of the European tourism industry and create more and better jobs through the sustainable growth of tourism in Europe and in the world as a whole.

RELATED POLICY ISSUES THAT AFFECT TOURISM

REMOVAL OF PHYSICAL BARRIERS

- **Legislation** Legislation to remove barriers to travel and the free movement of goods and services allows for the free movement of travellers between member states and implies the abolition of border controls and customs within the EU.
- **Transport policy** Transport policy has had a major effect upon tourism in two ways:
  - Firstly, through the creation of free movement by enhancing surface travel 'through routes' across Europe.
  - Secondly through the deregulation of transport. The major development here has been the three-stage deregulation of European air transport, with the effect of enhancing the role of regional airports, supporting budget and smaller airlines and changing the patterns of air travel across Europe.

REMOVAL OF TECHNICAL BARRIERS

- **Regional development** The different types of structural funds are designed to remove regional disparities across Europe. Tourism is a major beneficiary through the encouragement of small enterprises, the regeneration of rural, urban and declining industrial areas and through job creation.
- **Environmental legislation** A range of environmental initiatives have influenced tourism, in particular directives on water quality, environmental impact and auditing legislation and benchmarking exercises such as the 'Blue Flag' beach scheme.

- **Social legislation** Here tourism is affected through the provisions to enhance the working conditions of part-time and temporary workers and the mutual recognition of qualifications across member states. This will encourage labour mobility in tourism across the EU. However, some argue that restrictions on working hours, in an industry that is characterised by 'anti-social' hours, could make Europe less competitive with North America and the EAP region in maintaining its share of the international tourism market.
- **Consumer protection policy** This has important implications for tourism. The Package Travel Directive is designed to provide protection for those booking inclusive tours; the Timeshare Directive protects those purchasing timeshare accommodation and there is a range of information initiatives which involve tourism.

REMOVAL OF FISCAL BARRIERS

- **Economic and Monetary Union** The introduction of a Single European Currency (the euro) and the creation of a 'euro-zone' has facilitated travel throughout Europe by doing away with currency exchange. It also acts as a basis for fare construction and encourages pan-European travel companies. (Note that the 'euro-zone' is not co-terminous with the EU.)
- **Harmonisation of taxes and duties** Here there are a range of policies that aim to provide a 'level playing field' for competition across Europe. There are two areas where tourism is directly affected:
  - The removal of duty-free allowances for travellers between member states – a contentious issue as transport operators and terminals make a large profit on duty-free goods.
  - The harmonisation of value-added taxes (VAT) on the sale of goods and services across Europe will impact upon tourism enterprises and the government revenue of member states.

REFLECTIONS ON THE CASE

There is no doubt that tourism is a very important element of the EU's economy and society, and this is reflected in the fact that the EU is one of the few regions of the world to attempt a transnational tourism policy. However, the constitution of the EU has meant that tourism has been sidelined from a policy point of view and most significant decisions affecting tourism take place in other legislative areas of the EU such as transport and regional development.

DISCUSSION POINTS

1. Using UNWTO sources, draw a map of the key international tourism flows within and into Europe. Identify the major generating countries for Europe and the major destination countries on the map.

TOURISM IN CONTEXT

RESOURCES

CLIMATE

TRANSPORT

FUTURES

2. Choose one of the newly admitted countries to the EU and draft a checklist of the effects that EU entry will have on tourism in that country.

3. List the achievements of European tourism policy and rank the list in terms of (i) effective initiatives and (ii) significant initiatives. For example, the European Year of Tourism may or may not have been effective, but was it significant when set against other issues such as seasonality?

4. Draft a table with the most significant European policy initiatives for tourism that have been implemented as the columns, and the policy area (tourism, transport, consumer protection, etc.) as the rows. What does this table tell us about the difficulties of devising policy for a fragmented sector such as tourism?

5. What do you understand by the 'subsidiarity principle' and do you believe that it is right to apply it to tourism in the EU?

KEY SOURCES

Davidson, R. (1998) *Travel and Tourism in Europe*. Addison Wesley Longman, Harlow.

Horner, S. and Swarbrooke, J. (1996) *Marketing Tourism, Leisure and Hospitality in Europe*. International Thomson Business Press, London.

Jeffries, D. (2002) The European Union and European tourism: in search of a policy. *Travel and Tourism Analyst*, 3 (June), 1–23.

Montanaria, A. and Williams, A. (1995) *European Tourism: Regions Spaces and Restructuring*. Wiley, Chichester.

Robinson, G. (1993) Tourism and tourism policy in the European community: an overview. *International Journal of Hospitality Management*, 12 (1), 7–20.

UN World Tourism Organization (2004) *European Integration in the Era of the European Union's Enlargement and the Development of Tourism*. UNWTO, Madrid.

WEBSITE

http://ec.europa.eu/enterprise/services/tourism/index_en.htm

TOURISM IN CONTEXT

DEMAND

RESOURCES

CLIMATE

TRANSPORT

FUTURES

Redeveloped buildings at West India Quay in London.
© istockphoto.com/Christopher Steer

CASE 14

London Docklands – Waterfront Regeneration and Tourism Development

INTRODUCTION

This case presents the London docklands as an excellent example of the way that tourism has contributed to the regeneration of an urban area. On completion of this case you will:

1. Understand how the London Docklands has been regenerated.
2. Recognise the role of tourism in the regeneration of London Docklands.
3. Understand the role of transport in the development of London Docklands.
4. Be aware of the distinctive nature of the tourist attractions in the London Docklands, many of which appeal to the local community.
5. Be aware of some of the constraints upon Docklands from a tourism development point of view.

TOURISM IN CONTEXT

DEMAND

RESOURCES

CLIMATE

TRANSPORT

FUTURES

KEY ISSUES

The five key issues in this case are:

1. London Docklands is an example of urban regeneration with a significant tourism component.
2. The transport system of the docklands has been the subject of considerable development, but the main artery of the area – the River Thames – has been neglected.
3. A range of tourist attractions have been developed in the London Docklands and adjacent areas such as Greenwich, although the most significant – the Millennium Dome (now the O2 Arena) – was not a success.
4. Most of the tourism developments have been designed to attract the local community as well as visitors from outside the area.
5. The London Docklands has a number of problems as a location for tourism development including geographical location issues and the local authority management of the area.

BACKGROUND

London Docklands is an example of tourism on a local scale, focusing on a small area. On the other hand this is also one of the world's largest projects for inner city regeneration, involving the redevelopment of almost 90 kilometres of waterfront, mainly for commercial or residential use. Although tourism has been something of an afterthought rather than part of the original scheme, the new developments attract over 1.5 million visitors a year to a neglected part of London.

As officially designated, London Docklands extends along both banks of the River Thames. As well as Wapping, the Isle of Dogs and the Royal Docks – which are generally regarded as part of the East End – it also includes the former Surrey Docks and a substantial area extending south of the river from London Bridge to Deptford (see Figure 14.1). Although physically separate, these areas have a shared history of domination by the shipping industry, social deprivation and marginalisation from the rest of London.

The first enclosed docks were built in the early 1800s to alleviate the acute congestion of the shipping in the Pool of London (the section of the Thames between London Bridge and the Tower of London) and prevent theft of valuable cargoes. The last of the Royal Docks – the King George V – was not completed until shortly after the First World War. In the meantime the docks played a major role in Britain's overseas expansion and industry grew up nearby, along with low-grade housing to accommodate a vast pool of unskilled labour. Docklands – and the East End generally – had few amenities other than 'gin-palaces'. St. Saviour's Dock in Bermondsey was the setting for one of London's most notorious slums – Jacob's Island – described by Charles Dickens in *Oliver Twist*, while Whitechapel was the location for the *Jack the Ripper* murders in the 1880s.

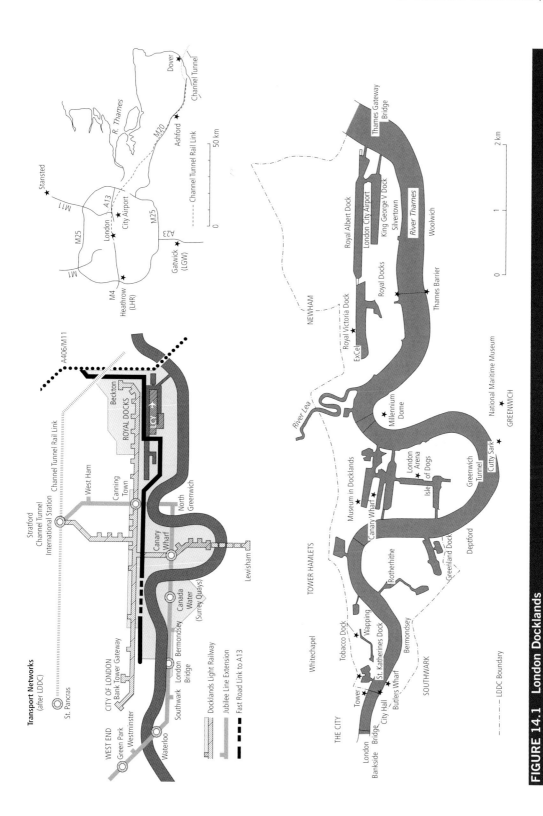

FIGURE 14.1 London Docklands

TOURISM IN CONTEXT

DEMAND

RESOURCES

CLIMATE

TRANSPORT

FUTURES

Docklands suffered severely from bombing during the Second World War, and although a considerable amount of slum clearance took place in the post-war period, the area remained visually unappealing and was shunned by tourists, partly because it was perceived to be crime-ridden. Also, the docks themselves had high fortress-like walls and security arrangements that prevented public access. The same was true of the waterfront of the Thames itself, an almost unbroken barrier of wharves and warehouses. The River Thames was no longer the transport artery for Londoners that it had been in the eighteenth century. Docklands was not easily accessible by public transport, with few underground and suburban railway services compared to Central London. By the 1960s, the enclosed docks had become obsolete due to the introduction of container ships requiring deepwater harbours. As a consequence, the East India, London, St. Katherine and Surrey Docks were closed between 1967 and 1970, followed by the West India, Millwall and Royal Docks in 1981. With the loss of an estimated 50 000 jobs, Docklands faced severe social and economic problems. More than 2200 hectares of wet docks, wharves and warehouses now lay derelict, but the private sector was reluctant to invest in redevelopment and the task of urban renewal was clearly beyond the resources of the local authorities for the area – the borough councils of Newham, Southwark and Tower Hamlets.

The Conservative government then in power was ideologically committed to the use of market forces rather than state intervention to reverse the process of inner city decline. Nevertheless it set up 13 Urban Development Corporations (UDCs) with wide-ranging powers to purchase land, prepare development plans and provide the necessary infrastructure. The sites were then sold or leased to private developers at market value. The London Docklands Development Corporation (LDDC) was the best known of these public agencies. Also of particular relevance to tourism were those UDCs responsible for large-scale redevelopment of inner city and waterfront areas in Bristol, Central Manchester and Liverpool. The LDDC was able to overrule any opposition to the scheme from the Labour-controlled local authorities for the area. Part of the LDDC area was designated by the government as an *Enterprise Zone*, where developers were granted generous tax relief and freedom from planning controls. With substantial financial backing from a Canadian corporation, this became the focus of a massive new office development project, centred on Canary Wharf and the former West India Docks.

TRANSPORT

Improved accessibility has been crucial to the success of London Docklands as a tourist destination and business venue. It has involved the following transport initiatives:

- **London City Airport (LCY).** This new airport, financed by the private sector, was designed to meet the needs of business executives, at a location much closer to London's financial district than congested Heathrow. However the site, between two of the former Royal Docks, is restricted and was originally intended to be a short take-off and landing (STOL) airport. The introduction of longer-range jet aircraft has enabled LCY to serve a growing number of destinations in

Europe, while a costly road scheme has improved access to the City of London and the motorway network.

- **The Docklands Light Railway (DLR).** This rapid transit system serving the new developments in Docklands was financed by the LDDC, London Transport and the private sector. Elevated above street level, and fully automated, the DLR was a novelty when it was inaugurated in 1987 and soon became a tourist attraction in its own right.
- **The Jubilee Line Extension**. This is part of the London Underground system, connecting Canary Wharf to the Channel Tunnel Rail Link terminal at Stratford and Waterloo Station. The Jubilee Line therefore improves the accessibility of Docklands and Greenwich, not only in relation to Central London, but also to the national and Continental rail networks. Canary Wharf Station – itself a masterpiece of civil engineering – is designed to handle 40 000 passengers an hour.

In contrast, the Thames is a neglected resource for transport. Although a variety of craft are used for floating restaurants, corporate entertaining, sightseeing tours and pleasure cruises, regular riverbus services, linking Docklands and Greenwich to the City and Westminster, have generally proved unprofitable, for the following reasons:

- It is difficult to find suitable craft, which are fast, manoeuvrable and yet produce the minimum of wash.
- Operating costs per passenger are much higher than for road transport.
- There are restrictions on the use of piers by the Port of London Authority, who control most activities on the river.
- There needs to be greater co-ordination with the public transport services operated by Transport for London.

ATTRACTIONS AND AMENITIES

London Docklands during the 1980s and 1990s was transformed from an industrial wasteland to a new 'city on the water' dominated by ultra-modern business and residential developments. Whereas the old docklands were a product of the Industrial Revolution, the new Docklands epitomise the 'Information Revolution' based on computer technology. Canary Wharf – boasting one of London's iconic buildings (Canada Tower) – is the flagship of the scheme, rivalling Frankfurt as one of Europe's most important financial centres. Not only has 'The City' spread eastwards, but also the newspaper publishing industry, formerly based in Fleet Street, has moved to Wapping and the Isle of Dogs. Many former warehouses of architectural merit have found new roles as restaurants, pubs, shops, artist's studios, apartments and museums. Some of the wet docks have become yacht marinas and provide facilities for a variety of water sports. These areas of open water, amounting to some 160 hectares – together with over 27 kilometres of waterfront now open to public access, are perhaps the most attractive feature of the new Docklands. There has been a significant increase to the capital's accommodation stock, including a new youth hostel at Rotherhithe, and a custom-built 'yacht hotel' at Royal Victoria Dock. However, jobs in the hotel and catering sectors

TOURISM IN CONTEXT

RESOURCES

CLIMATE

TRANSPORT

FUTURES

probably account for less than 10 per cent of the employment generated by the various development projects. Not all of these have proved to be successful; for example, Tobacco Wharf in Wapping was promoted as a Docklands version of Covent Garden, but its future as a leisure shopping centre is uncertain.

Most attractions and amenities in Docklands were designed primarily for use by local residents and the business community. Those of most significance to visitors include:

- **Leisure and shopping developments** such as Hay's Galleria, Butler's Wharf, and St. Katherine's Dock have benefited from their proximity to well-known tourist attractions such as Tower Bridge and the Tower of London. Canary Wharf is more isolated, but its shops and restaurants have now much more to offer the visitor than was the case in the 1990s.
- **Conference and exhibition venues** are represented by Cabot Hall and East Wintergarden at Canary Wharf, and by the ExCel Centre, which offers superior facilities to Earls Court or Olympia. Here transport links need improvement to overcome the disadvantage of a peripheral location, but thanks to ExCel, a business centre is developing in the Royal Docks area that is set to rival Canary Wharf.
- **Heritage attractions** – compared to other areas of Inner London, Docklands has relatively few historic buildings. There are a few eighteenth century churches, but these are far surpassed in tourist appeal by the riverside pubs in Wapping and Rotherhithe, which have traded on their past associations – real or imagined – with smugglers and pirates. More tangible reminders of the area's maritime heritage are the historic ships moored at the quays in St. Katherine's and West India Docks. The Museum in Docklands brings together materials relating to the development of London's port and its riverside communities from Roman times to the present day.
- **Sport attractions** include the London Arena, which is a major venue for concerts as well as sports events, drawing audiences from all over the capital. The Royal Victoria Dock is set to stage international water sports events, particularly in the light of London's successful bid for the 2012 Olympic Games.
- Two new universities, and City Hall, home of the Greater London Authority, have significantly raised the profile of this part of London, providing the impetus for other proposed visitor attractions, which include a world-class aquarium and a major arts centre.

Critics of the Docklands project allege that it has failed to benefit the local working-class communities in terms of job opportunities, as most of these are in the banking and financial sector. The new riverside apartments have been purchased by highly paid city executives and middle-class professionals, while the *gentrification* of the area is also shown by the type of restaurants and shops that have proliferated. The opportunity to re-plan a large part of London on the grand scale has been missed; although there are some interesting examples of modern architecture and engineering, most of the development has been piecemeal and of mediocre design.

Docklands has the following defects as a tourist destination:

- It is too spread out and lacks an overall focus, while the Greenwich Tunnel provides the only river crossing for pedestrians between Tower Bridge and Woolwich.

- Signposting for visitors is inadequate.
- Since the demise of the LDDC in 1998, Docklands has been the responsibility of the three local authorities in association with English Partnerships, the government's urban regeneration agency. As a result promotion of the area has been ineffective
- There is insufficient nightlife for visitors compared to other parts of London – for example, Canary Wharf, a hive of activity by day, is much less vibrant after office hours.

Docklands is likely to appeal to the type of visitor who is more interested in the 'new Britain' represented by the Design Museum at Butler's Wharf, than the 'theme park Britain' evident in London's more traditional tourist attractions. It is instructive to view Docklands as part of a wider area of London, focused on the riverside developments which are taking place along the south bank of the Thames from Waterloo to the Flood Barrier at Woolwich, and which are now within 15 minutes travelling time from Canary Wharf:

- To the west of London Bridge lies Bankside, another run-down area which in Shakespeare's time was the entertainment district for London. Attractions here include the reconstructed Globe Theatre, the Tate Modern Gallery and the Vinopolis wine museum.
- Downstream from the former Surrey Docks lies Greenwich, with such well-established tourist attractions as the *Cutty Sark*, The Royal Observatory and the National Maritime Museum, not to mention the effect of the O2 Arena (formerly known as the Millennium Dome) in regenerating the area.

A consortium of local councils and tourism enterprises has promoted the East End, including the whole of Docklands and Greenwich, as 'Eastside', in a bid to transform the image of the area for the American market. Such re-branding exercises have been tried for other parts of London. However, the future success of Docklands is more likely to depend on transport developments such as the Channel Tunnel Rail Link that affect the regeneration of other run-down areas, namely:

1. The 'Thames Gateway' to the south of the river estuary in north Kent.
2. The Lea Valley to the north, focusing on the major transport node of Stratford and set to become an important staging area for the 2012 London Olympics.

REFLECTIONS ON THE CASE

London Docklands is one of the world's most important urban redevelopments, located on the edge of what is arguably the world's most popular tourist city. For this reason, the urban regeneration has had a significant tourism component – a component that also appeals to the local population. However, political changes and the geographical situation of the docklands have acted as a severe constraint on the success of tourism in the area.

TOURISM IN CONTEXT

DEMAND

RESOURCES

CLIMATE

TRANSPORT

FUTURES

129

TOURISM IN CONTEXT

DEMAND

RESOURCES

CLIMATE

TRANSPORT

FUTURES

DISCUSSION POINTS

1. Draw up a balance sheet showing the costs and benefits of developing tourism on a 'brownfield site' (one reclaimed from industrial use), compared to a previously un-used 'greenfield site' in the countryside or on the edge of a city.
2. Working for an inbound tour operator with a predominantly North American clientele, draw up a one day itinerary in the docklands focusing on literary heritage.
3. Investigate the competitive advantages of ExCel as a venue for major exhibitions such as the World Travel Market or the Motor Show compared with the National Exhibition Centre in Birmingham.
4. Draft a plan (not more than two pages in length) to boost the use of the River Thames as a transport link for Docklands.
5. How might 'community tourism' be developed in the Docklands using the local knowledge of the residents?

KEY SOURCES

Beioley, S., Crookston, M. and Tyrer, B. (1998) London Docklands: the leisure element. *Leisure Management*, 8 (2), 30–31, 33

Law, C. (2002) *Urban Tourism*. Continuum, London.

Menzies, A. (1993) Tourism blueprint for Butler's Wharf. *Insights* (1), C1–C8.

Murphy, P. (1997) *Quality Management in Urban Tourism*. Wiley, Chichester.

Page, S. (1995) *Urban Tourism*. Routledge, London.

Page, S. and Hall, C. M. (2003) *Tourism and City Planning*. Prentice Hall, London.

WEBSITES

www.dockland.co.uk
www.visitlondon.com

New Forest pony grazing with foal.

The New Forest: Managing Tourism in an Environmentally Sensitive Area

INTRODUCTION

This case examines the New Forest – an environmentally sensitive area with a unique landscape in Hampshire in the south of England, designated as a national park in 2005. It is under severe pressure, not only from tourism and recreation, but also from other developments such as housing and transport. On completion of this case you will:

1. Understand the value of the New Forest as a resource for recreation and tourism.
2. Be aware of the components of tourism in the New Forest.
3. Recognise that the impacts of tourism on the New Forest are severe.
4. Understand that there are many stakeholders involved in the management of the New Forest National Park.
5. Be aware of the main elements of the New Forest's visitor and tourism strategy.

TOURISM IN
CONTEXT

DEMAND

RESOURCES

CLIMATE

TRANSPORT

FUTURES

KEY ISSUES

There are five key issues in this case:

1. The New Forest is a significant natural resource that faces many competing demands. Recreation and tourism create major impacts on both the resource and the local community, although the economy does benefit.
2. The New Forest tourism sector has a number of small attractions, a range of accommodation and road transport is the major means of access.
3. The New Forest is subject to strict visitor and traffic-management regimes to control both visitor volumes and impacts under national park designation.
4. A range of significant stakeholders have interests in managing the New Forest and there is some conflict between their respective objectives.
5. In an attempt to resolve conflict over the variety of tourism interests in the New Forest, a series of visitor and tourism management plans have been implemented.

THE NEW FOREST

Strictly speaking, the New Forest is neither *new*, nor a *forest*, but an area of open heathland, interspersed with woodland. The sandy soils were infertile and unattractive to early settlers, so that when William the Conqueror set the area aside in 1079 as a private deer hunting reserve, it was sparsely populated. William's 'new' hunting forest was much more extensive than the 56651 hectares that remains as the New Forest National Park, although its status as Crown land has undoubtedly protected the New Forest from development over the centuries. Today, the New Forest's landscape, flora and fauna are conserved under National Park Designation.

THE SCALE OF TOURISM

The New Forest is a very popular destination for both staying and day visitors. Visitor pressure in the Forest arises from the adjacent Bournemouth and Southampton conurbations, and the fact that it is easily accessible through the national motorway network. Tourism in the New Forest is estimated to:

- Support 3000 jobs in the area.
- Contribute £70 million annually to the local economy.
- Attract 10.5 million day visitors.
- Attract 3 million overnight visitors.

THE COMPONENTS OF TOURISM

ATTRACTIONS

The landscape, flora and fauna are the main attractions for visitors, even though less than half of the New Forest is wooded. There are three main landscape areas:

- The Avon Valley to the west, stretching from Salisbury to Christchurch.
- The Forest itself, a mosaic of open heathland, woodland and villages.
- The coast, stretching from Christchurch in the west to Southampton Water.

There is a range of visitor attractions either in or close to the New Forest:

- Beaulieu – featuring the National Motor Museum, Palace House and Abbey.
- Bucklers Hard – a preserved shipbuilding village from the era of the Napoleonic Wars.
- Breamore House and gardens.
- Paulton's Park – a small theme park close to the Forest.
- Gardens such as Exbury (with a steam railway), Lymington and Everton.
- Eling Tide Mill and heritage centre.
- Lyndhurst New Forest Museum and Visitor Centre.
- Rockbourne Roman Villa.
- Wildlife attractions such as the Otter, Owl and Wildlife Conservation Park and the New Forest Reptile Centre.
- A range of attractions based on farms and farm produce, vineyards, brewing and cider.
- Attractive villages with traditional thatched cottages such as Emery Down, Burley and Sway.
- The annual New Forest Show which is estimated to attract 100 000 visitors annually.

The flora and fauna are the main visitor attractions of the New Forest. ©istockphoto.com/ René Mansi

TOURISM IN CONTEXT

DEMAND

RESOURCES

CLIMATE

TRANSPORT

FUTURES

TOURISM IN CONTEXT

DEMAND

RESOURCES

CLIMATE

TRANSPORT

FUTURES

A key issue is the management of traffic in the New Forest. Most visitors arrive by car, although the area is well served by the main railway line between Weymouth and London Waterloo. Traffic management includes a 40 mph (65 kilometres/hour) speed limit on the unfenced roads of the Forest, and the use of landscaped verges, ditches and ramparts to prevent off-road parking. Visitors are directed instead to over 150 designated parking zones. Until 1999, parking in most of the New Forest was free, but since then visitors pay a car-parking fee. Other forms of transport include the ever-popular horse riding, cycle hire (although mountain bikes have caused damage in certain areas), horse-drawn wagon rides and regular bus and coach services. These alternatives to the car are coordinated in a series of networks in an attempt to reduce the number of car-borne visitors to the Forest.

ACCOMMODATION

Much of the accommodation for visitors to the New Forest is found in the neighbouring resort of Bournemouth. However, the Forest itself has a large number of camping and caravan sites providing over 20 000 bed-spaces. Serviced accommodation is in shorter supply, consisting of traditional bed and breakfast and small hotels/inns in the area's towns and villages. Self-catering cottages and apartments provide further bed-spaces.

MANAGING TOURISM

Managing the growing numbers of visitors is vitally important, given their possible impact on local communities and the sensitive wildlife habitats that visitors find so appealing. The New Forest District Council has regularly carried out visitor surveys and has in place a tourism and visitor management strategy for the Forest entitled *Our Future Together*. This followed an earlier strategy *Making New Friends* (NFDC, 1996) and a consultation document, controversially entitled *Living with the Enemy*, which mapped out the challenges for the New Forest tourism industry (NFDC, 1994). There is a plethora of agencies, committees and other bodies are involved in the management of the Forest under its national park status, including:

- The New Forest National Park Authority which works in partnership with these other bodies through coordinated and innovative policies and actions which are designed to:
  - Conserve and enhance the unique environment of the National Park, and in particular the special qualities of its landscape, wildlife and cultural heritage.
  - Encourage everyone to understand and enjoy the National Park's special qualities, while ensuring that its character is not harmed.
  - Support the social and economic well-being of local communities in ways that sustain the National Park's special character.
- Hampshire County Council – responsible for strategic planning and with a coordinating role.
- New Forest District Council – the local authority with day-to-day responsibility for the management of all elements of the New Forest and its population.

- New Forest Tourism – the local trade association representing over 250 private sector operators;
- Tourism South East, the regional tourist board.
- The Forestry Commission – primarily responsible for managing the woodlands, but with important recreation and tourism interests.
- Natural England – the government agency charged with designating national parks and protecting the landscape and managing recreation in the New Forest.
- The National Farmers' Union – representing practising farmers in the area.
- The Country Landowners' Association representing the interests of local landowners.
- The Court of Verderers – which administers the Forest's *commoners* – people who own or rent land and thus have the right to graze animals in the Forest. This ancient land management system means that around 5000 horses and ponies roam the New Forest and are part of its charm, though they are often to be found on unfenced roads and some are killed each year by traffic.

Clearly with so many interested and legitimate stakeholders, managing the New Forest is problematic, but this has been facilitated by the formation of the New Forest National Park Authority.

REFLECTIONS ON THE CASE

The New Forest is an internationally significant natural resource that attracts a large number of both recreation and tourism visitors. Whilst tourism and recreation provide jobs and income to the local economy, there is a view that their activities are having a detrimental effect on the resource. As a result, a range of agencies have been involved in complex management schemes in the Forest with a view to reducing both the numbers of visitors and their impacts.

DISCUSSION POINTS

1. In class, debate the positive and negative impacts of tourism in a destination known to the group.
   Define two clear groups: one group to argue that tourism is a positive force for the environment, economy and local community; and one group to argue that tourism is a negative influence upon these elements.
   Each side should appoint a spokesperson for each one of the three elements (environment etc) and speak for no more than 5 minutes on each

TOURISM IN CONTEXT

DEMAND

RESOURCES

CLIMATE

TRANSPORT

FUTURES

TOURISM IN CONTEXT

DEMAND

RESOURCES

CLIMATE

TRANSPORT

FUTURES

(i.e. 15 minutes in total) and then be questioned by the other side. Is it true that, in fact, there are no clear-cut answers to the debate?

2. Identify the stakeholders in tourism in the New Forest National Park. Can you classify them into those who might be expected to be pro-tourism and those who might be against it? Using this classification, can you now identify which of the stakeholders has the power to implement their views (for example the local authority) and those with less power (for example, a retired resident)?

3. Utilising the sources provided by this case study, and others that you can find, list the management approaches that the New Forest has adopted to control visitors, traffic and other activities (horse riding, trail bikes for example) in the New Forest National Park. Can you rank these management approaches in terms of effectiveness?

4. The New Forest is a popular tourism and recreation destination partly because of its location close to large conurbations and the motorway network. Using a map of the south of England, plot lines of equal drive times to reach the New Forest taking into account motorway speed limits. How might this map assist operators of attractions and accommodation in the New Forest?

5. The tourist authorities in the New Forest are concerned to maintain as much of the economic benefit from tourism as possible and this involves encouraging visitors to stay overnight in the Forest. Draw up a strategy to increase the number of overnight visitors in the Forest.

Key sources

Font, X. and Tribe, J. (1999) *Forest Tourism and Recreation*. CABI, Wallingford.
New Forest District Council (1994) *Living with the Enemy*. NFDC, Lyndhurst.
New Forest District Council (1996) *Making New Friends*. NFDC, Lyndhurst.
New Forest District Council (2003) *Our Future Together*. NFDC, Lyndhurst.
New Forest National Park Authority (2003) *Interim Management Plan*. NFNPA, Lyndhurst.

Websites

www.forestry.gov.uk/forestry/
www.hants.gov.uk/newforest/
www.nfdc.gov.uk
www.thenewforest.co.uk
www.visitsouthernengland.com
www.newforestnpa.gov.uk

Bird's eye view of Douglas, Isle of Man.
© istockphoto.com/Francois Sachs

The Isle of Man: Rejuvenating a Cold Water Destination

INTRODUCTION

The Isle of Man is an offshore island associated with, but not administratively part of, the UK. As a traditional resort at the end of its life cycle it has repositioned itself away from a typical British seaside destination and is a good example of a successful rejuvenated destination. On completion of this case you will:

1. Understand how the historic legacy of the Isle of Man's tourism has affected the island's tourism development.
2. Understand the significance of the Isle of Man's geographical position.
3. Be aware of the components of tourism in the Isle of Man.
4. Recognise the changing nature of market demand for the Isle of Man.
5. Understand how the Isle of Man has repositioned its tourism product.

TOURISM IN CONTEXT

DEMAND

RESOURCES

CLIMATE

TRANSPORT

FUTURES

KEY ISSUES

There are five key issues in this case:

1. Until the 1980s, the Isle of Man was a traditional British seaside destination in the final stage of the life cycle, but supplemented by business tourism from the offshore finance industry.
2. The Isle of Man authorities recognised the need to reposition the island to attract a new tourism market.
3. The island has all the necessary tourism attractions and facilities to succeed in the twenty first century tourism market.
4. The island's market for tourism has changed in the last 35 years both in terms of volume and the characteristics of the visitors.
5. The island has successfully transformed itself into a nature and heritage destination, supplemented by the remnants of the seaside holiday and supported by a strong business tourism market – effectively entering the rejuvenation stage of the life cycle.

THE ISLE OF MAN

The Isle of Man – 50 kilometres long and 20 kilometres wide – is situated in the Irish Sea, midway between Ireland, England and Scotland. The island's location is at once both an advantage and a disadvantage. On the one hand, it can draw upon the large population catchments of the Midlands and North of England, the Scottish Lowlands and the east coast of Ireland. However, to reach the island involves a short air journey or a sea crossing, often in unpredictable weather, as the island suffers from successive waves of Atlantic fronts passing over the Irish Sea.

The Isle of Man's Celtic legacy is shown by the persistence of the Manx language despite Viking invasions in the ninth century and long periods of first Scottish and then English rule. Since the mid-nineteenth century the island has regained its autonomy as a dependency of the British Crown and has its own parliament (Tynwald), civil administration and postal service.

The island has a long history of tourism, with peak numbers of visitors arriving by steamship in the early years of the twentieth century to enjoy a traditional seaside holiday. However, the Isle of Man's tourism success in the twentieth century has been one of mixed fortunes. There was a surge of visitors immediately following the Second World War, but by the 1950s the island began to experience the beginnings of a constant and sustained decline in visitor numbers. This was caused by the fact that holiday tastes and aspirations ceased to find the island's traditional holiday formula attractive. Since the 1970s, the island has undergone something of a renaissance with a thriving offshore finance industry. This has stimulated business tourism, and quality hotels and restaurants have been developed to serve this market. The island is now used as a setting for film and TV productions, with tours of the locations increasingly available. In 2001, tourism was worth 6 per cent of the island's GDP.

DEMAND FOR TOURISM

Demand for tourism on the Isle of Man was at its height in the late nineteenth and early twentieth centuries when visitors from the north of England, the Midlands and southern Scotland were attracted to the island's traditional seaside product and value-for-money accommodation stock. In the period following the Second World War, the island's tourism authorities were slow to respond to changing tastes in holiday taking and the structural shifts taking place in the UK domestic holiday market, resulting in falling visitor numbers. However, since the mid 1980s, strong political commitment and support for tourism have seen a rejuvenation of the island's products and facilities (partly driven by the demands of business travellers) and the demand has increased to over 300 000 visitors a year. The majority of visitors are from the UK, but the family market in the Republic of Ireland is also an important source. As a result, around half of all visitors arrive by sea.

SUPPLY OF TOURISM

ATTRACTIONS

As part of its repositioning strategy, the island's government has launched a grant scheme to assist visitor attractions to develop and become more professional and opened a new visitor reception centre. In addition to a developing programme of festivals and events the key attractions are:

- **Douglas and the coastal towns**   The main town on the Isle of Man is Douglas, with its sweeping Victorian promenade of guesthouses and terraced hotels. Douglas is the capital and main seaport, featuring the Manx Museum and 'The Story of Mann' exhibition. Douglas represents the main concentration of bed spaces, restaurants and other facilities for the visitor. Indeed, tourism supports many of the shopping and entertainment businesses that are used by residents. These include the restored Victorian Gaiety Theatre, and the restored £15 million Villa Marina – a leisure and conference centre. Other coastal towns, each with a range of small attractions, crafts, galleries and accommodation base, include:
  - Port Erin.
  - Peel – where Moore's Traditional Museum showcases the fishing industry and kippers – the Isle of Man's best known product.
  - Ramsey.
  - Castletown.
- **Cultural Heritage**   The island has a rich heritage, including many remains of both Celtic and Norse origin. The key features are:
  - The Laxey Wheel to the north of Douglas, an example of industrial heritage featuring the world's largest working waterwheel.
  - Historic buildings such as the castle and cathedral at Peel and Castle Rushen at Castletown – the island's former capital.

TOURISM IN CONTEXT

DEMAND

RESOURCES

CLIMATE

TRANSPORT

FUTURES

TOURISM IN CONTEXT

DEMAND

RESOURCES

CLIMATE

TRANSPORT

FUTURES

- The site of the island's first parliament at Tynwald Hill near Peel.
- Museums and craft centres including the Grove Rural Life Museum at Ramsey, the House of Manannan – a newly built heritage centre on the harbourside in Peel, and the Nautical Museum at Castletown.
- Cregneash Folk Village is a recreated rural life museum with original Manx cottages interpreting the crofting way of life of the islanders in the past.

- **Natural Heritage** The island has been likened to the landscape of northern England in miniature, as it features all the elements of beaches, fells, valleys and coast, yet within a small area. The natural heritage of the island is interpreted and developed for special interest holidays, and both walking and cycling trails are available – three long-distance footpaths have been designated with particular emphasis on the coast. The key features are:
- The Point of Ayre – a protected area of dune coast in the north of the island.
- The wetland habitats of the Ballaugh Curraghs with its wildlife park.
- The Calf of Man – a small rocky island which is a wildlife sanctuary to the south.
- A series of 17 mountain and coastal glens managed by the Manx Forestry Department with facilities for recreation.
- The *Cooil y Ree* (Nook of Kings) gardens in St. Johns.

Aerial view of Douglas in the Isle of Man. ©istockphoto.com/Francois Sachs

- **Transport Heritage** The Isle of Man is famous for a range of transport-based tourist attractions. These include:
- The annual Tourist Trophy (TT) motorcycle races, dating back to 1904. This event takes place on a road circuit around the island and fills the island's bed

spaces during 'TT Week'. The circuit is used for other race events throughout the year.

- The electric mountain railway from Laxey up the island's highest peak, Snaefell.
- The horse-drawn *toast-rack* trams that run along Douglas seafront.
- The Manx electric railway between Douglas and Ramsey.
- Groudle Glen steam railway.
- The Manx narrow gauge steam railway from Douglas to Port Erin in the south, with its railway museum at the Port Erin terminus.

ACCOMMODATION AND TRANSPORT

The Isle of Man has a varied accommodation base ranging from luxury country house hotels to value-for-money guesthouses. The Manx government has had a long-standing scheme to assist the accommodation sector both to adjust to the demands of the contemporary holidaymaker, and also to attract new accommodation stock. The tourism authorities also operate a compulsory registration and grading scheme for accommodation. Bed spaces stood at 6900 in 2003.

Traditionally, holidaymakers reached the Isle of Man by steamship, using the Isle of Man Steam Packet Company now sailing out of Liverpool, Heysham, Belfast, Larne and Dublin. The island is also attempting to break into the cruise stopover market. In recent years, fast catamarans have also been introduced, but the success of the island's airline – Manx – made it an important carrier for business and leisure passengers. The island's airport, Ronaldsway, has an aviation museum and is served by eight airlines with flights to UK regional airports, as well as to Ireland and the Channel Islands. Of course, as an island, it is very dependent upon its carriers for survival and the Tynwald closely monitors transport policy and scrutinises applications from new operators serving the route network.

THE ORGANISATION OF TOURISM

The Department of Tourism and Leisure has responsibility for both the promotion and development of tourism on the island as well as leisure and public transport. The department's policy is 'to develop and encourage tourism to optimise economic and social benefits to the Isle of Man'. The department works closely with other agencies that are responsible for heritage and planning. Manx National Heritage and the Manx Nature Conservation Trust are responsible for a number of the island's natural and historic attractions.

The Isle of Man has had to adapt its tourism product to the tastes of twenty first century holidaymakers through a number of plans and strategies. The most recent is the tourism strategy developed by the Department of Tourism and Leisure in 2004 aptly named 'Fit for the Future'. The island's traditional markets sought an English seaside product and while this still forms part of the island's appeal, other elements of the destination mix are now seen as more important in attracting visitors. These include the development of quality accommodation, the encouragement of activity holidays based upon the island's natural and cultural heritage, the

TOURISM IN CONTEXT

DEMAND

RESOURCES

CLIMATE

TRANSPORT

FUTURES

TOURISM IN CONTEXT

DEMAND

RESOURCES

CLIMATE

TRANSPORT

FUTURES

attraction of film and TV locations and the promotion of sport tourism utilising the island's eight golf courses, excellent fishing and other facilities. It is interesting that this approach also depends upon the provision of good quality, professionally managed tourist accommodation. Traditional establishments in Douglas have struggled to meet these standards and there has been a switch in demand towards, for example, country house hotels in rural parts of the island. The Isle of Man is therefore an excellent example of a destination that has successfully repositioned itself to become more competitive.

REFLECTIONS ON THE CASE

The Isle of Man is a classic example of the destination area life cycle. Having gone through the full life cycle from exploration to decline by the 1950s, the island authorities made a conscious decision to reposition the island as a heritage destination. This has been highly successful and the island is now entering the rejuvenation stage of the life cycle with new tourism products appealing to new markets.

DISCUSSION POINTS

1. Plot the locations of 'cold water' resorts on a map of the northern hemisphere. On the map identify those that have successfully maintained their role in tourism and those that have moved away from tourism. For this latter group, create symbols to identify the main economic activity that has replaced tourism – residential, health, education or other uses – and plot them on the map. Is there a pattern?
2. Thinking of stagnating 'cold water' resorts, have a class discussion as to how the characteristics and the needs of their tourism market have changed since 1900.
3. What do you think are the key elements that make a destination competitive? How many of these elements are present in the Isle of Man?
4. Access is the key to survival for island tourism destinations. Identify six island destinations with which you are familiar and list the means of access to each. Are any of these islands vulnerable to a transport link being removed?
5. One of the reasons that the Isle of Man has become a successful destination is the commitment of the public sector to tourism. What do you think are the main roles of the public sector in tourism in the twenty first century?

KEY SOURCES

Agarwal, S. and Shaw, G. (2007) *Managing Coastal Tourism Resorts*. Channelview, Clevedon.

Conlin, M. V. and Baum, T. (1995) *Island Tourism*. Wiley, Chichester.

Cooper, C. (1990) Resorts in decline: the management response. *Tourism Management*, 11 (1), 63–67.

Cooper, C. and Jackson, S. (1989) Destination life cycle: The Isle of Man case study. *Annals of Tourism Research*, 16 (3), 377–398.

Department of Tourism and Leisure (2004) *Fit for the Future*. Department of Tourism and Leisure, Douglas.

Drakakis-Smith, G. and Lockhart, D. (1997) *Island Tourism: Trends and Prospects*. Pinter, London.

WEBSITES

www.gov.im/tourism
www.isle-of-man.com/

TOURISM IN CONTEXT

DEMAND

RESOURCES

CLIMATE

TRANSPORT

FUTURES

Jan van Eyckplein, Bruges, Belgium.
© istockphoto.com/Oliver Malms

Bruges: The Impact of Tourism in the Historic City

INTRODUCTION

Bruges is one of the best-preserved medieval cities of northern Europe, a UNESCO World Heritage Site, and as such a considerable attraction to both day and staying visitors. This has created a range of issues for the city which are examined in this case. On completion of this case you will:

1. Be aware of the tourism significance of Bruges.
2. Recognise the tourism attractions and facilities of Bruges.
3. Understand the need for Bruges to achieve a balance between day and staying visitors.
4. Recognise the contribution of tourism to the significant traffic problems of this medieval city.
5. Be aware of the planning and strategy initiatives for tourism in Bruges.

KEY ISSUES

There are five key issues for this case:

1. Bruges is a well preserved and attractive medieval city, a UNESCO World Heritage listed site where tourism plays an important role in the economy.
2. The attractions of Bruges are based upon its heritage buildings, townscape and events, but the city's unique medieval layout creates problems for tourism management.
3. The tourism market for Bruges comprises both day and staying visitors. This raises the issue of achieving a balance between staying visitors who make a significant contribution to the economy, and day visitors who spend less but do have an impact upon the city.
4. The popularity of Bruges as a tourist centre has contributed to the significant traffic problems experienced by the centre of the medieval city.
5. Bruges has developed a strategy to alleviate traffic problems and develop tourism.

THE SETTING FOR TOURISM

Tourism is of major importance to Bruges, supporting an estimated 6500 jobs directly and indirectly in the city and its surrounding area, of which two thirds are in the hotel and catering sectors. Yet, the very popularity of this small city in West Flanders has brought severe traffic problems, threatening its unique heritage. These problems are now well on their way to being resolved through a number of planning and marketing initiatives.

Bruges (or Brugge as it is known in Flemish) is one of the best-preserved medieval cities of northern Europe. For this reason it has become a popular short-break destination as well as a long-established attraction on European touring circuits. Unlike modern conurbations, the townscape of Bruges is on a human scale, a picturesque composition of red-brick gabled buildings, church spires, cobblestone streets and squares and tranquil waterways set in the green Flanders countryside. A map of the city reveals the medieval street pattern threaded by a ribbon of canals which has led to Bruges being described, somewhat misleadingly, as the 'Venice of the North'. Beyond the ring road enclosing the old city lie the new residential and industrial districts, which attract relatively few tourists compared to the historic core.

There are two squares at the heart of the old city that symbolise its dual role as a trading centre and administrative capital:

- The Markt (market place).
- The Burg (the site of the fortress of the Counts of Flanders in medieval times).

Bruges grew rich in the Middle Ages on the wool trade with England, reaching the peak of its prosperity in the fifteenth century when it was chosen by the

TOURISM IN CONTEXT

RESOURCES

CLIMATE

TRANSPORT

FUTURES

Dukes of Burgundy as the capital of their extensive domains in France and the Low Countries. It was then the leading commercial centre of northern Europe, boasting the world's first stock exchange. Most of the important buildings and the art treasures date from this period. Later, Bruges lost wealth and population as the result of the silting up of the Zwin estuary and the shift of international trade to Antwerp. By the early nineteenth century Bruges appeared to be in terminal decline and was described in the Romantic literature of the time as the 'dead city', but this proved to be its salvation, as the citizens were too poor to replace the old buildings. The first tourists were attracted by the timeless atmosphere and encouraged the civic authorities to impose strict conservation measures that remain in force today. At the close of the century Bruges made an economic recovery, establishing a new port on the North Sea coast at Zeebrugge (Bruges on Sea). However, tourism continued to grow to become the basis for the city's prosperity.

THE TOURISM RESOURCES OF BRUGES

ATTRACTIONS

The tourist attractions of the old city include:

- The Hallen Belfry, the graceful bell tower which is the main landmark of Bruges. It dominates the Markt, and has played a major role in the events that shaped the city's history.
- The Stadhuis (town hall) dominates the Burg, and is another outstanding example of Gothic architecture.
- The medieval churches, of which the most famous is the Onze-Lieve-Vrouwekerk that boasts a sculpture by Michelangelo.
- The art galleries, which feature paintings by Van Eyck, Memling and other Flemish artists;
- The Begijnhof (beguinage) is the most visited of the medieval almshouses that give Bruges much of its peaceful charm.
- The Minnewater ('lake of love') was the harbour of Bruges in the Middle Ages but is now a romantic backwater.
- The new Concert Hall (Concertgebouw) is a modern landmark and an asset to the cultural product of the city.
- Boat trips on the canals are very popular with visitors, some going as far as Damme, a picturesque small town 7 kilometres to the north, which has been designated as 'Bruges in miniature'. Carriage rides in the old city are also popular.
- Event attractions are focused on the medieval period. The most famous example is the 'Procession of the Holy Blood' – one of Belgium's most colourful religious festivals – that has taken place annually since the time of the Crusades. Some purists accuse Bruges of being a 'medieval theme park' and question the authenticity of some of its traditions.
- The city has established a film office to facilitate the use of locations for film making.

TOURISM IN CONTEXT

DEMAND

RESOURCES

CLIMATE

TRANSPORT

FUTURES

TOURISM IN CONTEXT

DEMAND

RESOURCES

CLIMATE

TRANSPORT

FUTURES

- Apart from the heritage attractions, the city's shops, quality restaurants and markets are popular with visitors. The traditional lace industry would almost certainly have died out were it not for tourism, but is nowadays rarely carried on outside people's homes. Other industries less dependent on tourism are chocolate-making (an art form in Belgium) and brewing.

Boat trips on the canals are a very popular tourist attraction. ©istockphoto.com/jan kranendonk

Bruges is promoted jointly with Zeebrugge, which has a lively programme of events and entertainment during the summer. Attractions outside the old city in West Bruges include a theme park and dolphinarium, and a major sports complex, but these have limited international appeal, and the policy is to restrict any further development of tourism away from the historic centre.

Bruges is by no means a 'museum-city' or provincial backwater. Many of its residents commute to Brussels, while the College of Europe is a reminder of the city's important role in the development of the European Union. About 15 per cent of staying visitors are business travellers or conference delegates. Bruges is an important venue for international conferences, with many hotels providing facilities as well as the Congress Centre and historic Stadshallen.

TRANSPORT

The city has excellent transport links by road and rail to:

- Brussels airport.
- The ferry terminals at Ostend and Zeebrugge.
- Lille on the Eurostar route.
- The train (Thalys) connection between Bruges and Paris.
- The Channel Tunnel via the E40 motorway.

ACCOMMODATION

Bruges can offer the visitor an extensive range of accommodation. Hotels are the most important category with over 100 establishments, accounting for 70 per cent of bed capacity and approaching 90 per cent of tourist overnights in 2003. Almost 60 per cent of the hotels have less than 20 rooms, but there has been a large increase in recent years in the larger properties with over 80 rooms. The majority of hotels are in the 3 or 4 star categories offering en suite facilities, and are open for at least 10 months of the year. However, they face keen price competition from similar properties in Ghent, Antwerp and Brussels. As you might expect, the more expensive hotels are located near the city centre, while cheaper accommodation is generally found on the outskirts. This includes youth hostels – especially popular with young American visitors; campsites; private guest houses which attract a wide range of independent travellers; and holiday villages catering primarily for the Belgian and Dutch family markets.

THE DEMAND FOR TOURISM IN BRUGES

STAYING VISITORS

Bruges attracts visitors from all over the world. However, the majority of hotel guests come from neighbouring countries, with Britain contributing the largest numbers but the lowest spend per capita. Domestic tourists account for only 12 per cent of hotel stays, which is perhaps not surprising given the size of Belgium and the availability of cheaper types of accommodation. Spain is one European country that has shown significant growth since 2002, due in part to the success of promotion highlighting the historic cultural ties with Flanders. As for long-haul tourism, 9/11 and subsequent crises have had a severe impact on the Japanese and American markets.

DAY VISITORS

The biggest growth is in the numbers of day visitors, who are based mainly in the coastal resorts and cities of Belgium, and this has clear implications for the future direction of Bruges' tourism industry. By the middle of the first decade of the twenty first century the annual number of day visitors was well over three million, compared to three quarters of a million staying visitors, demonstrating the pressure on the city.

THE PROBLEMS

The majority of visitors arrive by car, and car ownership by Bruges residents is also increasing. The main problem, as in other historic cities all over Europe, is to find a balance between low-volume, high-spend staying tourists, and day visitors whose

TOURISM IN CONTEXT

DEMAND

RESOURCES

CLIMATE

TRANSPORT

FUTURES

TOURISM IN
CONTEXT

DEMAND

RESOURCES

CLIMATE

TRANSPORT

FUTURES

contribution to the local economy may be offset by their negative impact on the host community and the fabric of the historic town. Table 17.1 summarises the differences between these two types of tourism in Bruges.

As a result of the rapid growth of tourism, Bruges in the early 1990s faced severe traffic problems that threatened to devalue both the tourist experience and the quality of life for local residents. The main problems were:

- The concentration of visitors in a very limited area (430 hectares) of the old city. At peak periods there can be as many as 20 000 day visitors in addition to 8000 or so staying tourists.
- The large number of tourist coaches impeding traffic flow.
- The inability of the medieval street pattern to cope with the demands of the motor car.

A STRATEGY FOR TOURISM

As part of an integrated plan for tourism development, it was necessary to bring together the many small enterprises that make up the private sector in Bruges and

TABLE 17.1 Characteristics of tourism to Bruges in 2002 and 2006

Characteristics	Staying visitors	Day visitors
Volume trips	616 000 (723 500)	3 050 000
Volume nights	1 442 000 (1 333 000)	
Spend (in euros)	154 million – over half on accommodation, only 16% on shopping	100 million – one third on shopping
Transport:		
Car	43%	57%
Coach	13%	16%
Train	41%	23%
Seasonal distribution	75% of overnight stays in the period March–October	
Visitor origin:		
Domestic	12% (15%)	50%
Neighbouring countries	34% (34%)	26%
United Kingdom	32% (25%)	8%
Other countries	22% (26%)	16%

Source: West Flanders Economic Study Bureau (WES), 1995, updated to 2002 courtesy of Wim Vanseveren, the Director of Tourism Flanders; 2006 figures supplied courtesy of Saskia Desmidt of the Promotion Department Bruges Tourist Office

the local and regional authorities who formulate planning and marketing policies. To improve the quality of the tourism product, the first traffic control plan was implemented in 1992, with the following aims:

- To improve traffic flow within the historic centre.
- The diversion of through traffic away from the city centre.
- To discourage the use of the private car as the best means of transport to reach the historic centre.
- To encourage the use of the bicycle as a 'green' transport mode.
- To enable residents to access local services within the city centre.

The main features of the plan are:

- A circulation system consisting of five loops, which keeps superfluous traffic away from the city centre and diverts it to a number of large underground car parks on the periphery.
- Vehicles have been banned from certain streets and squares such as the Markt, which formerly acted as a traffic hub, and a one-way traffic system imposed elsewhere in the historic centre.
- At the same time, the traffic flow on the ring road has been improved.
- Tourist coaches are banned from the city centre, except to deliver tourists to and from their hotels.
- Restrictions on car use have gone hand-in-hand with an efficient and frequent bus service. Visitors who use the car park near the railway station (capacity 1600 spaces) also get free tickets for the bus into the centre.
- Cyclists are exempt from the one-way street system, and cycles are available for hire at the railway station and from many hotels.
- Signposting has been improved, and the promotional literature makes it clear to visitors that Bruges is easily accessible by public transport and can easily be explored by bicycle or on foot.

These measures have been supplemented since 2004 by a new traffic control plan, which is based on a 'park and ride scheme' encouraging drivers to leave their car at parking places just outside the city centre. The city centre can then be reached by a free bus service. Tourist coaches are directed to parking areas just outside the old city centre.

Traffic control is a means to the objective of creating a Bruges where tourism is in balance with the needs of residents and where the emphasis is on quality. This is to be achieved by:

- Restricting tourism to the historic centre.
- Encouraging repeat visitors by offering package deals, including public transport, to hotel guests from Belgium and neighbouring countries, who account for 70 per cent of the demand for hotel accommodation. Of these visitors, half choose Bruges as the sole destination for their trip.
- Promoting seminars and small to medium-sized conferences.

TOURISM IN CONTEXT

RESOURCES

CLIMATE

TRANSPORT

FUTURES

Worldwide Destinations Casebook

TOURISM IN CONTEXT

DEMAND

RESOURCES

CLIMATE

TRANSPORT

FUTURES

REFLECTIONS ON THE CASE

This case raises the key issue of how to develop tourism in historic cities whilst at the same time conserving the skyline and street scene, thus delivering a quality experience to the visitor. In Bruges there is the added issue of ensuring that tourism contributes to the economic well-being of the city by ensuring that staying visits are not displaced by large numbers of day visitors. There is no right answer to this dilemma as each of these issues requires trade-offs to be made.

DISCUSSION POINTS

1. You have been asked to plan a three-day tour of West Flanders based on Bruges for a group of 20 students from your college. Assess the suitability of each mode – road, rail, sea and air – for travel to Bruges, comparing costs and journey times. Provide a route plan from your group's point of departure to their accommodation in Bruges or Zeebrugge, and an itinerary for the three-day tour.
2. Compare the ways in which Bruges has managed visitors with other historic towns of similar size and popularity – such as York in the UK.
3. In class, debate whether a concentration on heritage can result in a 'museum-city' with little to offer young people in the local community. Use Bruges and other historic towns to support arguments both for and against the proposition.
4. Describe the ways in which architects, city planners and the local community can preserve a historic town's unique 'sense of place' in the face of the trend toward globalisation. Discuss how the shopping experience can avoid being dominated by obtrusive signage and the international brands in retailing, catering and entertainment.

KEY SOURCES

Ashworth, G. J. and Tunbridge, J. E. (1990) *The Tourist: Historic City*. Belhaven, London.

Drummond, S. and Yeoman, I. (2000) *Quality Issues in Heritage Visitor Attractions*. Elsevier, Oxford.

Law, C. (2002) *Urban Tourism*. Continuum, London.

Murphy, P. (1997) *Quality Management in Urban Tourism*. Wiley, Chichester.

Page, S. (1994) *Urban Tourism*. Routledge, London.

Richards, G. (2001) *Cultural Attractions and European Tourism*. CABI, Wallingford.
Vanhove, N. (2002) Tourism policy: between competitiveness and sustainability: the case of Bruges. *Tourism Review*, 57 (3), 34–40.

WEBSITE

www.brugge.be/toerisme/en/index.htm

Ski centre from a ski lift in fog in the Alps in Carinthia, Austria

CASE 18

The Impact of Winter Sports Tourism in the Austrian and Swiss Alps

INTRODUCTION

The Alps are a major tourism resource and destination on the world scene. This case introduces the development dilemma of tourism in the Alps. On completion of this case you will:

1. Be aware of the attraction of the Alps for tourism development.
2. Understand the potential social impacts of tourism as the Alps move away from an economy based upon agriculture.
3. Recognise the potentially damaging impacts of tourism development upon the Alpine environment.
4. Be aware of the development dilemma faced by the Alpine communities as they attempt to reconcile the economic benefits of tourism with its more negative impacts.
5. Recognise that the decentralised political system of Austria and Switzerland firmly places these development issues within the decision-making powers of local communities.

TOURISM IN
CONTEXT

DEMAND

RESOURCES

CLIMATE

TRANSPORT

FUTURES

KEY ISSUES

There are five key issues in this case:

1. The Alps are a significant tourism destination on the world scene and tourism makes important economic contribution to Alpine communities.
2. The development of tourism in the Alps has begun to replace agriculture as the economic mainstay of the region and this is having social consequences in the communities.
3. The development of tourism, particularly winter sports tourism, continues to have significant negative environmental impacts upon the fragile Alpine environment.
4. The key issue for this case is to understand the need for the Alps to develop tourism in such a way as to capitalise upon its economic benefits, whilst also minimising the negative social and environmental consequences.
5. The decentralised political system of Austria and Switzerland means that tourism development decisions are made by the local communities, making this a classic example of community-based tourism decision taking.

THE ALPS

The Alps must rank among the world's most visited destinations in terms of spending by international tourists. Other mountain regions can offer similar natural resources but do not have the advantage of a central location and proximity to some of the world's most prosperous cities and tourism-generating regions. Although the landforms are due to differences in geology and the effects of glaciation during the last Ice Age, much of the alpine landscape that tourists find so appealing is the work of mountain farmers over the centuries. The high Alps also provide a refuge for the marmot, the chamois and the edelweiss – symbolic of the fragility of alpine ecosystems. These resources are threatened by large-scale tourism, hydroelectric power generation, road building and more recently climate change. The region lies at the heart of Europe's north–south transit system and is faced with the seemingly inexorable growth of motor vehicle traffic, including the movement of vast quantities of freight through routes such as the upper Rhone Valley and the Brenner Pass. Air pollution is a serious problem, aggravated by the frequent temperature inversions that occur in enclosed mountain valleys in the winter months, and forests in some areas have been severely damaged as a result. The impact of tourism is greater in winter than in summer, due to the popularity of snow-based sports, particularly downhill skiing, and the need for high-capacity transport systems to convey skiers to the slopes. Over half the Alpine region is contained within Austria, Switzerland and the German state of Bavaria and together these accounted for about a quarter of the world total of skier visits (including domestic tourists) and the supply of skiing facilities in the late 1990s (Table 18.1).

TABLE 18.1	World distribution of skiing			
Destination country	**Skier visits (millions)**	**%**	**Number of ski lifts**	**%**
Austria	43		3473	
Switzerland	31		1762	
Germany	20		1670	
Sub-total	**94**	**24**	**6905**	**27**
France	56	14	4143	16
Italy	37	9	2854	11
Scandinavia	22	6	1860	7
North America	76	20	3644	14
Japan	75	19	3600	14
Australasia	4	1	203	1
Rest of the world	26	7	2605	10
World total	**390**		**25 814**	**100**

Source: Hudson (2000)

SOCIAL IMPACTS

Many Alpine communities have gradually changed in the course of a century from small farming villages on the margins of national economies to sophisticated ski resorts attracting a wealthy international clientele. Traditionally the local economy was based on a pastoral type of agriculture, with livestock being moved from the valleys to the high alpine pastures above the tree line in summer and back to the villages in autumn. Society was based on the peasant farmer and his extended family, accommodated in substantial farmhouses handed down through the generations. As agriculture yielded only a meagre livelihood, members of farming households supplemented their income with craft industries during the winter months or by temporary migration to find work in the cities. The advent of tourism in the late nineteenth century provided the opportunity to let rooms in the farmhouse to paying guests, and for farmers to work part-time as mountain guides, and later as ski instructors. Since the Second World War, tourism has developed from a profitable sideline to become the basis of most rural economies, to the extent that only 2 per cent of the population now make a living solely from agriculture. The farmhouse has become the family-run guesthouse or hotel. Instead of out-migration from rural communities there are now large numbers of incomers, mostly young people attracted by jobs in the tourism sector.

The ski resort of St Anton in the Tyrol is an example of this transformation. It has a population of only 2500 but accommodates a million tourist bednights a

TOURISM IN CONTEXT

DEMAND

RESOURCES

CLIMATE

TRANSPORT

FUTURES

TOURISM IN CONTEXT

DEMAND

RESOURCES

CLIMATE

TRANSPORT

FUTURES

year, of which 80 per cent take place in the winter season (late December to the beginning of April). The summer season (July and August) is not only shorter but much quieter, with a different type of clientele. There is a division of labour by gender in the tourism sector, with the running of the family-owned guesthouse or hotel being the women's responsibility. This involves very long hours during the winter season and often conflicts with the need for privacy with the family. Men, on the other hand, are much more likely to have jobs that are not centred on the home, are more varied and with working hours that allow more social contacts. This is particularly true of ski instructors who have prestige in the community and a glamorous image among foreign tourists. The difference between men's and women's roles in tourism has been blamed for difficulties in marital relationships, alcohol abuse and disruption to family life (McGibbon, 2000).

Winter tourism is replacing agriculture as the economic mainstay in the Alps.

ENVIRONMENTAL IMPACTS

Although tourism has helped to save the rural economy and many aspects of the traditional culture, the growth of winter sports has had a negative environmental impact on many parts of the Alps, in the following ways:

- **The preparation of ski runs** This entails the removal of vegetation and boulders to a depth of 20 centimetres to allow a good accumulation of snow, thereby causing damage to ecosystems and leaving unsightly scars on mountainsides to dismay summer tourists once the snow has melted. The deforestation of the lower slopes to create clear runs increases the risk of rockfalls, mudslides and avalanches.
- **The development of lift systems** The earlier lift systems necessitated road building that has caused erosion in formerly remote, unspoiled areas such as the Val d'Anniviers in the Valais. The use of helicopters to ferry in materials now makes it possible to develop previously inaccessible locations as high altitude

ski stations, sometimes with revolving restaurants and other tourist facilities that are inappropriate for their setting. Even glaciers can be used for summer skiing, causing damage to the watersheds of some of Europe's major rivers.

- **The use of artificial snow-making equipment** As climate change means that lower altitude resorts are faced with a shorter and less reliable season, operators increasingly rely on technology to guarantee a supply of snow. Thousands of snow cannons use up vast quantities of water – 200 000 litres for every hectare of *piste* (Holden, 2000, p. 84). The artificial snow melts slowly, reducing the already brief recuperation period for alpine vegetation. For example, due to the rigorous climate alpine grasses have a very slow growth rate, seeding once every seven years. Skiing on shallow snow can cause irreparable damage. Along with a lowering of the water table and noise pollution, there is the problem of soil contamination caused by the chemicals used to speed up the process of crystallisation.

- **The growth of motor vehicle traffic** Although Switzerland was the first European country to impose strict exhaust emission standards, it has little control over the millions of foreign vehicles that pass through the Alps each year, so that pollution remains a serious problem in a region once renowned for the purity of its air and water. Some ski resorts – notably Zermatt – have banned cars altogether in favour of 'green' modes of transport, but this still means that long-stay car parks have to be provided for visitors and residents further down the valleys.

- **The rise of off-piste skiing** More than half the world's avalanches occur in the Alps, and the problem is increasing as skiers and snowboarders push deeper into the mountains, away from the crowds and relative safety of the prepared ski runs. Vibrations can trigger the displacement of the snowpack from the unstable cornices overhanging smooth leeward slopes. Although communities have lived with the hazard they call 'the white death' for centuries, they have been protected to a large extent by the forests on the lower mountain slopes. Concrete barriers and rows of steel fences on the mountainsides are expensive, intrusive and a poor substitute for healthy forests, but they are often the only option available.

THE DEVELOPMENT DILEMMA

The decentralisation of planning in Austria and Switzerland means that decisions are made, not by central government or outside business interests, but by local communities, who can vote for large-scale development for winter and summer tourism (as in the case of Crans-Montana and Verbier), or perhaps shun the industry altogether. Only a small part of the Austrian and Swiss Alps has national park status, giving a full measure of state protection, while conservation bodies such as the Swiss League for the Protection of Nature lack the resources of their British equivalent, the National Trust. Ownership of the facilities in a typical Alpine resort may be divided between a dozen farmers, with the outcome of competing and non-integrated services, in contrast to the situation in North America where development is in the hands of large corporations who exercise uniform control. With the large number of resorts available, skiers are unlikely to tolerate lengthy queues at ski lifts as they can choose to go elsewhere. The decision to opt for large-scale expansion involves heavy capital investment in lift systems and the associated

TOURISM IN CONTEXT

RESOURCES

CLIMATE

TRANSPORT

FUTURES

TOURISM IN CONTEXT

DEMAND

RESOURCES

CLIMATE

TRANSPORT

FUTURES

facilities, and the risk of financial disaster for the community in the event of a poor season. Moreover, if the lift system is expanded, more skiers will be attracted, and more hotels will be needed to accommodate them. This will further reduce the area available for the traditional farming activities that give the Alpine landscape its appeal for summer tourists.

It is ironic that climate change, with the prospect of a shorter winter season, may drive communities to develop more sustainable forms of tourism. In the Alps, ski resorts are faced with the challenge of adapting to less reliable snow falls by either (a) taking the technological solution of engineering new slopes and the extensive use of snow cannons or (b) taking the business diversification route involving new products, new markets and year-round tourism. Here, the option of summer sports tourism inevitably means more investment in facilities such as golf courses and mountain bike trails, and ironically, further environmental damage. Hiking and other 'green' activities such as spas are another diversification option. Although some erosion would result from the widening of existing trails, summer tourism has a minimal impact on the Alps compared to the winter sports industry. Alternative tourism is now being promoted through an agreement between the seven countries that share the Alps, designating an international system of hiking trails that highlight the natural and cultural attractions of the region under the banner of "Via Alpina" (the Alpine Way). The work of pressure groups such as Alp Action is also important in persuading local communities to aim for more sustainable forms of development.

The environmental impact of road traffic using the Alpine passes should be reduced through a number of ambitious tunnel projects that use shuttle trains to replace trucks. These include a second St Gotthard rail tunnel linking Zurich to Milan and a tunnel under the Brenner Pass between Munich and Verona.

REFLECTIONS ON THE CASE

The Alps pose the classic development dilemma – how to develop tourism to capitalise upon its economic benefits whilst at the same time paying heed to the potential negative social and environmental consequences. The additional complication of climate change threatening the very resource upon which the winter sports industry depends is a new factor in the development equation. In the Alps, this issue is heightened by the fact that decision-making is devolved to the local communities who are left to wrestle with this complex issue, raising the question of whether it is wise to devolve internationally significant tourism development issues to community-based forums.

DISCUSSION POINTS

1. With the use of diagrams, describe the topography and facilities of two resorts at different altitudes in the Austrian or Swiss Alps, so that your client can make an informed choice on the best place to ski.

2. Select a resort in either Austria or Switzerland for a Canadian couple with two teenage children. They want to do 'some serious sightseeing' and visit a number of cultural attractions, as well as participating in winter sports. You should include the following considerations in your choice of resort:
   (a) accessibility to major cities and historic towns
   (b) altitude and topography, including slopes suitable for skiers with a range of abilities
   (c) natural attractions such as lakes and waterfalls
   (d) the transport infrastructure, including scenic highways, mountain railways, and the different types of lift systems – namely cable cars, gondola lifts, chairlifts and drag lifts
   (e) the type of accommodation available, recreation facilities for non-skiers, and *après ski* nightlife.
3. Describe the changes that have taken place in a typical alpine village since the nineteenth century, and discuss whether tourism has improved the 'quality of life' for the inhabitants along with living standards.
4. In class hold a debate about the pros and cons of going for large-scale development of winter sports tourism in a small alpine community, and assign roles to members of the class. These roles might include the local mayor, farmers, business people, school teachers and other members of the local community.
5. Assess the risk from avalanches and landslides in particular resorts in the Austrian and Swiss Alps, and evaluate the measures that have been carried out to minimise the danger to residents and visitors.

KEY SOURCES

Fuchs, M., Peters, M. and Weiermair, K. (2002) Tourism sustainability through destination benchmarking indicator systems: the case of Alpine tourism. *Tourism Recreation Research*, 27 (3), 21–33.

Goddie, P., Price, M. and Zimmerman, F. M. (1999) *Tourism and Development in Mountain Regions*. CABI, Wallingford.

Hinch, T. and Higham, J. E. S. (2003) *Sport Tourism Development*. Channelview, Clevedon.

Holden, A. (2000) *Environment and Tourism*. Routledge, London.

Hudson, S. (2000) *Snow Business*. Cassell, London.

Hudson, S. (2003) *Sport and Adventure Tourism*. Haworth Press, New York.

McGibbon, J. (2000) Family business: commercial hospitality and the domestic realm in an international ski resort in the Tirolean Alps, in M. Robinson (ed.), *Reflections in International Tourism: Expressions of Identity, Culture and Meaning*. Sheffield Hallam University, Sheffield, pp. 167–181.

Pechlaner, H. and Saverwein, E. (2002) Strategy implementation in the Alpine Tourism Industry. *International Journal of Contemporary Hospitality Management*, 14 (4), 157–168.

WEBSITE

www.alpseurope.com/

TOURISM IN CONTEXT

DEMAND

RESOURCES

CLIMATE

TRANSPORT

FUTURES

Mirror Reflection inside the Reichstag Dome, Germany's parliament building, Berlin.
© istockphoto.com/Dorit Jordan Dotan

Berlin: The Revitalisation of a European Capital

INTRODUCTION

Since the reunification of Germany in 1990, Berlin has begun to develop into one of the world's major tourist cities. This case examines the role of tourism in this development. On completion of the case you will:

1. Understand the background to the reunification of Germany and some of the issues involved.
2. Recognise how the tourism development of Berlin has been influenced by the contrasts between the former East and West Berlin.
3. Understand the development dilemmas surrounding the development of some of the historic features of Berlin.
4. Recognise that Berlin is competing with successful European capitals and tourist cities and that the ambitions of Berlin have not always been fulfilled.
5. Be aware of the economic issues involved in rebuilding the former East Germany and the impact that this has had on developing tourism in Berlin.

TOURISM IN CONTEXT

DEMAND

RESOURCES

CLIMATE

TRANSPORT

FUTURES

KEY ISSUES

There are four key issues in this case

1. Berlin is beginning to develop as a significant European capital and tourism city in Europe; however, it is finding it difficult to compete with other, more established tourism cities.
2. Berlin's attractions are primarily based upon its history, heritage and the institutions of a capital city. The reminders of the Second World War in particular create a tourism development dilemma in terms of the appropriate level of attention and interpretation to be provided to these 'dark tourism' resources.
3. The former East and West Berlin developed in very different ways and this legacy has been transmitted into the tourism developments of today.
4. The rebuilding of the former East Germany is a drain upon Germany's economy and this has affected the tourism development of Berlin.

THE HISTORICAL BACKGROUND

The reunification of Germany in 1990 brought together two major cities – East and West Berlin – that had evolved for 45 years under two very different political and economic systems. A year earlier, the Berlin Wall, which since 1962 had prevented free movement between East and West, ceased to exist except as a resource for souvenir-hunters from all over the world. At the time of the fall of the Berlin Wall the population of East Berlin was estimated to be 1.3 million, whereas West Berlin had a population of over 2 million. During the 1990s, both the administrative functions of the German Federal Government and embassies were gradually moved from Bonn to Berlin, which had been the capital of a united Germany from 1871 to 1945. The process of reinstatement was symbolised by the opening of the new *Reichstag* (Parliament Building) in 1998 with its symbolic glass dome, as part of a huge government complex on the eastern edge of the *Tiergarten* – Berlin's central park, which also includes the new Chancellery. Another landmark event was the ending of the four-power military occupation of the city by the wartime allies (the USA, Britain, France and Russia) in 1994. This allowed Lufthansa to operate flights to Berlin's Tegel Airport for the first time since Germany's defeat in 1945. The city now has its own regional airline – Air Berlin.

During the period of the Cold War, East and West Berlin used the medium of tourism to deliberately promote themselves as showcases for the achievements of socialism and Western democracy by their respective governments.

- In East Berlin, the *Alexanderplatz* was chosen as the centre of the DDR, the 350 metre high Television Tower symbolising the power of the Communist state. Before 1945, this impressive square had been the power centre of the Kingdom of Prussia and later of the Third Reich, and the East German regime was determined to obliterate this legacy of the past. East Berlin also contained what had been the most fashionable street of the pre-war capital – the *Unter den Linden* – which had suffered massive destruction as a result of Allied bombing in the Second World War. The majority of Berlin's cultural attractions – its great museums, cathedrals, universities, palaces and art galleries – were likewise in the Communist zone.

- In contrast, West Berlin focussed on the *Kurfurstendamm*, which had been a secondary centre in the pre-war capital. This became noted for its shops, restaurants, cabarets and hotels, while West Berlin as a whole generated cultural dynamism and prosperity under a free market economy, aided by generous subventions from the federal government in Bonn. The Europa Centre epitomised this commercial success in contrast to the greyness and the restricted shopping and nightlife of East Berlin. West Berlin was also multi-cultural, not only in comparison to East Berlin, but also to the rest of the Federal Republic, attracting immigrants from all over Europe. It was also a major tourist centre, whereas East Berlin placed restrictions on Western tourists.

Checkpoint Charlie was the entry point to East Berlin for Western visitors. ©istockphoto. com/Carsten Madsen

You should remember that West Berlin was an enclave, 'an island of democracy' completely surrounded by the Soviet-controlled DDR throughout the Cold War period. This made the city a vulnerable target for economic blockade since its surface transport links could be cut at any time. When in 1948 Stalin tried to starve the city into submission, the Western allies responded with the Berlin Airlift (which indirectly led to the rise of the air charter entrepreneurs, using the surplus aircraft, once that crisis was over). The need for NATO military protection also made West Berlin a potential flashpoint in any dispute between the two superpowers – The USA and the Soviet Union.

The heart of pre-war Berlin – the *Potsdamerplatz* – remained a wasteland throughout the Cold War period due to its location on the border between East and

TOURISM IN CONTEXT

DEMAND

RESOURCES

CLIMATE

TRANSPORT

FUTURES

TOURISM IN CONTEXT

RESOURCES

CLIMATE

TRANSPORT

FUTURES

West. Since the late 1990s, this area has become the focus of one of the world's greatest urban rebuilding projects, with the aim of making Berlin the European metropolis of the twenty-first century. The *Potsdamerplatz* is a new commercial centre, with a mix of theatres, hotels, shopping malls and restaurants. Most of the projects are taking place in the former East Berlin – specifically in the historic area of the city known as *Mitte* lying to the east of the *Friedrichstrasse*. This contains what little is left of the medieval nucleus of Berlin and the elegant Baroque city, centred on the *Unter den Linden*, laid out by Frederick the Great and other kings of Prussia in the eighteenth century.

The rebuilding programme is controversial in that it raises questions as to which elements of the city's heritage should be preserved or restored. Here ideological considerations play a major part, given Berlin's role in shaping European history during the twentieth century. For example, the ruined church – Kaiser Wilhelm Gedachtniskirche – stands as a stark memory of the Allied bombing of Berlin. Other examples include:

- Of Hitler's Chancellery and wartime Bunker, no trace remains, and even the sites are left unmarked, to avoid the possibility of them becoming neo-Nazi shrines. In contrast, a museum and memorial to the Jewish Holocaust now stand in the locality. Just to the north of Berlin, the Sachsenhausen concentration camp is also a memorial to the Holocaust.
- Similarly many Germans would like to see the monuments of the East German regime removed. In 2002, the Reichstag voted to demolish the *Palace of the People* (the DDR Parliament). This had been built on the site of the *Stadtschloss*, the former palace of Kaiser Wilhelm II and the kings of Prussia, which is to be reconstructed as a heritage attraction.
- The Communist regime neglected the Baroque heritage of East Berlin for many years, but in the 1970s initiated a massive restoration programme following a re-appraisal of the role of Frederick the Great as a national leader. Since reunification there has been controversy around the restoration of Berlin's most well-known landmark – the *Brandenburg Gate* – as the Prussian Eagle and Iron Cross surmounting this monument were regarded by many as symbols of the old militaristic Germany.
- The medieval nucleus of Berlin is unlikely to be restored on an intimate scale, given the high cost of land in the city centre and the need to yield economic returns.

The new Berlin has become a centre for fashion, music and the performing arts, boasting one of the world's largest street parties – the annual 'Love Parade'. This recalls the avant-garde role of Berlin cabaret in the 1920s, and as a short-break destination the city exerts a special fascination because of its recent history. It is also a green city, with a great deal of recreational space in the form of parkland, woods, lakes and canals. It has hosted many international events, including the final of the 2006 Football World Cup.

Transport facilities are excellent with Berlin acting as both a rail and air hub, and it is worth noting that the *U-bahn* and *S-bahn* networks, which functioned efficiently even during the division of the city, have now been extended. Tours along the River Spree give unrivalled views of the city. Founded in 1993, the city's tourism organisation, Berlin Tourismus Marketing is charged with the worldwide promotion of Berlin as a tourist destination. It acts as a tourism management agency and booking agency for the city's 300 hotels. Berlin's attractions include 170 museums and galleries, a zoo and a world-class aquarium, but the following are those most visited by foreign tourists:

- **The Berlin Wall**: Only a segment remains of the original 160 kilometre-long Wall, but this is now the world's largest open-air art gallery. Near *Checkpoint Charlie* on *Friedrichstrasse* (the former entry point to East Berlin for Western visitors) a museum now commemorates the attempts made by East Berliners to escape to freedom in the West.
- **Museum Island**: This historic area of East Berlin, bounded by the Spree and the Kupfergraben canal, has some of Europe's finest museums and art galleries, the most famous being the Pergamon Museum, which is a collection of art objects from the ancient civilisations of the Middle East, the most spectacular being the Ishtar Gate from Babylon. The Neues Museum will be the new home for one of Europe's finest collections of ancient Egyptian artefacts, including the bust of Nefertiti.
- **The Charlottenburg Palace** was a favourite residence of Frederick the Great, along with his ornate summer palace at Sans Souci, in the western suburb of Potsdam.

Nevertheless, the new Berlin is only partially a success story. The population stands at 3.4 million, much lower than the expected 5 million. This is because Berlin has to compete against a number of well-established regional capitals, and the city is no longer eligible for generous subsidies from the federal government to attract and retain businesses. Nonetheless, Berlin attracts significant numbers of tourists (almost 16 million bednights), with the UK, the USA and Italy as the leading markets.

REFLECTIONS ON THE CASE

Berlin is unique as a tourism city in that it is re-inventing itself after decades of division into East and West Berlin. Tourism is playing an important role in this re-invention, but there are issues surrounding the very different natures of the former East and West Berlin, and also the appropriate development of features associated with previous regimes. At the same time, the rebuilding of Berlin is being affected by the cost of developing the economy of the former East Germany. Berlin is also finding the competitive environment difficult as other capital cities in Europe are making significant tourism investments.

TOURISM IN CONTEXT

DEMAND

RESOURCES

CLIMATE

TRANSPORT

FUTURES

TOURISM IN CONTEXT

DEMAND

RESOURCES

CLIMATE

TRANSPORT

FUTURES

DISCUSSION POINTS

1. Explain the appeal of Berlin for art and music lovers.
2. You work for a tour operator which is proposing to add Berlin to its city breaks programme aimed at the 20–35 age group. Which aspects of Berlin would you include in the brochure and why?
3. Define what is meant by 'dark tourism', and discuss the ethics of including places associated with disaster and human suffering under the Nazi and Communist regimes in a tour programme.
4. Unlike London and Paris, Berlin has a number of serious rivals as the nation's primary city. Find out the reasons for this, and discuss ways in which Berlin can deal with the competition from Munich, Hamburg and Frankfurt.
5. Describe one of Berlin's site or event attractions in detail, and relate this attraction to a particular market.

KEY SOURCES

Hausserman, H. and Colomb, C. (2003) The new Berlin, marketing the city of dreams, in L. Hoffman (ed.), *Cities and Visitors*. Blackwell, Oxford, pp. 200–218.
Irving, C. (1998) The new metropolis. *Conde Nast Traveler* (November), 96–108, 174–178
Law, C. (2002) *Urban Tourism*. Continuum, London.
Murphy, P. (1997) *Quality Management in Urban Tourism*. Wiley, Chichester.
Page, S. (1995) *Urban Tourism*. Routledge, London.
Page, S. and Hall, C. M. (2003) *Tourism and City Planning*. Prentice Hall, London.

WEBSITES

www.visitberlin.de

A gondolier navigating the Grand Canal of Venice.
© istockphoto.com/MBPHOTO

Venice: Heritage in Danger

INTRODUCTION

Venice is a unique tourist city. This case examines the development of tourism in Venice and focuses on the challenges facing the city in the twenty-first century. On completion of the case you will:

1. Understand the significance of Venice as a tourist city.
2. Be aware of the attraction of Venice and its tourism resources.
3. Recognise the consequences for the community and the environment of developing tourism.
4. Understand that many of the challenges facing Venice are due to its exposed waterland location and are outside the control of the tourism sector.
5. Recognise the urgency of planning and managing for the future of the city if it is to be preserved.

TOURISM IN CONTEXT

DEMAND

RESOURCES

CLIMATE

TRANSPORT

FUTURES

KEY ISSUES

There are five key issues in this case:

1. Venice is a unique tourist city due to its waterland location, canals, art and architectural treasures where almost every building is listed.
2. The development of tourism in Venice has to be achieved sensitively and is highly constrained by the nature of its site and situation.
3. The scale of tourism in Venice has brought about negative social and environmental impacts due to the massive growth in the numbers of both visitors and motor vessels.
4. The survival of Venice is threatened by its low-lying location and a range of engineering and pollution issues.
5. Urgent planning and management solutions are needed if Venice is to survive.

VENICE: THE TOURIST CITY

Venice is truly unique, an irreplaceable resource and designated as a UNESCO World Heritage site. Here we see a city without the problems of the motor car; this is due largely to the city's location on a cluster of low-lying islands in the middle of an extensive shallow lagoon. Venice has few rivals in its wealth of historic buildings and art treasures, but it is not so much individual attractions that define this city's appeal, as its waterland setting and townscape which have changed remarkably little over the centuries. We need to remember that Venice is not just this historic island-city, but also includes a sprawl of industrial suburbs on the mainland, and it is here that most Venetians actually live and work.

ATTRACTIONS

The best-known tourist attractions of Venice are to be found in and around the Piazza di San Marco (St Marks Square), one of Europe's finest meeting places. Like the rest of this city it has evolved over the centuries without planning, but somehow seems of a piece. Here you can see the Basilica of St Marks, which is architecturally quite unlike any other cathedral, and the Doge's Palace, which was the seat of government for the powerful Venetian Republic. The palace is lavishly decorated with paintings by Titian and other famous artists, and is connected by 'The Bridge of Sighs' to the former prisons. Venice's other well-known bridge is the Rialto that dates from medieval times. Many of the 200 or so palaces lining the Grand Canal were built by rich merchants between the 13th and 16th centuries, when Venice controlled the Eastern Mediterranean and the trade in luxuries from Asia. By Casanova's time in the eighteenth century, Venice had declined as a business centre, but had found a new role as a resort for gamblers and pleasure-seekers from all over Europe. The Venice Carnival, when people dress up in elaborate masks and costumes, is a reminder of this period. It is during Carnival that the timeless quality of this city can best be appreciated, long after the hordes of summer tourists have departed. In addition to the Carnival Venice has developed a range of event attractions, including the Venice Film Festival.

To escape the crowds you can visit the other islands in the Lagoon. These include:

- Murano – famous for its glass industry based on traditional craftsmanship and exclusive design.
- Burano – noted for lace making.
- Lido di Venezia (Venice Lido) – Venice's own beach resort, built on a sandspit (lido) separating the Lagoon from the Adriatic Sea. Venice Lido is famous for its casino and international film festival.

TRANSPORT AND ACCOMMODATION

Between Mestre and Treviso, Venice has its international airport, named after Marco Polo, the famous Venetian merchant-adventurer. Relatively few tourists arrive by sea, other than cruise passengers, although Venice ranks as Italy's fifth largest port. You can also reach the city by road or rail. The most stylish way to arrive is by the Orient Express, where the standards of service and the decor of the carriages recall the 'golden age of travel' before the Second World War. But whatever your mode of transport, once you have crossed the causeway linking the island-city to the mainland, and arrived at the bus terminal or car park in the Piazzale Roma, or the Santa Lucia rail terminus, all onward travel to your destination must be on foot or by boat. Confronting you is a maze of narrow streets and alleys, sometimes opening out onto small squares known as *campi*, and superimposed on an intricate network of canals. The S-shaped Grand Canal, four kilometres in length, is the main artery of Venice, bisecting the city and crossed by only three

The Grand Canal is one of the major tourist attractions, but this has caused issues for the city. ©istockphoto.com/Živa Kirn

bridges, with the project for a fourth, designed by the Spanish architect Santiago de Calatrava, proving controversial. The Venice Card allows tourists to pay one price for transport around the city and admission to some museums. Motor vessels such as the *vaporetto* (waterbus) and water taxi provide passenger transport, and have largely replaced the traditional gondola which is expensive and nowadays used by Venetians only on special occasions. Nevertheless, gondolas are very much part of the city's romantic image, and the gondoliers' expertise as guides is appreciated by tourists. Accommodation is expensive everywhere in Venice, so that many visitors prefer to stay at Lido di Jesolo, the principal resort of the 'Venetian Riviera', 30 kilometres to the north. The situation eased somewhat in 2007 with the opening of the largest hotel in Venice – the Molino Stucky Hilton in a converted mill. However, most tourists to Venice are day excursionists.

THE PROBLEMS

As a destination Venice has many strengths but it also has weaknesses. Opportunities for developing the tourism product are strictly limited, and the unique qualities of the resource are under threat. We will now look at the relevant issues and some of the solutions that have been proposed.

THE SOCIAL IMPACT OF TOURISM

- **The issue**   Venice's popularity is itself a major problem. More than 60 000 visitors arrive in the historic city each day during the summer, totalling 12 million over the year. The great majority are excursionists or tourists on a tight budget, whose contribution to the city's economy may be minimal while adding to its costs in litter disposal and policing; for example, attempts by the civic authorities to fine visitors for inappropriate dress and behaviour have so far proved ineffective. Moreover, Venice is in danger of becoming a 'museum-city' for tourists. Venetians allege that the regional culture is being neglected in favour of Neapolitan music which foreign tourists regard as more 'typically Italian'. The tourist influx has been blamed for the closure of the everyday shops on which residents depend and their replacement by souvenir shops and boutiques. The resident population of the historic city is now 60 000, half what it was in the sixteenth century, and the decline is accelerating as Venice's environmental problems increase. The social composition of the population is also becoming less balanced. Middle income families continue to move to Mestre on the mainland, where most of the job opportunities outside tourism are to be found. This leaves the historic city to the wealthy, who can afford the upkeep of expensive palazzo-apartments, the elderly and those on low incomes, who are unable to leave.

TRAFFIC CONGESTION

- **The issue**   Venice may be car-free but faces traffic problems of a different kind. The influx of visitors has led to a rapid increase in the numbers of motor boats using the canals, with severe congestion occurring at the Rialto and Santa Lucia landing points. Speed limits are widely flouted, causing waves that undermine buildings and endanger passengers. Not surprisingly, gondoliers have demanded strict traffic control measures and the restriction of water taxis to the Grand Canal.

THE THREAT OF FLOODING AND SUBSIDENCE

- **The issue**   Venice is built on foundations consisting of billions of timber pilings driven many centuries ago into the mud of the lagoon – these pilings are slowly eroding. Venice has always been subject to flooding, but the problem is getting worse due to the rise in sea level brought about by climate change. The combination of high tides and storm surges in the Adriatic has led to St Marks Square being flooded much more frequently than was the case earlier in the twentieth century. Although Venetians have coped with the flood risk by, in effect, abandoning the lower floors of their dwellings, great damage has already been done to the fabric of many buildings, which are slowly sinking into the Lagoon. The 1966 flood disaster alerted the world to the possibility that the city would have to be abandoned. The *Venice in Peril Fund* was set up to co-ordinate international efforts in the work of restoration and salvage, and to galvanise the authorities into action. In 2003 the Italian government proposed the MOSE project – the construction of huge movable inflatable floodgates across the three entrances to the Lagoon, saving Venice by closing it off from the Adriatic. This has attracted widespread criticism as a 'quick-fix' solution because:
  - The project is not cost-effective, as the savings in the costs of flood damage do not justify the vast expense.
  - It would disrupt navigation into the port of Venice. Considerable investment has taken place to improve port facilities, including the dredging of a deep-water channel for oil tankers (which itself has upset the balance between salt and fresh water in the Lagoon). The scheme would accelerate the silting up of the shipping channels.
  - It would aggravate the build-up of pollution in the Lagoon.

THE IMPACT OF POLLUTION ON THE LAGOON ECOSYSTEM

- **The issue**   The Lagoon is a fragile ecosystem. It is a patchwork of marshes, small islands, slow-flowing rivers and sandbanks, acting as a sponge-like barrier between the city and the Adriatic Sea. Pollution is the most deadly and insidious threat to Venice. Venetians have, for centuries, been aware of the need to protect their water resources and the Magisterio alla Acqua, financed by the city government, is probably the world's oldest environmental protection agency, with regulatory powers over the canal system and the Lagoon. The scale of the problem is probably much greater now than in the past with pollution coming from the following sources:
  - Waste from the city's households, hotels and restaurants. Venice has no sewers and domestic sewage is simply dumped in the canals. Regulations

TOURISM IN CONTEXT

DEMAND

RESOURCES

CLIMATE

TRANSPORT

FUTURES

TOURISM IN CONTEXT

DEMAND

RESOURCES

CLIMATE

TRANSPORT

FUTURES

that hotels and restaurants should install biological water treatment works have been largely ignored. Sewage treatment works around the Lagoon have themselves contributed to the problem and a city-wide system of sewage disposal is required.

- Discharges of effluents from industrial plant on the mainland at Porto Marghera. Factories were built here in the early 1900s to solve Venice's unemployment problem, but they were sited in the wrong place, far from the cleansing action of the tides. Pollutants include concentrations of heavy metals and ammonia. Limits for discharges are set by the Magisterio alla Acqua, but penalties for non-compliance are limited to a fine. Industrialists prefer to pay this rather than install waste treatment facilities; in effect a polluter's charter. This is true of Murano's glassworks that emit arsenic; here the individual enterprises are much smaller than on the mainland and financially unable to carry out the treatment required.

- The drainage into the Lagoon of pesticides and fertiliser from agriculture, much of it taking place on reclaimed land. An excess of nitrates and phosphates has contaminated fish and shellfish resources, to the extent that fishing is now prohibited over wide areas of the Lagoon. These conditions favour the spread of algae, which in turn decompose, giving off a foul stench in the process. With the absence of natural predators, swarms of chironomides (insects similar to mosquitoes) have become a plague, at times even threatening to disrupt air and rail communications. No effective solution has been implemented, partly because it is difficult to track down the polluters. A long-term solution would be for farmland to revert to marsh, restoring the original ecosystem.

THE FUTURE

These problems are not just the concern of the environmentalists, but clearly threaten the viability of Venice as a tourist destination, unless both the private and public sectors can agree on drastic anti-pollution measures. In the public sector, closer co-operation is needed between the three levels of government – the city of Venice, the region of Veneto, and the Italian State, to formulate a policy of sustainable development for the area.

REFLECTIONS ON THE CASE

The simple fact that Venice is a unique city draws millions of visitors every year. Whilst these visitors themselves create a range of problems for the local community, 'bigger picture' problems threaten the survival of the city, including subsidence, flooding and pollution. Unless these can be addressed, the city may not survive the twenty-first century.

DISCUSSION POINTS

1. Draw up a chart that identifies the stakeholders in Venice's tourism industry and shows the different ways in which they are involved.
2. Obtain a large-scale map of Venice and locate a selection of major and lesser known attractions. Identify three special interest tourism markets (e.g. food and wine lovers, opera-goers). Suggest alternative tourist routes for each of your markets.
3. Discuss the practical measures that could be implemented to protect the more popular attractions and art treasures of Venice from the pressure of excessive numbers of visitors.
4. Design a holiday brochure for cultural tourists that focuses on the life and work of famous Venetians such as Vivaldi and Titian, and the buildings or sites in Venice and the Veneto region that are associated with them.
5. Debate in class the two radical proposals that *either* (i) Venice should be managed as a 'Disney-style' theme park with an entrance charge *or* (ii) Enough money has been spent on saving Venice and it should be simply abandoned to the waves.

KEY SOURCES

Ashworth, G. J. and Tunbridge, J. E. (1990) *The Tourist: Historic City*. Belhaven, London.

Dove, J. (1991) Venice: the environmental challenge. *Geography Review*, 5 (2), 10–14.

Drummond, S. and Yeoman, I. (2000) *Quality Issues in Heritage Visitor Attractions*. Elsevier Butterworth-Heinemann, Oxford.

Law, C. (2002) *Urban Tourism*. Continuum, London.

Murphy, P. (1997) *Quality Management in Urban Tourism*. Wiley, Chichester.

Page, S. (1994) *Urban Tourism*. Routledge, London.

Richards, G. (2001) *Cultural Attractions and European Tourism*. CABI, Wallingford.

Russo, A. P. (2002) The "Vicious Circle" of tourism development in heritage cities. *Annals of Tourism Research*, 29 (1), 165–182.

Van der Borg, J. (1992) Tourism and urban development: the case of Venice, Italy. *Tourism Recreation Research*, 17 (2), 46–56.

Van der Borg, J. and Costa, P. (1993) The management of tourism in cities of art. *Tourist Review*, 48 (2), 2–10.

WEBSITES

www.turismovenezia.it

TOURISM IN CONTEXT

DEMAND

RESOURCES

CLIMATE

TRANSPORT

FUTURES

Sanaa, the old city, is the capital of Yemen and a UNESCO world cultural heritage.
© istockphoto.com/arne thaysen

CASE 21

Tourism Issues in Yemen

INTRODUCTION

Yemen is one of the world's poorest countries and has a complex history. This case examines the issues surrounding the development of tourism in Yemen. On completion of this case you will:

1. Understand Yemen's historical and social background.
2. Recognise that Yemen was a divided country until recently and this is reflected in its tourism development with security concerns as a major issue.
3. Be aware of Yemen's tourist resources and facilities.
4. Understand the constraints on tourism development posed by the cultural and religious traditions of Yemen.
5. Recognise that Yemen is a country in the early stages of the tourist destination life cycle, and that planning and management are needed to sustain the archaeological resources.

TOURISM IN CONTEXT

DEMAND

RESOURCES

CLIMATE

TRANSPORT

FUTURES

KEY ISSUES

There are five key issues in this case:

1. Yemen is a country in the early stages of the destination area life cycle.
2. Yemen has significant archaeological attractions, as well as cultural resources that attract the more adventurous visitor.
3. As one of the poorer countries in the world, Yemen needs the economic benefits of tourism, but there are significant social and cultural constraints on tourism development in the country.
4. Yemen's political background and incidents of attacks on tourists mean that safety and security issues act as a further constraint on its tourism development.
5. Yemen must plan for the sustainable management of its major tourist attractions – particularly its archaeological resources.

BACKGROUND

Yemen occupies the south west of the Arabian Peninsula with a coastline along the Red Sea and the Gulf of Aden. High mountains offer a cooler climate and provide the country with a more abundant water supply than the rest of Arabia. In ancient times this supported the Sabaean (Sheba) civilisation which grew rich on the trade in frankincense and myrrh. However, Yemen nowadays is classified by the UN as one of the world's poorest countries. It is an example of a complex tribal society that is slowly opening up to Western investment and tourism. In this respect the kidnappings and deaths of tourists in the late 1990s and the more recent association of Yemen with terrorism were a major setback for the fledgling tourism industry. The fascination of the country for Westerners is that it still retains the lifestyles of bygone centuries and a feeling of isolation from the rest of the world.

The situation for tourism development is complicated by the fact that until 1990 there were two Yemens reflecting wider Cold War divisions:

- **The People's Republic of South Yemen** came into being when the British protectorate based in Aden ended in 1967. South Yemen was a hard-line Marxist–Leninist regime supported by the Soviet Union whereas.
- the **Yemen Arab Republic** based in Sana'a in the north remained a deeply traditional and strongly Islamic tribal country after centuries of despotic rule.

Unification as the **Republic of Yemen** with a population approaching 20 million failed to reconcile two very different political and economic systems, resulting in civil war in 1994. It was not until the return to a more stable political situation that tourism could be seriously considered.

Tourism is in the very early stages of development in Yemen – a good example of the involvement stage of the tourism area life cycle. Although a small amount of business travel took place during the colonial era in Aden, due to its role as a staging point on the British P&O shipping route to India, organised international tourism did not begin until the 1970s. Two international hotels were built in the 1980s; yet even at the beginning of the twenty first century volumes of tourism remain small, fluctuating considerably according to the levels of security in tribal areas – where the writ of the central government does not always run – and the political situation in Sana'a and Aden.

TOURISM DEMAND

The majority of visitors either arrive in organised groups to see the antiquities and the lifestyle of the Yemeni people, or are on oil-related business trips. Demand has been affected by the widely publicised kidnappings in 1998 (resulting in the deaths of four tourists in a shoot-out between government troops and the hostage-takers). This was followed by the suicide bombing of an American warship in Aden harbour and the heightened tensions post-9/11, when Yemen was suspected of harbouring Al-Quaeda terrorists. Nevertheless, Yemen now receives around 400 000 international visitors a year with a spend of US$309 million.

Yemen has a developing tourism industry.

The gateways are the international airports at Sana'a and Aden. Leisure tourism to Yemen has the following characteristics:

- The focus is on north Yemen, based on Sana'a where touring circuits for the antiquities/heritage sites have been developed.
- Visitors stay on average 4 or 5 days.
- West Europeans dominate the market.

TOURISM IN CONTEXT

DEMAND

RESOURCES

CLIMATE

TRANSPORT

FUTURES

TOURISM IN CONTEXT

DEMAND

RESOURCES

CLIMATE

TRANSPORT

FUTURES

- Most visits are by organised groups, often with a military escort for security reasons.
- Demand is highly seasonal, concentrated in the cooler months of December to March.

Domestic tourism is important, contributing between one half and two thirds of bed-nights in Yemen. Apart from visits to friends and relatives it includes adventure excursions to the desert. Here there is a contrast with international tourism as domestic trips are less seasonal and tend to focus on the south of the country.

TOURISM SUPPLY

TOURISM RESOURCES

These are based on the culture and lifestyle of the people, the unique architectural heritage and a fledgling festival industry. Apart from cultural tours and trekking, Yemen offers the potential for snorkelling and scuba diving off the Red Sea coast and the outlying island of Socotra in the Indian Ocean. Socotra's recently opened airport will boost tourism to the island, although cultural attitudes mean that beach tourism is not really an option, in contrast to the situation in Dubai.

The traditional culture and lifestyle is all-pervasive, as shown by the *souks* of Sana'a which sell all manner of merchandise, including *qat* – a narcotic widely used in Yemen – and the highly decorated daggers worn by Yemeni tribesmen. Yet it is strangely difficult for the international visitor to access. In contrast, the architecture is accessible and is of international significance – as for example the central area of the capital – Old Sana'a, which is a UNESCO World Heritage Site. The impressive tower houses made of mud-brick, featuring stained glass windows and alabaster decorations, give many of the towns and villages a medieval atmosphere. That so much remains from previous centuries is due to Yemen's poverty, in contrast to the situation in the Gulf States where the traditional architecture has been swept away as a result of the oil boom. However, lack of funding also means that many buildings are in a poor state of repair and some are being lost, while the illicit trade in artefacts from archaeological sites further endangers the country's heritage.

The archaeological resources are found mainly to the north east of Sana'a, at Marib – site of a spectacular Sabaean irrigation dam – and at Baraqish. Although there are many ground handlers in Yemen designing tourist circuits, two companies dominate the market. The circuits are mainly in north Yemen, in the triangle between Sana'a, Hudaydah and Ta'izz, although unification has allowed tour operators to include the Hadramaut Valley in the south east, focusing on Shibam – another UNESCO World Heritage Site. However, the infrastructure to support tours is primitive, the roads are dusty and in poor repair, and this has led the tour operators to invest in hotels and other facilities en-route.

ORGANISATION OF TOURISM

Overall, the Ministry of Tourism co-ordinates tourism, with the Tourism Promotion Board in charge of marketing and tourist information.

Tourism priorities for Yemen are as follows:

- Developing sustainable tourism for the benefit of the community.
- Enhancing and preserving Yemen's cultural, historic and natural assets.
- Promoting the unified Yemen internationally.
- Facilitating tourism and removing constraints.
- Assisting in the construction and upgrading of the accommodation sector.
- Improving the level and output of tourism training.

In addition to these priorities, there is a need to address the regional imbalance between the north – which receives the bulk of international tourism – and the south. In part, international assistance will achieve these aims through the two tourism master plans carried out since unification. However, tourist's fears regarding their safety and security may render these plans meaningless.

ACCOMMODATION

In the past, the state has intervened in the accommodation sector – in the former South Yemen the government owned and operated hotels, whereas in the north government incentives were provided. A number of projects demonstrated how historic buildings could be converted and managed as hotels. Since unification, the government has leased its own hotels to the private sector. This means that the accommodation sector remains dominated by locally owned small hotels and *funduks* (traditional-style inns, often with outdoor sleeping quarters for the very hot summers) at the lower end of the market. However, this situation is slowly being addressed as a number of international chains have opened hotels in the main tourist centres. These chains include Accor, Movenpick, Sheraton and Taj. At the beginning of the twenty first century there were around 12 000 bed-spaces in Yemen.

REFLECTIONS ON THE CASE

Yemen is a complex country. For one of the poorer countries in the world tourism offers both income and employment opportunities. However, the development of tourism in Yemen is far from straightforward as there are issues of religion and culture, as well as security concerns stemming from the political situation in Yemen. In addition, Yemen's unique archaeological resources are in danger of being lost unless effective planning and management is put into place. Tourism therefore has the potential to make a significant contribution to the national economy and the quality of life for the people of Yemen, but religious and cultural constraints remain problematic, and much will depend on the maintenance of political stability.

TOURISM IN CONTEXT

DEMAND

RESOURCES

CLIMATE

TRANSPORT

FUTURES

TOURISM IN CONTEXT

DEMAND

RESOURCES

CLIMATE

TRANSPORT

FUTURES

DISCUSSION POINTS

1. Investigate why Western-style beach tourism is not really an option for development in Yemen and most of the Middle East region, whereas it has been successfully developed in Dubai.
2. Give possible reasons why Western visitors find it difficult to access the lifestyle and culture of the Yemeni people.
3. Explain why it is so important to protect the architectural heritage of Yemen, and then list the difficulties facing those responsible for carrying out conservation measures.
4. Describe the challenges desert travellers face from the climate and terrain, and the type of equipment needed for trekking and other types of adventure tourism in Yemen.
5. Design a three-day tourism circuit for a group of American tourists interested in archaeology, and entering Yemen through Sana'a.

REFERENCES

Burns, P. and Cooper, C. (1997) Yemen. *Tourism Management*, 18 (8), 555–563.

Daher, R. (2006) *Tourism in the Middle East*. Channelview, Clevedon.

Gietzelt, M. (2005) *Does Cultural Tourism in Yemen have a Future*. NHTV Breda University of Professional Education, Breda.

Kia, B. and Williams, V. C. (1989) Saving Sana'a. *Geographical Magazine*, 61 (5), 32–36.

Kopp, H. (1989) Tourism and recreation in Northern Yemen. *Tourism Recreation Research*, 14 (2), 11–15.

Thomas, K. (2002) High hopes. *Geographical*, 74 (8), 30–35.

WEBSITE

www.yementourism.Com

Docked at Kom Ombo, a cruise ship provides easy access to the Temples of Sobek and Haroeris on the west bank of the Nile.
© istockphoto.com/Heather Faye Bath

Managing Nile Cruise Tourism

INTRODUCTION

The Nile is the world's longest river, and Nile cruises are one of Egypt's best-known tourism products. This case outlines the Nile cruise product and identifies some of the issues surrounding Nile cruises. On completion of the case you will:

1. Understand the history and development of Nile cruises.
2. Be aware of the scale of the Nile cruise product.
3. Recognise the characteristics of the Nile cruise.
4. Be aware of some of the problems surrounding the organisation of the Nile cruise sector.
5. Recognise that Nile cruises are dependent on the health of the tourism sector in Egypt and the political situation in the Middle East region as a whole.

TOURISM IN CONTEXT

DEMAND

RESOURCES

CLIMATE

TRANSPORT

FUTURES

KEY ISSUES

There are four key issues in this case

1. Nile cruises are a well-known tourism product in Egypt, based on the resource of the Nile and allowing visitors to access a variety of archaeological sites from a 'floating hotel'.
2. Nile cruises have a number of distinctive characteristics that make their management and organization difficult.
3. The Nile cruise industry faces a number of challenges, not the least of which are over-crowding and chaotic organization at the landing sites.
4. The Nile cruise industry faces a number of challenges in the future including safety/security issues and problems relating to water levels and pollution in the Nile.

Cruises are one of the best-known tourist products in Egypt. ©istockphoto.com/Susanna Fieramosca Naranjo

THE NILE

The Nile is the world's longest river at 6700 kilometres (although the Amazon far exceeds it in terms of volume), and Nile cruises are probably Egypt's best-known tourism product. A cruise is a romantic way of seeing many of Egypt's best-known 'antiquities' – the sites of its ancient civilisations – which include the temples at Luxor and Karnak, the Colossi of Memnon, Tutankhamun's Tomb and the Valley of Kings. Cruising has the advantage of providing an accommodation base in a floating hotel, avoiding the often arduous journeys by road or air otherwise involved in sightseeing.

The Nile is synonymous with Egypt and for thousands of years it has been a vital resource and the transport lifeline between the north and south of the country. Until recently, the river used to flood extensive areas regularly between July and October, following the rains at the source of the Blue Nile in the highlands of Ethiopia. These floods renewed the fertility of the soil by depositing a layer of silt on the fields. With the construction of the Aswan High Dam in 1971, a gain of 20 per cent in the area of cultivatable land and a boost to power supplies has been offset by ecological changes and a reduction in water levels, which has impeded cruise operations. When Thomas Cook inaugurated steamship services on the Nile in the 1870s, thus opening up Egypt to modern tourism, the entire length of the river was navigable to Aswan throughout the year. Since the early 1990s, cruises no longer operate on the lower Nile between Cairo and Luxor, as silt has built up in the river, aggravating the problem of low water levels during the winter months.

THE DEVELOPMENT OF NILE CRUISES

Since the days of Thomas Cook, tourism on the Nile has grown steadily. Initially, small groups of independent, adventurous tourists were attracted, and the Agatha Christie novel "Death on the Nile" exemplified the upper class, predominantly British, image of Nile cruising before the Second World War. More recently, larger groups on inclusive tours, drawn from a wider range of countries and socio-economic groups have become the norm. Many Nile cruises are young couples in their twenties, although the over 50 age group is also well represented. All-inclusive packages are now common, bringing the price of a Nile cruise within reach of budget travellers. The international hotel chains have entered the cruise market; Hilton, for example, began operating five star cruise vessels in 1988, while Sheraton and Marriott soon followed. The number of vessels grew considerably during the 1990s from a total of 55 in 1990, to 290 by 2005. This probably represents the Nile cruise industry at its peak (see Table 22.1). Although, numbers of visitors to Egypt and thus numbers of cruise customers fluctuated dramatically during the 1990s due to terrorist attacks, tourist arrivals to Egypt have recovered in the new millennium to reach over 8.6 million in 2006. The downside to this success is the fact that these visitors place more pressure on sensitive archaeological and ecological sites.

Table 22.2 clearly shows that on average the higher quality 'floating hotels' are much larger than the two star vessels, with three times as many cabins. The majority of cabins have two berths, indicating the importance of the 'couples' market. Most of the vessels have air conditioning and water purification systems. On-board facilities for those in the higher price range include sundecks, bars, games areas, swimming pools, entertainment lounges, restaurants and boutiques.

CHARACTERISTICS OF NILE CRUISES

- Nile cruises are a unique product, using shallow-draft four-deck vessels. Most are of a standardised 'shoebox' design, but some have been modelled on the

TOURISM IN CONTEXT

DEMAND

RESOURCES

CLIMATE

TRANSPORT

FUTURES

TOURISM IN CONTEXT

DEMAND

RESOURCES

CLIMATE

TRANSPORT

FUTURES

TABLE 22.1 Growth of floating hotel capacity (1991–1/7/2006)

Year	Units		Cabins	
	No.	% growth	No.	% growth
1991	169	–	8584	–
1992	181	7.1	9297	8.3
1993	188	3.9	9763	5.0
1994	205	9.0	10339	5.9
1995	206	0.5	10532	1.9
1996	215	4.4	11184	6.2
1997	214	−0.5	11322	1.2
1998	224	4.7	11673	3.1
1999	229	2.2	12258	5.0
2000	250	9.2	13391	9.2
2001	259	3.6	14135	5.6
2002	261	0.8	14564	3.0
2003	269	3.1	15188	4.3
2004	275	2.2	16010	5.4
2005	290	5.5	16897	5.5
1-/7/2006	282	–	16564	–

Source: Hotels Supervision Sector/Egyptian Ministry of Tourism (2006)

TABLE 22.2 Breakdown of floating hotel capacity by category (1/7/2006)

Category	Units	%	Cabins	%	Beds	%
5 stars	193	68.4	12706	76.7	25412	76.7
4 stars	53	18.8	2556	15.4	5112	15.4
3 stars	18	6.4	734	4.4	1468	4.4
2 stars	5	1.8	148	0.9	296	0.9
1 star	0	0.0	0	0.0	0	0.0
Under Classification	13	4.6	420	2.5	840	2.5
Total	**282**	**100**	**16564**	**100**	**33128**	**100**

Source: Hotels Supervision Sector/Egyptian Ministry of Tourism (2006)

paddle steamers used in Cook's time. The emphasis is on comfort and sight-seeing rather than speed. The newest vessels can cruise at 16 kilometres/hour upstream against the Nile current, and 22 kilometres/hour downstream.

- The major cruising stretch of the Nile is between the Valley of the Kings, the site of ancient Thebes, Luxor and Karnak in the north, and Aswan to the south. En route, passengers visit the temples at Edfu before arriving at Aswan to see the three-kilometre-long High Dam and the Temple of Philae.

- To the south of Aswan, another cruising area has been opened up as a result of the High Dam on the 500 kilometre-long Lake Nasser. Known locally as the 'Nubian Sea' its attractions are less well known, with the exception of the temples of Abu Simbel, which were rescued from inundation by UNESCO.

- Most cruises have a duration of between 3 and 11 nights. In the shorter version, clients cruise in one direction only – from Luxor to Aswan or vice versa – with domestic flights based on Cairo forming the other 'legs' of the trip. Longer cruises allow more quality time for sightseeing with short excursions on both banks of the Nile. Sometimes, tour operators offer 'cruise and stay' arrangements with one or more nights in a hotel at Luxor and/or Aswan, adding an extra dimension to the holiday.

- The high season for cruising is from October to April when the climate is ideal for sightseeing. The vessels also operate in the low season, when the heat can be extreme, at considerably reduced prices.

- Crews tend to be recruited locally, with the length of training varying from a few weeks to a few months according to job description.

- Ground-handling of cruise passengers at the sites tends to be organised by Egyptian travel agencies who provide transport and guides for the visiting groups, often under contract to the larger inbound tour operators.

- The base for the Nile cruise industry is at Luxor, which has a long history as an international tourist centre. It was made world-famous by Howard Carter's discovery of the tomb and treasures of the boy Pharaoh Tutankhamun in 1922. Until recently, The West Bank of the Nile opposite Luxor was difficult to reach except by boat. The construction of a new road to the Valley of the Kings in 1995, followed by a bridge linking the city to the West Bank two years later, has improved access considerably. The floating hotels moored on the East Bank complement other accommodation in and around Luxor.

THE ISSUES

- **Overcrowding**   The Nile cruise industry is poorly organised and visits to the sites when a vessel has berthed can be chaotic with guides, taxi drivers and traders vying for tourists' attention. At Luxor for example, most guided tours are arranged to meet tour buses and the arrival of cruise ships at certain times of the day, resulting in considerable congestion as visitors and vehicles converge. There is a case for phased visits and good visitor management as the focused visitor pressure is threatening the integrity of the sites. Some idea of the pressures can be gauged from the numbers of visitors at the key sites shown in Table 22.3. To mitigate threats to the sites and to enhance the visitor experience, the

TOURISM IN CONTEXT

DEMAND

RESOURCES

CLIMATE

TRANSPORT

FUTURES

TABLE 22.3	Visitors to the main historic sites and museums in Egypt, 2005	
Historic Sites	**Foreigners**	**Egyptians**
Cairo		
Egyptian Museum	1 678 203	331 222
Coptic Museum	264 199	69 957
Other Tourist Sites	2 275 145	918 708
Total Cairo	**4 217 547**	**1 319 887**
Opera Theaters	11 057	262 306
Alexandria	52 6091	477 765
South Sinai	396 162	42 804
Fayoum	10 487	5014
Beni-Suif	10 197	16 466
Luxor	4 693 314	295 233
The Pyramids	1 716 364	781 865
Sakara	658 484	19 096
Meet Rehena	473 914	5688
Dahshour	107 956	611
Pharaonic Village	45 863	52 322
Sound and Light Show	320 579	1818
Sohag	42 244	8853
Menia	17 016	51 180
Aswan	4 770 832	358 385
Total	**18 018 107**	**3 699 293**
Grand Total	**21 717 400**	

Source: Tourist and Antiquities Police (Ministry of Interior Affairs)

Supreme Council of Luxor has initiated a comprehensive urban and social planning exercise for both the East Bank, where the Luxor and Karnak temples are located, and the West Bank, where the tombs of the famous ancient Egyptian kings and queens were discovered. The plans are designed to reduce the threat of residential expansion encroaching on the monuments and sightseeing areas. Whilst environmental improvements and management programmes have been implemented at the monuments, as for example at the Karnak temple, the issue

TOURISM IN CONTEXT

DEMAND

RESOURCES

CLIMATE

TRANSPORT

FUTURES

of managing large numbers of visitors and respecting carrying capacities continues to be a challenge.

- **Terrorism**   The Egyptian government has stepped up security in the Luxor area, since the terrorist attacks in November 1997 at the Temple of Hatshepset received wide international publicity. This led to a severe downturn in the number of visitors, particularly from European countries, with hotel occupancy rates in Luxor falling to 25 per cent during most of 1998. In response, the Egyptian government has launched an initiative to encourage Egyptians to visit the antiquities in greater numbers, but the success of this campaign adds to congestion at the sites.

- **Port facilities**   The main overnight berthing points for cruise vessels are Luxor, Esna, Kom Ombo and Aswan, where docks and other facilities are of a poor standard. Travel agents and cruise operators are developing their own quays in the absence of official provision. For example, at any one time there can be between 30 to 80 vessels moored at the dock on the east bank at Luxor, with as many as seven moored side by side. This means that passengers have to cross from vessel to vessel to reach the shore, at some risk and inconvenience to themselves. As part of the planning exercise referred to above, a marina accommodating 180 floating hotels will be completed by 2009, aiming to reduce pollution, provide better docking facilities and improve the management of berthing.

- **Pollution**   The vessels are mainly diesel powered, causing pollution in the Nile and corrosive fumes at the sites.

- **Low water levels**   Low water levels in the Nile can disrupt cruise schedules at a certain time of the year. This is nowadays due to controls by the authorities on the amount of water leaving Lake Nasser through the Aswan High Dam. A more insidious problem is the run-off of the fertilisers that farmers are forced to use, now that the annual cycle of Nile floods has been disrupted. This encourages the growth of algae and weeds that not only upsets the ecological balance of the river, but causes damage to the propellers of the vessels.

REFLECTIONS ON THE CASE

This case has shown that Nile cruises have a long pedigree and are a significant part of the Egyptian tourism sector. As such they are viewed as a romantic way to view the Nile and the antiquities of the region. However, the Nile cruise industry suffers from poor organization, particularly at the landing points and this detracts from the tourism experience. In addition, the cruise sector is vulnerable to changes related to water levels and pollution in the Nile as well as security issues in the region.

Note: We are grateful to Dr. Eman Helmy for her help with this case.

TOURISM IN CONTEXT

DEMAND

RESOURCES

CLIMATE

TRANSPORT

FUTURES

DISCUSSION POINTS

1. Debate the issue as to whether regulating the somewhat chaotic Nile cruise industry would in fact remove the charm and local colour of the experience.
2. There are some real issues of safety and poor management at many of the cruise ports of call – how might you solve these problems without detracting from the experience of the tourist?
3. The Nile is a complex tourism product. Using a large-scale map, plot the itineraries of the Nile cruise boats and their major ports of call. You may need to use brochures and Internet sites of the companies and tour operators to do this. Looking at the completed map, identify potential congestion points and areas of concern for the future.
4. The Nile cruise is a classic example of an element of tourism – transport – being the product. Can you think of other examples where transport is the product? Are there any lessons that can be learnt from these other products that might assist the Nile cruise industry to be more efficient?
5. Debate whether the popularity of an Egyptian antiquity site results from its accessibility, or from its historic value.

KEY SOURCES

Fawzy, A. (2001) The potential for corporate meetings on Nile cruises. *Hospitality Review*, 3 (3), 52–55.

Pakkala, L. J. (1990) Egyptian tourism: cruising for growth. *The Cornell Hotel and Restaurant Association Quarterly*, 31 (2), 56–59.

Rivers, J. (1998) Thebes (Luxor, Egypt) traffic and visitor flow management in the West Bank of the Necropolis, in M. Shackley (2000), *Visitor Management: Case Studies from World Heritage Sites*. Elsevier Butterworth Heinemann, Oxford, pp. 161–181.

WEBSITES

www.idsc.gov.eg
www.egypt.travel/sitemap

A village in the nature reserve in Matobo National Park, Zimbabwe.
© istockphoto.com/Poula Hansen

CAMPFIRE: Local Community Involvement in Safari Tourism

INTRODUCTION

This case study introduces an innovative tourism programme that involves the management of wildlife by local communities in Africa so that they can benefit directly from tourism and reduce poverty. On completion of this case you will:

1. Be aware of some of the wildlife management issues in Africa.
2. Understand the principles of the management of wildlife by local communities under the CAMPFIRE (Communal Areas Management Programme for Indigenous Resources) programme.
3. Be aware that the key elements of the programme involve hunting and safari tourism for the economic benefit of local communities.
4. Understand that there is opposition to the programme from those who oppose hunting.
5. Recognise that the CAMPFIRE project is a good example of community-based tourism that assists in poverty alleviation.

TOURISM IN CONTEXT

DEMAND

RESOURCES

CLIMATE

TRANSPORT

FUTURES

KEY ISSUES

There are five key issues in this case:

1. Tourism in Africa faces a number of challenges, two of which are the imperative for sustainable wildlife management and the need to deliver the benefits of tourism to the local community in order to reduce poverty.
2. The CAMPFIRE programme is focussed upon hunting and safari tourism.
3. The CAMPFIRE programme is a partnership between local authorities, communities and the tourism sector to allow local people to manage and benefit from the tourist exploitation of wildlife.
4. There is opposition to the CAMPFIRE programme from those who oppose hunting.
5. The CAMPFIRE programme is a classic example of successful community-based tourism.

CAMPFIRE

CAMPFIRE was founded in the 1980s in Zimbabwe and has since spread to other countries in Southern Africa. It involves the management of wildlife resources by local African communities to earn money from tourism and so reduce poverty. Wildlife conservation is no longer an end in itself – it must be seen to pay its way.

Zimbabwe is suffering from inflation and a political dictatorship. Over one-third of the population live below the poverty line. Around 12 per cent of the area of Zimbabwe is protected as national park land. The rural areas of Zimbabwe, as elsewhere in Africa, are experiencing the following problems:

- A demographic crisis, with the population in some areas doubling every 20 years.
- A fall in real incomes.
- A decline in investment.
- Climatic change, with droughts becoming more frequent – this particularly hits subsistence farmers who make up more than 80 per cent of the population.

At the same time wildlife habitats are dwindling. This causes:

- Environmental degradation in the existing game reserves through overgrazing.
- Damage to African farms outside the reserves – for example, by elephants trampling crops, or predators killing livestock.

Traditionally, wildlife in Zimbabwe had been utilised by the African tribes as a community resource controlled by the chief and his council. Under British colonial rule, wildlife was declared the property of the state and hunting was outlawed. The best agricultural lands were reserved for the white settlers. The designation of the Hwange and Gonorezhou National Parks in the 1950s and 1960s involved the eviction of thousands of villagers of the Shangaan tribe from their lands without compensation, and relocation to communal lands outside the parks. When independence under African majority rule brought no improvement to their situation, the Shangaan reacted with a poaching campaign directed against the national park system. The government responded by transferring ownership of wildlife from the state to the local community. The CAMPFIRE programme is a partnership between local councils and the public and private sectors in tourism. Recently, the World Wildlife Fund for Nature has become involved, by advising on wildlife management. The programme is designed to encourage local communities to take decisions about wildlife management. The overall approach is to encourage responsible management of the ecosystem and in doing so provides a legal means for communities to benefit from wildlife resources. There are five sources of income form the CAMPFIRE programme – trophy hunting, selling live animals, selling meat, harvesting natural resources and tourism.

In terms of tourism, although a few CAMPFIRE communities are involved with white-water rafting companies operating on the Zambezi, and in managing luxury camps for ecotourists, the bulk of their income is from hunting safaris, as follows:

- Safari companies pay rent for the use of communal lands, and employ local people as trackers.
- Hunters pay hunting and trophy fees, amounting to approximately $12 000 for a mature elephant, the most sought-after game. While the hunter retains the trophies, the meat is shared out amongst the villagers, whose everyday diet lacks protein.

The district council decides on an annual quota of animals to be killed, with the advice of the World Wildlife Fund for Nature as to sustainability. The revenue is distributed to the local villages, each of which has a CAMPFIRE committee that decides how the money should be spent. Twenty per cent of the income goes to the district council for administration; the remainder goes to the communities.

From an African viewpoint CAMPFIRE is justified for the following reasons:

- It encourages high income, low volume tourism. Although fees are high there is no shortage of wealthy clients, including hunting enthusiasts from the USA.
- Big game hunting is beneficial for the conservation of wildlife, as numbers are kept within the ecological capacity of the area by selective culling. Elephant numbers have actually increased in CAMPFIRE managed areas, as poachers no longer gain support from the local community.
- Hides and ivory are valuable wildlife resources in marginal areas where little else can be produced. The lifting of the 1989 ban on the export of ivory by CITES (The UN Convention on International Trade in Endangered Species) has allowed Zimbabwe and other Southern African countries to earn as much as $50 million a year in revenue from Japan, and more recently, China. This ivory would be from legally culled elephants.
- Hunting benefits the local community, bringing in revenue for much-needed schools, clinics and infrastructure. It encourages enterprise and involvement by local people. The revenue from sport hunting is four times more profitable per

TOURISM IN CONTEXT

DEMAND

RESOURCES

CLIMATE

TRANSPORT

FUTURES

TOURISM IN CONTEXT

DEMAND

RESOURCES

CLIMATE

TRANSPORT

FUTURES

hectare than raising cattle on the same land. Not surprisingly, one-third of all land in Zimbabwe is now given over to wildlife conservation, including privately owned game reserves and game ranches as well as national parks.

Opposition to the CAMPFIRE programme has come mainly from environmentalists in the USA. The powerful animal rights lobby – the Humane Society – oppose hunting in principle. The future of this type of tourism hangs in the balance because the CAMPFIRE project is funded as part of the package of foreign aid that has to be approved each year by the US Congress, and the political situation in Zimbabwe continues to deteriorate.

The issue here for discussion is whether the Western world is justified in imposing its own value systems regarding hunting on a different culture, thereby denying the people an opportunity of becoming more self-reliant on the basis of their own resources.

REFLECTIONS ON THE CASE

This case has demonstrated a successful example of community-based tourism. The CAMPFIRE programme succeeds in the twin aims of delivering tourism benefits to indigenous communities whilst at the same time contributing to the sustainable management of Africa's wildlife resources. Whilst it is criticised by those who oppose recreational hunting, there is no doubt that the African tourism sector needs more of these types of initiatives.

DISCUSSION POINTS

1. Discuss whether the Western world is justified in imposing its own value systems regarding wildlife conservation on African communities.
2. Debate the ethics of hunting and safari tourism in Southern Africa from the viewpoints of the various stakeholders involved. These might include representatives of African rural communities, NGOs (non-governmental organisations) working in the region, tour organisers, the pro-animal welfare lobbyists and the tourists themselves.
3. Design publicity material for distribution at 'grass roots' level that would convince African villagers of the case for regarding wildlife as an asset to be conserved, rather than as a liability.
4. Explain why, despite initiatives such as CAMPFIRE, the future of wildlife in Southern Africa remains under threat.
5. Investigate the methods of transport and the types of accommodation used by tourists visiting the game reserves of Southern Africa, and suggest ways in which the safari experience could be made more sustainable.

Key sources

Dieke, P. (2000) *The Political Economy of Tourism Development in Africa.* Cognizant, New York.

Gamble, W. P. (1989) *Tourism and Development in Africa.* Murray, London.

Kester, J. (2003) International tourism in Africa. *Tourism Economics*, 9 (2), 203–221.

Websites

www.unsystem.org/ngls/documents/publications.en/voices.africa/number6/vfa6.08.htm

www.worldbank.org/wbi/sourcebook/sbxc05.htm

http://povertyenvironment.net/files/CASE%20Zimbabwe.pdf

TOURISM IN CONTEXT

DEMAND

RESOURCES

CLIMATE

TRANSPORT

FUTURES

Essaouira port on the Moroccan coast, blue fishing boats and white buildings of walled city.
© istockphoto.com/Sean Randall

Vision 2010: A Tourism Strategy for Morocco

INTRODUCTION

Morocco along with Tunisia accounts for a high proportion of the tourist arrivals for the continent of Africa. However, the past model of tourism for both countries has been over-dependent on inclusive tours and beach tourism with a low economic yield. Yet Morocco's economy depends to a large extent on tourism for income and employment. In response, the government has devised a wide-ranging plan to upgrade tourism and attract more high-spending visitors. This case study outlines Morocco's Vision 2010. On completion of the case you will:

1. Understand the importance of tourism to Morocco and other North African countries.
2. Be aware of the main objectives of Morocco's Vision 2010.
3. Understand how Morocco is targeting new markets with the Vision.
4. Be aware of the range of new products, including substantial investment in beach tourism, involved in the Vision.
5. Understand the issues surrounding the implementation of strategies such as Vision 2010.

TOURISM IN
CONTEXT

DEMAND

RESOURCES

CLIMATE

TRANSPORT

FUTURES

KEY ISSUES

There are five key issues in this case:

1. Tourism can play a major contribution to the economies of northern Africa, given that the countries involved have growing populations with high rates of unemployment and poverty. However, if tourism is to play an effective role in underpinning these econo- mies, it will need to be redesigned to deliver positive economic benefits.
2. The Moroccan government has decided to design a disciplined strategic framework for tourism to guide its future and to ensure that economic benefits can be delivered.
3. The first element of Vision 2010 is the diversification of Morocco's tourism market to ensure that it is not overly dependent upon France and that it can attract high-yield tourists.
4. The second element of Vision 2010 involves redesigning the tourism product to deliver the type of tourism demanded by the new markets. These products include an ambi- tious investment programme in beach tourism, as well as both rural and cultural tourism.
5. Crafting and implementing a plan for Morocco's tourism future raises a number of issues – in particular the danger of exceeding the capacity of Morocco's built and natu- ral heritage to receive large numbers of tourists.

TOURISM IN MOROCCO

Only a 15-kilometre wide stretch of water separates it from Spain, yet Morocco is very different from Europe, and the Western tourist arriving at, say, Tangier experi- ences something of a culture shock. The timeless scenes in the countryside and the crowded, tortuous *medinas* (old Arab districts) of the cities have a particular appeal, making the country a favourite location for film-makers. The country is a blend of African and Middle Eastern influences, where the Islamic heritage is dom- inant, particularly in the architecture. Traditional lifestyles persist in mountain areas such as the High Atlas and in the semi-desert south, where the Berbers have a language and culture which is distinct, and to an extent marginalised, from the Arab-speaking majority and the Western-educated, French-speaking elite of mod- ern cities such as Casablanca. In its physical geography and climate, Morocco is different from sub-Saharan Africa, and the Atlas ranges are fold mountains geologi- cally similar to those of southern Europe. The High Atlas ranges are snow-covered during the winter months, while the Atlantic coast of southern Morocco enjoys a sub-tropical climate, making it an ideal winter sun destination.

On the basis of its natural and cultural resources Morocco has developed a sig- nificant tourism industry, but one that is dominated by beach tourism and tour operators based in northern Europe. Tunisia is Morocco's main North African competitor, offering similar products but on a less extensive resource base.

Morocco, like all North African countries, has a high birth rate and a growing number of young people (over half the population are under 25 years of age). This

TOURISM IN CONTEXT

DEMAND

RESOURCES

CLIMATE

TRANSPORT

FUTURES

'demographic time bomb' means that the Moroccan economy cannot support them and unemployment is high. As a result, tourism is seen as a major contributor to both the economy and employment, representing 8 per cent of gross domestic product and employing well over 600 000 people. However, the tourism model of the past, with its dependence on inclusive tours and overseas tour operators, tends to generate low-yield tourism. Morocco is therefore reconsidering its approach and has developed 'Vision 2010', a far reaching tourism strategy for the twenty-first century.

'Vision 2010' was launched in 2001 on the personal initiative of King Mohammed VI, and is linked to a series of reforms to modernise the economy, tackle illiteracy and raise the status of women. The Vision is a partnership between the government, headed by the monarch, and the Moroccan Employers Federation, which recognises that tourism development is a national priority. The Vision became law in October 2001 and has the twin aims of transforming tourism in Morocco and enhancing its economic contribution (to a target of 20 per cent of GDP by 2010). The Vision uses tourism as a means to reduce poverty and unemployment in Morocco and to contribute to social goals.

Vision 2010

The Vision has three main themes:

Diversifying the market

The Vision hinges upon removing Morocco's dependence upon the inclusive tour and moving to a more up-market tourism. The French, mainly due to the old colonial ties between France and Morocco, and to a lesser extent the Spanish (through the proximity of the two countries rather than their historical associations), dominate the market for tourism to Morocco. Part of the strategy is designed to diversify Morocco's markets away from this dependency upon France and Spain. In particular, the strategy targets tourists from the emergent markets of China, India and other Asian countries.

In addition, the Vision targets the domestic market for growth by offering discounts and promotional packages to Moroccan nationals and developing social tourism schemes for the disadvantaged. This approach is based upon detailed market research into the domestic market.

The targets in the strategy are ambitious:

- ten million tourists by 2010 (7.4 million visited in 2007 compared to just over 3 million when the Vision was launched in 2001)
- six million domestic tourism nights by 2010.

Developing the product

Currently over 40 per cent of international tourists go to the main beach resort of Agadir, and 30 per cent visit Marrakech for its cultural tourism attractions. The

TOURISM IN CONTEXT

DEMAND

RESOURCES

CLIMATE

TRANSPORT

FUTURES

key aim of the Vision is to develop the Moroccan tourism product away from these two key locations by promoting and developing other destinations. The four main development themes of the Vision 2010 are:

1. Beach tourism
2. Cultural tourism
3. Rural tourism
4. Niche tourism

The targets on the supply side for the Vision are equally ambitious and demand substantial investment:

- increasing the supply of accommodation by 160 000 beds (of which two-thirds will be located on the coast and the remainder at destinations attracting cultural tourism) to take the total to 230 000 beds
- six major new coastal resorts to be developed under the 'Plan Azur'
- building 1000 kilometres of new roads
- creating 600 000 new jobs (almost doubling the total in tourism)
- training 70 000 tourism professionals.

These ambitious targets are being achieved through a series of measures:

- improving air access and levels of service to Morocco and liberalising air transport to open up routes to low-cost carriers such as Ryanair; this initiative is designed to ensure that the new accommodation developments are co-ordinated with access arrangements
- restructuring the public sector organisation of tourism, boosting promotional budgets, developing partnerships with the tourism industry and utilising new technology
- developing training schemes to increase human capacity for tourism in the country; this is particularly focused upon customer service training, and includes an expanded role for the police to ensure that the *medinas* are more 'tourist-friendly'
- developing a new financial and taxation strategy to encourage new investors in tourism.

BEACH TOURISM

A major part of the plan deals with beach and coastal tourism and this comprises two themes:

1. Firstly, upgrading facilities and reinvesting in the existing resorts of Agadir and Tangier, which have both suffered from a lack of investment in facilities and infrastructure for some time.
2. Secondly, the construction and development of six 'new-generation' resorts. Of these, one is located on the Mediterranean coast and the rest on the much more extensive Atlantic coast. These resorts are designed to attract up-market tourism with both a regional and international clientele, and marinas are an

important feature of these developments. The resorts are designed to blend in with the local environment and strict building codes are in place. The initiative aims to generate 'intelligent seaside' tourism. Each new resort is close to an existing historic or cultural tourism site, as shown below:

- **Plage Blanche (Guelmim)** – partly an ecotourism resort, situated in the deep south of Morocco and positioned as an 'oasis by the sea'
- **Taghazout (Agadir)** – a resort for sport and leisure
- **Mogador (Essaouira)** – close to the established destination of Essaouira where the medina of this historic seaport is a World Heritage Site
- **Mazagan (El Haouzia, El Jadida)** – a business-oriented resort for training and seminars along with sporting facilities
- **Lixus (Larache)** – a spa product with health fitness and sports
- **Saidia (Berkane)** – this is the only resort on the Mediterranean coastline and focuses on leisure and sports; it is designed to compete with Tunisia, Turkey and Spain's Costa del Sol.

CULTURAL TOURISM

Morocco has a rich resource base for cultural tourism with 7 World Heritage Sites, over 300 listed sites of antiquities and a wide range of handicrafts. A real issue in the development of cultural tourism is the relationship between the Ministry of Tourism, responsible for promoting and managing visits to cultural sites, and the Ministry of Culture, which is responsible for the conservation and management of these sites. There is a danger here that the success of tourism to these sites, encouraged by larger promotional budgets, will swamp the resources of the less well-funded Ministry of Culture. This is particularly the case when a site gains World Heritage listing, as tourist volumes tend to increase dramatically. Indeed, many of Morocco's historic sites and buildings are in poor condition, and where the Ministry of Culture does not have the funding to preserve and restore them, private foundations and international agencies such as the World Bank often step in.

RURAL TOURISM

Rural tourism is seen as an important means to spread the benefits of tourism to poorer areas and to spread the load of tourism away from the coast and fragile heritage sites. This is being done through the development of routes and trails with associated infrastructure and accommodation. Rural tourism has the potential to increase employment in the countryside and remote mountain communities, particularly for women, and to improve the living conditions of the rural poor. Destination management plans are being implemented to not only open up new areas for tourism, namely Chefchaouen in the Rif, Ifrane and Immouzer Ida Outanane in the Middle Atlas, but also to strengthen areas where tourist activities are well-established and need to be enhanced. These include Berber communities in the High Atlas, where trekking is already an important tourist activity, and the oasis towns on the fringes of the Sahara, such as Er Rachidia, Ouarzazate (a major location for film-making) and Zagora.

TOURISM IN CONTEXT

DEMAND

RESOURCES

CLIMATE

TRANSPORT

FUTURES

NICHE TOURISM

Niche products are also being developed to attract particular market segments. These include:

- the improvement of port facilities to accommodate cruise ships at Tangier, Casablanca, Safi and Agadir
- windsurfing and kite surfing at Dakhla on the coast of the Western Sahara
- parachuting in Beni Mellal in the Middle Atlas mountains
- surfing on the Atlantic coast at Mirleft, south of Agadir, and at Safi
- hunting in Arbaoua and Bin El Ouidane-Azilal (Province of Kenitra)
- the tourist 'train of the desert' in Bouarfa
- water sports in Laayoun
- sea canoeing off the Mediterranean coast near Nador, Al Hoceima and Chefchaouen.

DESTINATION MANAGEMENT

In addition to these two key themes, the Vision also has a significant destination and image management element for each of the major cities and destinations in Morocco. Morocco's cities have not benefited from professional destination management and this will change with implementation of tourist regional development programmes (PDRT) for the leading cities of Fez, Casablanca, Agadir, Tangier and Tetouan.

SOME ISSUES

If Morocco's Vision is to be successful then a number of additional factors will need to be dealt with. These include the danger of exceeding the carrying capacity at Morocco's fragile heritage sites, balancing the ambitious wave of property development involved in Plan Azur with environmental considerations, ensuring that the marketing and development plans are underpinned by detailed and accurate research and statistics, boosting the limited infrastructure provision in the remoter areas of the country, and finally, ensuring that the new developments and investment incentives for tourism development benefit local businesses as well as the larger international companies.

REFLECTIONS ON THE CASE

This case has shown how Morocco has decided to take its tourism sector into the twenty-first century using an ambitious and far-reaching strategy – Vision 2010. The Vision is a blend of market diversification and product development designed to boost the contribution of tourism to Morocco's economy. The case is an excellent example of how disciplined tourism planning and strategy can deliver real benefits to a country.

DISCUSSION POINTS

1. Draw up a checklist of the main economic benefits of tourism at the national scale. Do you think that Morocco's Vision 2010 will be able to deliver on these benefits?
2. Draw up a five-day itinerary for a group of tourists travelling by coach who are interested in the main cultural attractions of Morocco. Annotate the itinerary with the main points at which the tour group would deliver an economic benefit to the local community through shopping, dining in restaurants or staying in accommodation.
3. Morocco's beach tourism will be dependent upon high environmental standards at the coast. Draft a list of potential threats to that coastal environment that could be potentially caused by Plan Azur, and for each threat suggest a solution. Which of these threats and solutions is in the control of the tourism sector?
4. What are the main benefits of a strategic plan for tourism?
5. Some commentators on Vision 2010 have argued that the massive growth of tourism envisaged, along with the encouragement of low-cost carriers, is difficult to reconcile with 'quality tourism'. In class, debate whether their fears of an influx of tourists who are less culturally sensitive than previous visitors to Morocco, and a decline in the tourism experience, are justified.

Key sources

Ambrose, T. and Weeks, J. (2002) Eastern promise: cultural tourism opportunities in Morocco. *Locum Destination Review*, Winter 2002, 26–28.

Caffin, A. and Jobbins, G. (2003) Governance, capacity and stakeholders in the development and management of coastal tourism: examples from Morocco and Tunisia. *Journal of Sustainable Tourism*, 11 (2&3), 224–245.

Dieke, P. U. C. (2000) *The Political Economy of Tourism Development in Africa*. Cognizant, New York.

Websites

www.essentialmorocco.com
Morrocanway/vision.html
www.tourism-in-morocco.com

TOURISM IN CONTEXT

DEMAND

RESOURCES

CLIMATE

TRANSPORT

FUTURES

Dubai Marina at dusk, the largest Marina residence in the world.
© istockphoto.com/Alex Jeffries

Dubai: Where the Future of Tourism Begins

INTRODUCTION

Dubai is set to become a significant destination of the future, thanks to meticulous planning and the vision of its leaders, who are determined to deliver a high-quality tourism experience. Dubai is now an established brand and one of the city's hallmark hotels – the Burj Al Arab, with its distinctive sail-like outline – has become a world famous icon. This case examines the scale and character of tourism in Dubai and the basis of its planning. On completion of this case, you will:

1. Be aware of the extraordinary scale and complexity of Dubai's vision for tourism.
2. Understand the role of tourism in diversifying the economy of Dubai.
3. Be aware of Dubai's advantageous location.
4. Understand the blend of endowed and purpose-built attractions that make up its tourism product.
5. Recognise the range of high-quality tourist facilities and the scale of organisation supporting tourism in Dubai.

KEY ISSUES

There are three key issues in this case:

1. Dubai is set to become one of the most significant destinations in the future. This is being achieved through a meticulously planned strategy of economic diversification with tourism playing a key role. This vision for Dubai is being driven through a strategic plan and is strongly supported by the emirate's leaders and explains the success of the destination.
2. Dubai offers an environment sympathetic to business enterprise where the state plays a leading role. Public sector-led development projects are delivering a high-quality and exciting tourist destination based upon a mix of traditional Arabic heritage attractions and visionary purpose-built developments within a crime-free environment.
3. The emirate's tourism agency is pursuing a strong quality management policy to ensure that Dubai creates a memorable visitor experience.

GENERAL BACKGROUND

Tourism to the Middle East has suffered at the hands of a turbulent political environment, in addition to poor access to some countries. Dubai is a notable exception to this tendency, where tourism is seen as a major strategic thrust to diversify the economy. This looks forward to the time when the country's petroleum resource runs out. Dubai is achieving strong economic growth through a long-term plan and vision for the emirate – a vision that is clearly articulated in the 'Dubai Strategic Plan, 2015 – Dubai Where the Future Begins'. In Dubai, bold and visionary leadership is creating not only a significant city of the twenty-first century, but also a tourism destination of the future where investment in attractions, high-quality accommodation, state-of-the-art infrastructure and a well-articulated strategy are set to attract 15 million visitors by 2015.

The United Arab Emirates (UAE) was established in 1971. Although only the size of Luxembourg, Dubai is the second largest of the seven emirates and was originally little more than a strip of desert and a small fishing settlement noted for its pearls. In the 1830s, it was taken over by a tribe led by the Maktoum family, which still rules the emirate. Due to its location, the UAE has been able to act as a connecting link between Europe and the Indian subcontinent, the Far East and Africa, and it has acquired a reputation for trading and business flair. For example, in the 1950s Dubai captured a large share of the Asian gold market after the government of India imposed severe restrictions on the trade.

DUBAI

Dubai is a city of 1.4 million people, of whom less than 20 per cent are UAE nationals. The majority are expatriates from a wide range of countries, of which three – India, Pakistan and the Philippines – provide the bulk of the unskilled workforce in

TABLE 25.1	Accommodation and demand statistics for Dubai, 1997–2006			
Year	Hotels	Hotel rooms	Hotel beds	Hotel visitors (millions)
1997	246	14 223	25 228	1.79
2000	265	20 315	33 364	2.83
2001	264	21 428	35 483	3.06
2002	272	23 170	38 386	4.11
2003	271	25 574	41 226	4.34
2004	276	26 185	42 812	4.72
2005	290	28 610	47 001	5.23
2006	302	30 850	50 009	5.47

Source: Ministry of Planning/Department of Economic Development/Department of Tourism and Commerce Marketing, Dubai

the construction and service industries. The city is divided into two parts by Dubai Creek, with the old port district of Deira on the northern side and Bur Dubai to the south. Dubai is a good example of a destination that has built upon its natural and cultural heritage whilst investing heavily in purpose-built attractions. Even the climate, where summer temperatures frequently exceed 40 °C (104 °F) hardly acts as a constraint, thanks to air conditioning; indeed hotels report occupancy rates of over 80 per cent in the hottest months. Dubai offers the tourist a secure and crime-free environment, high standards of service, with the attraction of an Arabian experience. This has led to a boom in tourism where receipts account for close to 30 per cent of gross domestic product (compared to 6 per cent from oil revenues). The city attracted almost 5.5 million visitors to hotels in 2006, each staying for an average of 2.5 nights (Table 25.1). The main markets for Dubai are neighbouring countries in the Middle East, the UK, India, Germany, Russia and the USA.

Tourism in Dubai is part of the emirate's strategic plan which is designed to accommodate the sector's growth, investment and physical planning. This includes attractions, accommodation and transport, infrastructure and the marketing and management of tourism.

We can classify Dubai's attractions as 'endowed' (based on the country's natural and cultural heritage), or as 'artificial', that is purpose-built for tourism and recreation:

ENDOWED ATTRACTIONS

- *Archaeological sites* – the three main archaeological sites in Dubai are Al Ghusals, Al Sufooh and Jumeirah.
- Burj Nahar city with its three watchtowers.
- Dubai Museum housed within the Al Fahidi Fort.
- Sheikh Saeed Al Maktoum House Museum
- Desert experiences and Bedouin camps.

TOURISM IN CONTEXT

DEMAND

RESOURCES

CLIMATE

TRANSPORT

FUTURES

- The spice and gold souks.
- Mosques.
- The Al Maha eco-tourism project and resort where the endangered Arabian oryx has been re-introduced to become one of the showpieces.

ARTIFICIAL ATTRACTIONS

- Al Boom Tourist Village.
- *Shopping* – with over 20 shopping malls, including the Mall of Arabia.
- Nightlife (although gambling is prohibited).
- Wild Wadi Park, a water adventure theme park.
- Festivals and events, including the Dubai World Cup, the Dubai Desert Classic Golf Tournament and the Dubai Shopping Festival.
- *Sport* – the Dubai tennis centre, golf courses, water-sports, power boating, sand skiing, horse racing, polo, falconry, camel-racing, deep sea fishing and dune driving (sometimes known as dune or wadi bashing).
- Palm Jumeirah, the first man made island in the UAE, where the fronds of the 'palm' provide sites for prime real estate developments.
- Artificial ski slopes.
- Spa and medical facilities for health and 'wellness' seekers.

It is these artificial attractions which are helping to create the distinctiveness of Dubai as a tourist destination. By 2015, a range of new significant new developments are planned which will change the face of the city even further. These include:

- The Dubai Waterfront development.
- The Dubai Marina.
- The World project whereby 200 off-shore artificial islands create a map of the world.

Palm Jumeirah, the first man made island is a major artificial attraction. ©istockphoto. com/Haider Yousuf

- Sports City.
- Theme parks including Universal City, Dubailand and the Falcon City of Wonders.
- The Lagoons development set around the Dubai Opera House, planetarium, museums and theatres.

TRANSPORT

Dubai operates an open skies policy, and its national airline – Emirates – has been remarkably successful, even post-9/11. As a result, Dubai is the most accessible destination in the Middle East with Dubai International Airport accommodating 107 airlines, connecting to over 160 destinations in 2004. The airport was opened in 1960 and, located only four kilometres from the city, is now the airline hub for the region and ranked 10th in the world for passenger movements. Growth in passenger numbers has been dramatic, rising from 4.3 million in 1988 to reach 18 million in 2004. The airport's growth is being accommodated by the development of a new terminal and concourse which will increase the airport's capacity to almost 70 million passengers a year.

The Dubai Cruise Terminal was opened in 2001 at Port Rashid to capture this lucrative market. The terminal can handle up to two ships simultaneously with a unique mobile design to enable customisation of passenger and baggage flows.

Internal transport around Dubai is facilitated by the excellent infrastructure, including a metro. Tourist-specific transport includes helicopter and light aircraft tours, Wonder Bus (the first amphibious bus in the Middle East), and cruises by water taxi and dhow (the traditional Arab sailing vessel).

ACCOMMODATION

Dubai has a reputation for luxury hotels and has created a favourable investment environment for hotel companies. Growth has been impressive (Table 25.1), and a number of new properties are planned, including Intercontinental, Movenpick and Ritz-Carlton. In 2006 Dubai had just over 300 hotels and 50 000 bedspaces.

GOVERNMENT ORGANISATION

The main public sector agency for tourism is the Dubai Department of Tourism and Commerce Marketing (DCTPB). It was established in 1997 with the vision to position Dubai as the leading tourism destination and commercial hub in the world. Its mission is one of economic diversification through:

- The development of sustainable tourism.
- The provision of a unique visitor experience combining quality service and value for money.
- The innovative promotion of Dubai's commerce and tourism opportunities.
- The further development of partnership with industry stakeholders.

TOURISM IN CONTEXT

RESOURCES

CLIMATE

TRANSPORT

FUTURES

219

The DCTPB has two main areas of responsibility:

1. The international promotion of Dubai's commerce and tourism interests. The DCTPB plans and implements an integrated programme of international promotions and publicity activities, including participating in exhibitions, marketing visits, presentations and road shows, familiarisation and assisted visits, advertising brochure production and distribution, media relations and enquiry information services.
2. The planning, supervision and development of the tourism sector in the emirate. This includes the classification and licensing of hotels, hotel apartments, tour operators, tourist transport companies and travel agents. Its supervisory role also covers all tourism, archaeological and heritage sites, tourism conferences and exhibitions, the operation of tourist information services and the organisation and licensing of tour guides.

The DCTPB has a quality policy designed to satisfy tourists' requirements. This has been achieved through a quality management system (QMS) complying with the international standard ISO 9001:2000, and includes special policies for visitors with special needs. The licensing and classification of hotels is designed to enhance the levels of quality service in the emirate and ensure that the availability of services and facilities are in accordance with the expectations of visitors.

PROBLEMS FOR THE FUTURE?

Despite Dubai's undoubted success as a haven of stability and tolerance amid the turbulent Middle East, the destination and its government have been criticised by environmentalists, who question its sustainability credentials, and by human rights campaigners. For example, the artificial ski slopes consume enormous quantities of water and power, while Dubai citizens have some of the world's largest ecological footprints. It is claimed that large-scale dredging for port facilities and all those artificial islands has already caused serious damage to the marine ecosystems of the Gulf. The desert vegetation, which is slow to regenerate, is under threat from four wheel drive vehicles and quad bikes which leave the designated trails.

The treatment of the Asian workforce on which the economy largely depends is also proving to be controversial. Many of these people suffer from short-term contracts, abuse by recruitment agencies, overcrowded barrack-like accommodation, limited leisure facilities and inadequate protection at the workplace. Furthermore, there is evidence of widespread trafficking in women for sex tourism, mainly from Eastern Europe and the CIS.

REFLECTIONS ON THIS CASE

Dubai is set to become one of the most exciting and visionary destinations of the future. This vision is being realised through a disciplined strategic planning process and public sector-led investment in major projects as part of an economic diversification process. The emirate's tourism success lies in delivery of a safe and secure experience of an Arabic culture, combined with stunning purpose-built attractions. The government's tourism agency is augmenting this approach with a quality management plan designed to ensure a high-quality tourism visit to the emirate.

DISCUSSION POINTS

1. Using the Dubai Department of Tourism and Commerce Marketing website (www.dubaitourism.ae), identify Dubai's top five markets. For each of these list the main threats that Dubai may face in attracting this market in the future.
2. Draw up a two-day sight seeing itinerary for a specialist group of amateur historians, interested in the emirate's Arabic heritage.
3. Currently, the seven emirates – Abu Dhabi, Ajman, Dubai, Fujairah, Ras Al Khaimah, Sharjah and Umm Al Quwain – promote tourism separately. Draw up a proposal outlining the benefits of the emirates co-operating to create a pan-Arab tourism body.
4. In class, debate the possible conflict between promoting and displaying Dubai's Arabic heritage and the glamorous new developments in the city which may detract from this heritage.
5. Draw up a two-day sightseeing itinerary for a group of architects keen to see the new buildings being constructed in Dubai.

KEY SOURCES

Anwar, S. A. (2004) Festival tourism in the United Arab Emirates: first-time versus repeat visitor perceptions. *Journal of Vacation Marketing*, 10 (2), 161–170.

Henderson, J. C. (2006) Tourism in Dubai: overcoming barriers to destination development. *International Journal of Tourism Research*, 8 (2), 87–99.

Hickman, L. (2007) *The Final Call: In Search of the True Cost of our Holidays*. Transworld Publishers, London.

Sharpley, R. (2002) The challenges of economic diversification through tourism: the case of Abu Dhabi. *International Journal of Tourism Research*, 4 (3), 221–235.

WEBSITES

www.dubaitourism.ae
www.dubaiairport.com

TOURISM IN CONTEXT

DEMAND

RESOURCES

CLIMATE

TRANSPORT

FUTURES

Shacks in Soweto South Africa.
© istockphoto.com/Steven Allan

Township Tourism

INTRODUCTION

Tours to the townships of South Africa have been developed in recent years as a form of pro-poor tourism and to meet the demand for authenticity from the 'new tourist'. However, this type of tourism is controversial and raises a number of issues exemplified by this case of the township of Soweto. On completion of the case you will:

1. Understand the nature of, and background to, township tourism.
2. Be aware of the structure of township tourism.
3. Recognise the consequences for the local community.
4. Understand the many challenges facing township tourism.
5. Be aware of the need for township tourism to be more closely linked to the tourism sector.

TOURISM IN
CONTEXT

RESOURCES

CLIMATE

TRANSPORT

FUTURES

KEY ISSUES

There are four key issues in this case:

1. Township tourism has a particular structure based upon small groups, short stays and 'local' guides. This structure is preventing tourism reaching its full potential in townships such as Soweto.
2. The current infrastructure in Soweto is not adequate to support a major increase in township tourism.
3. There is a real dilemma with township tourism in that if it grows beyond a certain point, authenticity will be lost.
4. Township tourism in Soweto is not currently engaged with the conventional tourism sector in South Africa and this has reduced its potential economic contribution to the township communities.

TOWNSHIP TOURISM

The townships of the post-apartheid South Africa have embraced pro-poor tourism as a means of alleviating deprivation in their communities, while for the tourist seeking authenticity these have become very distinctive destinations.

The townships of South Africa developed in the early 1950s as a result of the planning policy of racial segregation imposed by the former apartheid system of white supremacy. This has left these communities with a legacy of poor-quality housing such as corrugated iron shacks and 'matchbox houses', unemployment, overcrowding, high crime rates and poor infrastructure caused by the lack of investment in the apartheid years. Since 1994, in the new South Africa, these issues are slowly being tackled as the government is greening the townships with trees and parks, and upgrading the infrastructure with electricity and running water.

SOWETO

Soweto is the largest and most populated of South Africa's townships with around 900 000 people. It is the most influential of the townships in terms of the arts and politics, famed for its resistance to apartheid and its association with internationally known personalities such as Nelson Mandela and Desmond Tutu. As a result, it has become the symbol of the new South Africa, poverty and the legacy of apartheid providing a contrast with the prosperity of Johannesburg and the new South Africa.

The name Soweto is derived from 'South Western Townships' and was coined in the 1960s. It is a sprawling, unplanned group of townships, with some middle class 'extensions'. The first of the Soweto townships, Orlando, was created in 1930 for black labourers in Johannesburg's mines and other industries and located 25 kilometres from the elite white residential areas of the city. Until 1994, the area was a virtual 'no go' area for white people, but since the ending of apartheid Soweto has become the focus for not only tourism, but also major development projects which include:

- The Orlando Ekhaya Project – a shopping and entertainment centre.
- Taxi rank upgrades.
- Providing the roads with an all-weather surface.
- Installing electric street lights.
- Upgrading hostels.
- Upgrading the Five Roses Bowl entertainment centre.
- A centre for disabled children.
- Upgrading local parks.
- Upgrading the water supply.
- Building a tourism information centre.
- Building an international standard hotel.

ATTRACTIONS

The main attraction of the townships is the spontaneity of the everyday life and culture of the community with its music, dancing, art, music, galleries, craft centres and shops. There are also a number of dedicated tourist attractions. These include:

- The Hector Pieterson Museum and Memorial, named to commemorate the children who died in the 1976 uprising.
- Archbishop Tutu's house.
- The Nelson Mandela Museum.
- The Regina Mundi Catholic Church.
- Freedom Square.
- Themed routes such as the 'struggle route tour'.

ACCOMMODATION

Accommodation in Soweto is mainly in bed and breakfast guesthouses, of which there are more than 30. However, despite winning tourism awards and being totally authentic, the guesthouses are struggling to remain viable, as many tourists prefer to stay in more luxurious accommodation in the suburbs of Johannesburg such as Sandton. In addition, a Holiday Inn has opened in Soweto creating more competition for the indigenous accommodation owners. The lack of success of the guesthouses is partly due to:

1. Poor marketing of the guesthouses by the tourism authorities and the owners themselves.
2. Inadequate signposting once tourists are in Soweto.
3. The fact the guesthouses are small and cannot accommodate large groups.
4. Lack of interest on behalf of the inbound tour operators.

TOURISM IN CONTEXT

RESOURCES

CLIMATE

TRANSPORT

FUTURES

TOURISM IN CONTEXT

DEMAND

RESOURCES

CLIMATE

TRANSPORT

FUTURES

Authenticity can also equate to an amateur approach to hospitality. To combat this the government is providing training courses for guesthouse owners and their staff.

TRANSPORT

Transport around Soweto is mainly by guided tour with a large number of 'local' guided tours available, many of which arrange for tourists to meet local people and to visit their homes. One of the first tour companies to be established, in 1985, was 'Face to Face Tours', which uses the 'Soweto knowledge' of locals to guide tourists. There is also a road train that runs through the township.

ADMINISTRATION

Tourism in Soweto is managed by a number of agencies, leading to the danger of duplicated roles and confusion in the minds of visitors:

- The local agency is Soweto Tourism.
- The regional agency is the Gauteng Tourism Authority.
- The township falls under the umbrella of the Johannesburg Tourism Company (JTC), a 'not for gain company' created by the city government to increase the importance of tourism as an economic sector.

DEMAND

Visitor numbers to Soweto have grown rapidly, doubling between 2000 and 2005 to place Soweto as one of the top 20 destinations in South Africa. Demand is dominantly from overseas visitors with around two thirds of all visits, with the USA and the Netherlands as the leading markets. Tourist flow is still small by international standards at around 100 000 visitors a year, but most are excursionists staying in Soweto for around three hours on average. As a result, they do not deliver the economic benefits to the community of an overnight stay. In addition, most visitors come as part of an organised tour with a pre-determined itinerary. For the authorities, attracting domestic tourists is therefore a major challenge to prevent overdependence on international visitors.

THE ISSUES RAISED BY TOWNSHIP TOURISM

- The potential social and cultural impact of township tourism is great if visitors are not well-managed. This will be a particular issue if the volume of visitors grows substantially.

- The environment of the townships is not well suited to tourism. The geographical configuration of the township means that there is no critical mass of attractions that cluster together and which link to support facilities such as accommodation and food and beverage services. There remains a lack of infrastructure and tourists are warned not to go into Soweto alone, not only because of the risk of crime, but also because roads and venues are not signposted and many roads are potholed and badly surfaced; indeed car hire companies do not insure vehicles that go into Soweto. In addition, language barriers and differences in culture constrain the opportunity for businesses to sell art and crafts and to engage with the visitor; moreover the townships operate on a cash economy where neither credit cards nor automated teller cash machines (ATMs) are available.
- A particular issue related to township tourism, and one that is acute in Soweto, is the fact that the operation of tourism is both small-scale and not embedded within the tourism sector. Most of the businesses are small and this brings particular problems:
  - They find it difficult to link into the tourism supply chain.
  - Quality and product satisfaction are often not considered.
  - Products are often narrowly focused and not creative.
  - They have weak bargaining power and as a result often sell their products on price rather than authenticity.

  The solution here is for businesses to work together, forming cooperatives to bargain for better supply prices, market themselves and access the supply chain.
- Yet despite these issues, township tours do provide tourists with a genuine learning experience about the way of life of these communities. Soweto also benefits from the corporate social responsibility of tourism companies such as KDR tours and Southern Sun. They are developing pro-poor tourism schemes by re-investing profits into Soweto development schemes and assisting with training and human capacity development.

REFLECTIONS ON THE CASE

Township tourism is a particularly twenty-first century form of tourism, based on authenticity, delivering pro-poor tourism to the host community on a small scale. However, it is clear that not only does the spatial configuration of the townships make it difficult to develop tourism clusters, but also the dominance of amateur, small businesses means that some of the benefits of tourism to the townships are not being realized. In the future, the key will be to manage the impacts of tourism carefully, to ensure that the scale and authenticity of township tourism will not be compromised and that it will deliver tangible benefits to the hosts.

TOURISM IN CONTEXT

DEMAND

RESOURCES

CLIMATE

TRANSPORT

FUTURES

TOURISM IN
CONTEXT

DEMAND

RESOURCES

CLIMATE

TRANSPORT

FUTURES

DISCUSSION POINTS

1. Draft an itinerary for a half-day township tour of Soweto for a group of social historians.
2. As the marketing manager for Soweto Tourism, develop a marketing strategy to attract domestic tourists and develop a short PowerPoint presentation of the highlights.
3. Draft the key elements of a training programme to assist guesthouse owners in Soweto to develop professional hospitality skills.
4. Design a brochure for cultural tourists that focuses on the life and work of famous residents of Soweto such as Nelson Mandela and the buildings or sites that are associated with them.
5. Debate in class the pros and cons of township tours – on the one hand they are a means of effecting pro-poor tourism, on the other hand they exploit the culture and history of the townships.

KEY SOURCES

Binns, T. and Etienne, N. (2002) Tourism as a local development strategy in South Africa. *The Geographical Journal*, 168 (3), 235–247.

Dieke, P. U. C. (2000) *The Political Economy of Tourism Development in Africa*. Cognizant, New York.

Nemasetoni, I. and Rogerson, C. M. (2005) Developing small firms in township tourism: emerging tour operators in Gauteng. *South Africa Urban Forum*, 16 (2–3), 196–213.

Rogerson, C. (2004) Transforming the South African tourism industry: the emerging black-owned bed and breakfast economy. *GeoJournal*, 60 (3), 273–281.

Rogerson, C. M. (2004) Urban tourism and small tourism enterprise development in Johannesburg: the case of township tourism. *GeoJournal*, 60 (3), 249–257.

WEBSITES

www.soweto.co.za
www.joburg.org.za
www.guateng.net
www.face2face.co.za

Mountaineers climbing Everest.
© istockphoto.com/Sandeep Subba

Adventure Tourism in Nepal

INTRODUCTION

Nepal offers an attractive environment for Western tourists seeking wilderness adventure, and has built upon its legendary mountain climbing legacy. This case analyses the organisation and impacts of adventure tourism in Nepal. On completion of this case you will:

1. Understand the tourism resources of Nepal and their use as a basis for adventure tourism.
2. Understand the organisation and management of trekking in Nepal.
3. Be aware of the economic benefits of adventure tourism in Nepal.
4. Recognise the significant impacts of tourism upon the Nepalese environment and communities.
5. Be aware of strategies to manage the impacts of adventure tourism in Nepal.

TOURISM IN CONTEXT

DEMAND

RESOURCES

CLIMATE

TRANSPORT

FUTURES

KEY ISSUES

There are four key issues in this case:

1. Nepal offers an ideal resource base for adventure tourism products such as mountain climbing, trekking, mountain biking and river-running.
2. Trekking is a major industry in Nepal and along with other adventure tourism products contributes to the Nepalese economy.
3. However, adventure tourism across Nepal has brought with it significant negative impacts to both the environment and the host community.
4. There have been a number of initiatives to alleviate these impacts including projects such as that for the conservation of Annapurna.

ADVENTURE TOURISM IN NEPAL

Nepal offers an attractive environment for Western tourists seeking wilderness adventure. In fact, surprisingly little of this mountainous but quite densely populated country is uninhabited wilderness in the North American sense. Adventure tourism includes the following related activities:

- **Mountain climbing** Nepal forms part of the central Himalayas and boasts the majority of the world's highest summits over 8000 metres. The expedition to climb Annapurna was the first group of Western visitors allowed into Nepal. It was followed three years later by Hillary and Tenzing's successful ascent of Mount Everest in 1953, which attracted worldwide attention. Climbing the Himalayas is exceptionally hazardous, because of the extreme weather conditions and the lack of oxygen at high altitudes; even the base of a mountain like Annapurna is at a higher level than any summit in the Alps. In view of these conditions, most expeditions have been organised on a lavish scale, involving teams of climbers, sophisticated equipment and a small army of Sherpa porters to provide logistical support. The accumulated waste left by successive expeditions, particularly on Everest, has been an environmental disgrace, necessitating a major clean-up operation. However, more climbers are adopting the minimalist approach, pioneered by Reinhold Messner, who proved it was possible to climb peaks at over 8000 metres without the use of supplementary oxygen.
- **River-running** Nepal's fast-flowing rivers, including the Trisuli, Sun Kosi and Karnali, offer ideal conditions for white-water rafting and kayaking, particularly the first two, which are more accessible from Kathmandu.
- **Mountain biking** like river-running, is often combined with trekking by younger Western tourists, and takes place at relatively low altitudes.
- **Trekking**, which provides the main focus for this study.

TREKKING

TOURISM IN CONTEXT

DEMAND

RESOURCES

CLIMATE

TRANSPORT

FUTURES

INTRODUCTION

Trekking is the most popular tourist activity in the Himalayan zone of Nepal. During the late 1990s trekkers accounted for over a quarter of all visitors. Trekking originally developed as a separate activity from climbing in the 1960s, and the treks were based on the approach routes used by the Everest and Annapurna expeditions. Trekking is a way of visiting locations 'off the beaten track', but differs from hiking in a number of ways. Trekkers usually walk in organised groups escorted by a *sirdar* (guide), with a back-up team of cooks and porters who carry food supplies and equipment between the stopping places on the route. Although itineraries can be tailor-made to meet the requirements of small groups of clients, most treks differ little in organisation from other types of inclusive tour. Western-based tour operators carry out the marketing, bring together the clients in their country of origin and arrange for the trekking permits, which for independent travellers involves a time-consuming hassle with Nepalese bureaucracy. Like other tour operators, they may opt for consolidation if there is not enough demand for a particular trek. Some also allege that trekking is not really a sustainable, alternative type of tourism, and as we shall see, there is some evidence to support this view.

Nepal offers an attractive environment for Western tourists seeking widerness adventure. ©istockphoto.com/Jason Maehl

THE ORGANISATION OF TREKKING

Nepal offers a great variety of trekking opportunities including some of the world's most spectacular scenery, the ethnic groups who have modified this landscape over the centuries and a wide selection of routes and types of trek to suit most clients:

TOURISM IN CONTEXT

DEMAND

RESOURCES

CLIMATE

TRANSPORT

FUTURES

- The longer treks, such as the Annapurna Circuit, take up to three weeks and involve tackling steep gradients at altitudes ranging from 1000 to over 5000 metres above sea level. These require a high standard of fitness, and *hypoxia* (altitude sickness) is a risk at the higher levels even for experienced hikers.
- On the other hand, short treks lasting three days or so are available at lower altitudes on less rugged terrain.

The trails – based on established trading routes – are well maintained and trekkers are rarely far from a village. Moreover, large numbers of lodges providing overnight accommodation and *tea houses* offering basic catering facilities have sprung up along most routes to meet their needs.

However, trekking in Nepal shows a high degree of seasonality. Climatic conditions largely dictate that the majority of treks take place between October and December (when snow blocks the high mountain passes) and from March to May, prior to the monsoon rains.

Although new areas are being opened up to meet the demand, trekking also shows a high degree of concentration in particular areas of central and eastern Nepal, including:

- The Annapurna region west of Pokhara, with its well-developed infrastructure of trails and lodges, is the most popular with trekkers and tour operators. It includes among its attractions the Kali Gandaki Valley, reputed to be the world's deepest gorge, and the Annapurna Sanctuary. The region is particularly rich in plant and animal species, including more than 100 species of orchid and the endangered snow leopard.
- The Everest route, from Lukha to the base camp at the foot of Mount Everest, is more demanding for trekkers than the Annapurna circuit and acclimatisation to high altitudes is even more essential. It includes the Khumba region with its Sherpa villages, the famous Thyangboche monastery and the Khumbu glacier that marks the approach to the world's highest mountain. Most of the region has been designated as the Sagarmatha National Park.

Economic impacts of trekking

Trekking is estimated to provide about 24 000 full time jobs and another 20 000 on a part-time basis. In the Annapurna region, 60 per cent of the population rely on tourism for a livelihood. Here the Thakali ethnic group has been particularly successful in taking advantage of the trekking boom, since they run most of the lodges on the Annapurna Circuit. Nevertheless the local economy is too poorly developed to supply most of the goods and services needed by Western tourists, so these have to be imported, often from India. As a result, only an estimated 20 cents out of the 3 dollars spent daily by the average trekker actually contributes to the local village economies. In the Khumba region, one of the least fertile and highest areas of Nepal, the Sherpa lifestyle has changed within a generation, from subsistence pastoralism based on the yak to a cash economy. With a long tradition as traders over the high mountain passes into Tibet, the Sherpas are very much in demand as guides and porters for at least part of the year. Others work in tea houses, shops selling local handicrafts and tourist lodges. Income from tourism allied to Sir Edmund Hillary's fundraising from international donors, has provided schools and basic infrastructure. These impacts are most apparent in Namche Bazar, once a small hamlet and now an important tourist centre, where almost every other building is a hotel or curio shop.

SOCIAL/CULTURAL IMPACTS

The economic opportunities presented by trekkers and mountaineering expeditions have stemmed the previously high rates of out-migration from Himalayan villages, while improved medical care and greater prosperity have encouraged a high rate of population growth. Nevertheless, as in other Third World countries, the contrasts between the lifestyles and altitudes of affluent Western tourists and the poverty of the village communities has resulted in a number of impacts, including:

- The breakdown of traditional social structures due to the differentiation of earning power between those involved in the tourism sector as compared to agriculture.
- The demonstration effect as younger Nepalis strive to emulate Western lifestyles.
- The high incidence of begging from tourists, particularly by young children.
- The loss of the cultural heritage. This can be direct, as in the desecration of religious artefacts that are stolen and sold on the international art market, or indirect, through craftsmen adapting their designs to suit the preferences of Western tourists, for example in the sale of *thankas*, Buddhist temple scrolls, which are highly decorative.

ENVIRONMENTAL IMPACTS

Although national parks and other protected areas demonstrate Nepal's commitment to conservation, the country's forest resources were already dwindling before trekking arrived on the scene to make matters worse. In a country without cheap renewable sources of energy, firewood is used by villages for fuel and cooking. Forest clearance on steep slopes means accelerated soil erosion. In Nepal, 400,000 hectares of forest are cleared each year, resulting in devastating floods and landslides. Trekkers have contributed to Nepal's environmental problems in the following ways:

- The lodges along the major trek routes demand firewood for heating, often from virgin rhododendron forest which is slow to regenerate at high altitudes.
- Large quantities of litter are discarded by trekkers, including plastic water bottles and a trail of toilet paper.
- Water sources are contaminated by human waste from trek campsites.

On the other hand, strict conservation measures, as applied in the Sagarmatha National Park, may put additional strains on traditional agricultural systems already under threat from tourism.

TOURISM IN CONTEXT

DEMAND

RESOURCES

CLIMATE

TRANSPORT

FUTURES

TOURISM IN CONTEXT

DEMAND

RESOURCES

CLIMATE

TRANSPORT

FUTURES

Trekking, perhaps more than other forms of tourism, is characterised by an insatiable demand for new 'unspoiled' locations, which may well be in countries other than Nepal. Despite tourism's impact on the culture and environment of the host community, there is little to show for it in economic terms, as Nepal remains one of the world's poorest countries.

THE ANNAPURNA CONSERVATION AREA PROJECT

Measures involving local communities would appear to provide one solution to the problem, as in the Annapurna Conservation Area Project. This is a partnership between tour operators and local entrepreneurs to encourage sustainable development and prevent ecological disaster along Nepal's most popular trekking routes. The project covers an area of 2600 square kilometres. Its conservation strategy includes:

- The levy of a permit fee on each visitor which goes towards conservation projects.
- The substitution of solar power or kerosene as alternative fuels to firewood.
- A programme of re-afforestation and forest management that allows local villagers to make sustainable use of these resources.
- The raising of environmental awareness among visitors and the local communities.

POLITICAL UNREST

Despite its calm and peaceful image, Nepal has undergone significant political unrest since the mid-1990s. After centuries of rule by a Hindu absolute monarchy it has experienced many changes of government, becoming a republic in 2008. In large areas of the country Maoist revolutionary insurgents fought the Nepalese army for control. Trek operators have often made informal agreements with the rebels, but events such as the massacre of the royal family in 2001, and an uncertain security situation have had a negative impact on tourist arrivals.

REFLECTIONS ON THE CASE

This case has demonstrated how the resource-based and mountain climbing legacy of Nepal has been developed to support a range of adventure tourism products. However, despite the positive economic benefits to the Nepalese economy, adventure tourism is having a number of significant social and environmental impacts in Nepal. These have raised international concern and have become the focus for 'clean-up' tourism and conservation projects such as that for Annapurna.

DISCUSSION POINTS

1. Investigate ways in which trekking could become more sustainable, such as the recycling of discarded materials.
2. Draw up a code of conduct for tour organisers that will respect porters' rights and improve their working conditions, taking into account the economic and social realities of life in Nepal.
3. Differentiate between 'soft' and 'hard' adventure. Account for the growth in demand for activities such as trekking, climbing and river-running in developed Western countries. Which particular groups in Western society generate most of the demand?
4. Using the Internet and a range of holiday brochures, select suitable trekking routes and give appropriate advice to (i) a group of college students who have experience of the 'great outdoors', but who have never visited an Asian country and (ii) a retired bank manager with a family history of heart and pulmonary illnesses.
5. What strategies might the tourist authorities in Nepal utilise to reassure trekkers that the region is safe to travel in?

KEY SOURCES

Baral, E. (2004) Marketing Nepal in an uncertain climate: confronting perceptions of risk and insecurity. *Journal of Vacation Marketing*, 10, 186–192.

Deegan, P. (2003) Appetite for destruction. *Geographical*, 75 (3), 32–36.

Goddie, P., Price, M. and Zimmerman, F. M. (1999) *Tourism and Development in Mountain Regions*. CABI, Wallingford.

Godwin, S. (2003) Trekking into trouble. *Geographical*, 75 (3), 22–27.

Holden, A. and Sparrowhawk, J. (2002) Understanding the motivations of ecotourists: the case of Trekkers in Annapurna, Nepal. *International Journal of Tourism Research*, 4 (6), 435–446.

Nepal, S. K. (2000) Tourism in protected areas: the Nepalese Himalayas. *Annals of Tourism Research*, 27 (3), 661–681.

WEBSITES

www4.gu.edu.au/ext/unesco/theme_c/mod10/uncom10t03s02.htm
www.tourism.gov.np/ministry.php

Hammock under palm trees at the beach of a Maldives island.
© istockphoto.com/Harald Bolten

The Maldives: Tourism in an Island Nation

INTRODUCTION

The Maldives are a pristine marine environment in the Indian Ocean. This case study examines the nature of tourism in the Maldives and the associated development issues. On completion of the case you will:

1. Understand the characteristics of the Maldives and the scale of tourism.
2. Be aware of the fragility of the Maldives' marine environment and its value for tourism.
3. Be aware of the tourist resources and facilities of the Maldives.
4. Be sensitive to the religious and cultural character of the islands and the implications for tourism.
5. Understand the issues surrounding the development and marketing of resorts on the Maldives.

TOURISM IN CONTEXT

DEMAND

RESOURCES

CLIMATE

TRANSPORT

FUTURES

KEY ISSUES

There are five key issues in this case:

1. The islands of the Maldives are set in a pristine marine environment over a large expanse of the Indian Ocean, which causes both access and logistical problems for tourism.
2. The main tourism resource of the Maldives is the marine environment of coral atolls, although the culture of the Maldives is also a potential attraction.
3. Tourism development is sensitive to the cultural and religious traditions of the islands.
4. The Maldives find themselves in the classic dilemma of gauging how much tourism development to allow in order to ensure the conservation of the marine environment.
5. The Maldives authorities have drafted development and marketing plans to control the development of tourism and to ensure that the Maldives attract upmarket tourists.

THE MALDIVES

The Maldives is an independent republic located in the Indian Ocean, south west of the Indian subcontinent. Geographically, the Maldives is a unique collection of 26 coral atolls, containing 1190 coral islands and hundreds of small sandbanks. The Maldives was formed by volcanic eruptions millions of years ago, leaving behind coral reefs as the volcanic cones subsided. All the islands are low lying, on average less than 2 metres above sea level, making them vulnerable to long-term changes in sea level. The islands are scattered over a large expanse of the Indian Ocean, more than 820 kilometres from north to south and 130 kilometres from east to west. This makes transfer to the tourist resorts a logistical problem – indeed in the early days of tourism, experts recommended that the distances involved made tourism development impossible. The climate is hot and humid, with a rainy season between May and November and sea temperatures between 26 and 31 °C, perfect for both beach tourism and the marine life.

Resorts have only been developed on islands not inhabited by the local people. This has the following advantages:

- the privacy of visitors is assured
- Arguably, it minimises negative impacts on the culture of the islanders
- It minimises competition for scarce resources between the tourism industry and other sectors, although resorts do compete for access to marine resources such as the reefs.

Of course, this does mean that cultural tourism in any meaningful sense is minimal. The islanders are devout Muslims and no alcohol is allowed except in the resorts. Mosques are found on many islands and visitors are expected to respect the traditions of Islam in terms of modest dress when visiting the capital, Malé. English is the second language to the local *Dhivehi* tongue.

Apart from tourism, the Maldives also have an important fishing industry. However, tourism is the driving force in the economy as it:

- supports 45 per cent of the jobs in the islands
- brings the islanders an enhanced quality of life
- provides amenities and facilities both for tourists and locals alike through the taxes levied on tourists (there is both a bed tax and an airport tax)
- contributes 30 per cent of the gross domestic product and 70 per cent of foreign currency earnings
- represents almost a quarter of capital investment.

TOURISM DEMAND

The Maldives receives around 600 000 international visitors annually, predominantly from Italy, the UK and Germany, but other important source markets are France, Japan and China. The North American market is in its infancy for the Maldives but holds considerable potential. Growth of demand has been steady and is expected to increase in line with greater bed capacity to the year 2012.

TOURISM RESOURCES

- **The marine environment** The prime tourism resource of the islands is the pristine marine environment where the quality of the coral reefs and marine life is unrivalled anywhere in the world. The majority of visitors arrive in the Maldives to experience this marine environment and also for water sports. Each of the resort islands (many of which are very small) has a diving base and the resort *house reef* is commonly within wading or swimming distance from the accommodation. Scuba diving and snorkelling (night dives and drift dives are a speciality), fishing, underwater photography and a variety of water sports are popular and many resorts have both indoor and outdoor sports facilities, swimming pools and other activities to supplement the attractions of the reef. Spa developments are also emerging in line with international trends. However, this does raise the question as to whether hard engineering, air conditioning, gyms and swimming pools are compatible, in terms of their energy use, with truly sustainable tourism.
- **Malé** The capital is a small town with many shops and restaurants, but little else to attract the visitor, although it contains two thirds of the Maldivian population. Moreover, it is the gateway to the islands through Hulhulé International Airport.
- **Resorts and safari vessels** Tourism is a relatively new development in the Maldives, with the first resort opening as recently as 1972. By the late 1990s, tourism was developed on 73 islands. Tourists have the choice of either basing themselves on one of the resort islands or using safari vessels with 'floating beds'. In the early 2000s, the resorts had almost 15 000 bedspaces, and the safari vessels a further 1700 bedspaces.

The resort islands are self-contained, but far from self-sufficient, as almost all the produce needed for visitors (other than fish) has to be imported. However, a

TOURISM IN CONTEXT

DEMAND

RESOURCES

CLIMATE

TRANSPORT

FUTURES

241

TOURISM IN CONTEXT

DEMAND

RESOURCES

CLIMATE

TRANSPORT

FUTURES

few resorts are experimenting with growing their own vegetables. Water is desalinated and each resort island has its own fleet of boats. Apart from the very distant resorts, staff tends to work on the islands for short intensive periods before returning to Malé for a few days to be with their families. This highlights the isolation of each of the resort islands – visitors are effectively trapped on the island of their choice for the duration of their stay unless they opt for an 'island-hopping' excursion for a day. There are two trends in the accommodation sector:

- the growing popularity of 'all inclusive resorts'
- a number of international hotel companies are now active in this area (namely Hilton, Four Seasons, Shangri-La and Club Méditerranée), although most of the accommodation is leased by local resort operators from the Government of the Maldives, which retains ownership of the islands.

TRANSPORT

As with all island destinations, air access is the key to success or failure. The Maldives are a difficult destination to reach. There are charter flights from Europe (the UK and Germany), and scheduled services include:

- Srilankan Airlines
- Emirates
- Singapore Airlines
- Indian Airlines
- Qatar Airways

However, scheduled services are routed through the respective hub of the airline, so that there are no direct scheduled flights to the Maldives from its main generating markets.

The main gateway to the islands is Hulhulé International Airport at Malé, with a second airport in the South Maldives. Hulhulé is a short speedboat or *dhoni* (sailboat) journey to Malé. Each resort island or safari vessel has to be reached by transfer from the airport. These transfers are sometimes lengthy and thus expensive, as many resorts are over 120 kilometres from Malé. Transfers are by:

- traditional sailboat or *dhoni* (slow and rarely used)
- speedboat (becoming less popular as reaching some resorts from Hulhulé involves a journey of up to three hours)
- seaplane (more commonly used today because of the distances involved).

In the early 1990s, Russian-built helicopters were used for transfers but safety issues led to them being withdrawn from service. Maldivian Air Taxi and Trans Maldivian Airways operate seaplanes. However, seaplanes cannot land at night, so visitors arriving or departing on night flights have to spend one night in a hotel in Malé or Hulhulé before being transferred in the daylight hours. For the remoter islands, there are four domestic airports which allow landing at night, as well as stimulating investment.

In the Maldives it is imperative that tourism development and conservation are balanced.

TOURISM POLICY AND ORGANISATION

It is imperative that tourism development in the Maldives does not threaten the marine environment. Although global warming and rising sea temperatures have affected the coral, these events are outside the control of the islands themselves. The government has designated marine reserves and implemented tourism codes of conduct. Tourism development is being used as a regional development tool for the remoter islands, although this does mean visitors have to undergo long transfers from Malé.

The Ministry of Tourism and Civil Aviation oversees tourism development and regulates the tourism resorts. In the late 1990s the Maldives Tourism Promotion Board was created to market the islands internationally. The islands are the subject of rolling tourism master plans and marketing plans. These plans and policies will determine the future direction of tourism in the Maldives:

Marketing The islands are attempting to position themselves as the premium eco-tourism destination and to diversify their markets – for example into the meetings, incentives, conference and exhibitions (MICE) market.

Development For tourism development in the Maldives the key phrase is *the highly managed expansion of tourism*. The target is to have around 37 000 bedspaces in resorts by the year 2012. This will be achieved on a geographical basis as follows:

- Expansion of development to all the atolls from north to south in the country. Malé and Ari Atoll do not have any suitable islands anymore for resort development.
- In the southern region the development of Vilingili Island as a Shangri-La resort.
- In the remoter atolls, the development of regional airport gateways to stimulate investment.

TOURISM IN CONTEXT

DEMAND

RESOURCES

CLIMATE

TRANSPORT

FUTURES

TOURISM IN CONTEXT

DEMAND

RESOURCES

CLIMATE

TRANSPORT

FUTURES

REFLECTIONS ON THE CASE

This case has shown how the Maldives have to balance the demands for tourism development with the imperative to conserve the pristine marine environment – which is after all why the tourists visit the islands. The tourism product is one of high quality and has been developed with the social and religious traditions of the islands in mind.

DISCUSSION POINTS

1. A consideration in developing tourism in the Maldives is the transfer time to the various resorts from the airport at Hulhulé. Using an atlas with large-scale maps and tour operator's information, plot the transfer routes to the major resorts and draw up a table of transfer times by different craft (seaplane, speedboat, etc.). Do you think that the transfer times act as a constraint upon development on the remoter islands or are part of the attraction?
2. The Maldives is dependent upon their pristine marine environment. Draft a list of potential threats to that marine environment and for each threat, suggest a solution. Which of these threats and solutions is in the control of the tourism sector?
3. The Maldives is a predominantly Islamic society, but one which has traditionally been tolerant of other cultures. It is increasingly under pressure from growing demands for a more democratic government and from Muslim fundamentalists. How might this affect tourism development?
4. Specify the main destinations competing with the Maldives for tourists in the following generating countries:
   (a) The USA
   (b) Europe
   (c) Australia
   (d) South Africa
   How does each competitor rate against the Maldives in terms of attractions, support facilities (such as accommodation) and access?

ACKNOWLEDGEMENT

We are grateful to Aishath Shakeela who provided additional material for this case study.

KEY SOURCES

Athukorala, P.-C. (2004) *Trade Policy Making in a Small Island Economy: The WTO Review of the Maldives*. Blackwell Publishing Ltd, Oxford.

Bryant, N. (2004) Maldives: paradise soon to be lost. BBC Online, viewed 15th September 2006, available at http://news.bbc.co.uk/2/hi/south_asia/3930765.stm.

Dowling, R. K. and Wood, J. C. (2003) Ecotourism development in the Indian Ocean region: the case of shared learning, in R. N. Ghosh, M. A. B. Siddique and R. Gabbay (eds), *Tourism and Economic Development: Case Studies from the Indian Ocean Region*. Ashgate Publishing Ltd, England, pp. 42–62.

Garrod, B. and Wilson, J. (2003) *Marine Ecotourism*. Channelview, Clevedon.

Sathiendrakumar, R. and Tisdell, C. (1989) Tourism and the economic development of the Maldives. *Annals of Tourism Research*, 16 (2), 254–269.

UNWTO (2000) Maldives study points the way for small islands, available at http://www.world-tourism.org/newsroom/Bulletin/archives/son2000/B0007015.html.

UNWTO (2004) *Indicators of Sustainable Development for Tourism Destinations: A Guidebook*. World Tourism Organization, Madrid.

WEBSITES

www.airports.com.mv/
www.aviainfo.gov.mv/
www.employment.gov.mv/
www.meteorology.gov.mv/
www.mv.undp.org/index.aspx
www.planning.gov.mv/en/
www.tourism.gov.mv/
www.visitmaldives.com/

TOURISM IN CONTEXT

DEMAND

RESOURCES

CLIMATE

TRANSPORT

FUTURES

Cape Du Couedic lighthouse on Kangaroo Island of Australia.

Kangaroo Island: Debating Tourism Development

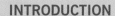

INTRODUCTION

Kangaroo Island is the third largest of Australia's offshore islands, and, as an important wildlife site, tourist destination and home to local communities, it has become a classic case study in the debate about the future development of tourism. On completion of this case you will:

1. Understand the location of and characteristics of Kangaroo Island.
2. Be aware of the natural resource base of Kangaroo Island.
3. Understand the organisation of tourism on Kangaroo Island.
4. Recognise the potential conflict between nature conservation and tourism development.
5. Understand the innovative planning approach taken on Kangaroo Island.

TOURISM IN CONTEXT

DEMAND

RESOURCES

CLIMATE

TRANSPORT

FUTURES

KEY ISSUES

There are five key issues in this case:

1. Kangaroo Island is situated off the southern coast of Australia and is rich in flora and fauna which have been designated as nature reserves.
2. The island has become a classic example of the development dilemma between tourism, the local community and nature conservationists.
3. The island's natural resources have been developed as tourism products in a number of cases.
4. The island's market is changing with improved access from the mainland of South Australia, with more overseas visitors arriving and considerable numbers of day visitors.
5. Kangaroo Island has approached its development dilemma by implementing an innovative planning regime, the Tourism Optimisation Model (TOMM) that is a model for monitoring and managing the health of Kangaroo Island's tourism industry and resources.

KANGAROO ISLAND

Kangaroo Island is situated off the coast of South Australia, 150 kilometres from the capital Adelaide. Its main feature is a low plateau rising to 300 metres resulting in a spectacular coastline. It is thinly populated even by Australian standards with only 4566 inhabitants occupying an area of 4350 square kilometres. Most of these live in the coastal towns of Kingscote and Penneshaw, and inland around Parndana. From the 1980s visitor arrivals steadily increased, so that the island has become a significant tourist destination in South Australia, second only to Adelaide. In the early years of the twenty-first century tourism has become the major contributor to the island's economy, which was based on sheep and cattle raising, and the local farmers have benefited from the additional income gained by developing farm-stays, bed and breakfast, camping and sales of local produce. The authorities and the community therefore have to meet the challenge of sensitively developing tourism in a fragile environment. As part of the South Australia tourism region, the island is committed to sustainable tourism development.

TOURISM RESOURCES

Kangaroo Island's tourist appeal is based upon its rural lifestyle and the fact that, although the island gives the impression of isolation, it provides easier access to Australia's wildlife resources than the outback of the continental interior. Although only a narrow stretch of water separates it from the mainland, this has been sufficient to protect the native wildlife from introduced species such as the dingo, fox and rabbit. Wildlife includes a range of marsupials as well as marine species

TOURISM IN CONTEXT

DEMAND

RESOURCES

CLIMATE

TRANSPORT

FUTURES

representative of the Southern Ocean, such as penguins, seals and sea lions. The main attractions are the Flinders Chase National Park – a wilderness area of *mallee* scrub and woodland, and the Seal Bay Conservation Park, both receiving over 100 000 visitors annually. Other tourism resources include:

- The dramatic coastal scenery, featuring natural attractions such as Remarkable Rocks, Cape Coudic, Admiral's Arch and sea caves.
- The opportunities for sailing, scuba diving and surfing. Fishing charters are available from the north coast.
- Bird watching.
- The natural bushland is ideal for nature retreats, wildlife viewing and 'bush walking' (hiking).
- An interesting heritage, including historic lighthouses and shipwreck sites.
- Niche agricultural products, local gastronomy and wine.
- An expanding events programme – including horse races and local markets.

The natural resources on Kangaroo Island include the dramatic coastal line.
©istockphoto.com/Harris Shiffman

TRANSPORT AND ACCOMMODATION

- Kangaroo Island is easily accessible from Adelaide.
- Kangaroo Island is served by a vehicle ferry from Cape Jervis, the nearest point on the South Australia mainland.
- Small plane services are available.

Touring on the island is mainly by coach, or more tailor-made tours using four-wheel-drive vehicles. At Penneshaw, the island's gateway visitor centre acts as an orientation and interpretation point for newly arriving visitors.

Accommodation is mainly in the form of apartments, small motels and hotels and ranges from informal camping sites, through farm stays and holiday houses,

TOURISM IN CONTEXT

DEMAND

RESOURCES

CLIMATE

TRANSPORT

FUTURES

to low impact holiday villages and 'heritage house accommodation' (historic cottages) in the Flinders Chase National Park.

Limited water resources and fire risk to the native vegetation have to be considered in tourism development.

DEMAND

Most visitors arrive in the summer months and during school holidays. Visitor numbers approached 150 000 in 2002. Around 95 per cent of visitors are overnight travellers and stayed an average of 3.9 nights as the majority of the island's visitors are from interstate or international in origin (above 65 per cent). As a result of this growing number of international and interstate visitors, intrastate visitors have declined by almost 7 per cent since 2004. Domestic tourists are more attracted to the recreational activities on the island, while foreign visitors find the viewing of wildlife and scenery, and the experience of staying in a rural area of Australia, more appealing. The majority of visitors have been satisfied with their experience overall.

ORGANISATION

There are a number of agencies involved in managing tourism on Kangaroo Island:

- At local level:
  - Kangaroo Island Council
  - Tourism Kangaroo Island
  - Kangaroo Island Development Board
  - Kangaroo Island Natural Resources Management Board
- At state level:
  - South Australia Tourism Commission
  - Department of Environment and Heritage

It is the nature of Kangaroo Island as a significant natural resource (30 per cent of the area is protected, with national or conservation park status) and also as a thriving rural community, that has given rise to the debate over the island's future, particularly in terms of tourism. In response, a range of planning and management initiatives have been implemented:

- As tourism expanded, a tourism policy for the island was implemented in 1991 dividing Kangaroo Island into 11 tourism zones, identifying the resources in each of the zones, and the potential for future development.
- The tourism policy stimulated considerable debate and community consultation that eventually culminated in a Sustainable Development Strategy for the island in 1995. The mission statement of this strategy was:
  - 'Kangaroo Island will be one of the world's pre-eminent nature-based tourist destinations with a strong rural industry selling its products to tourist, mainland and overseas markets, a high quality of life for residents and well managed natural resources'.
  - In order to achieve this strategy an innovative approach to monitoring the island's tourism was developed, known as the TOMM. TOMM involves

extensive consultation as to the future of the island; identification of key indicators and benchmarks to monitor progress towards future conditions; and a system of monitoring to ensure the island is on track to achieve these conditions. TOMM has become internationally recognised as an effective approach to planning and managing sustainable tourism.

- In 2002 the South Australian Tourism Commission and Planning South Australia launched a consultation document on environmentally sustainable tourism development.
- In 2006 the Kangaroo Island Strategic Tourism Plan was prepared to provide a clear vision and direction for tourism growth for Kangaroo Island over the next 20 years in conjunction with the TOMM process.

Kangaroo Island is therefore an excellent example of a disciplined and professional community-based approach to the management of tourism in a sensitive area.

REFLECTIONS ON THE CASE

Kangaroo Island is an important wildlife site, tourist destination and home to local communities and, as such, it has become a classic case study in the debate about the future development of tourism. The island has solved the problem by adopting an innovative planning and monitoring regime, which adjusts to changing circumstances, and places development decisions firmly in local control. This approach could act as a model for other destinations facing similar development issues.

DISCUSSION POINTS

1. Devise a class debate focusing on the issue of conservation versus development on Kangaroo Island.
2. Draft a set of recommendations to the local authority on Kangaroo Island as to how the local community can be fairly represented in decisions about the island's future.
3. Kangaroo Island has utilised a number of its natural resources as tourism products. An example here would be bird watching. Design a tourism product based upon one other element of the island's ecology or ecosystems. Draft a brochure and brief marketing campaign for the product.
4. It is important to encourage more visitors to stay overnight on the island. What incentives can be put in place to encourage overnight visitors and reduce the number of day visitors?

RESOURCES
CLIMATE
TRANSPORT
FUTURES

TOURISM IN CONTEXT

DEMAND

RESOURCES

CLIMATE

TRANSPORT

FUTURES

Acknowledgement

We are grateful to Charles Lim for his help with this case study.

Key sources

Hall, C. M. (1997) *Introduction to Tourism in Australia*. Longman, Harlow.

Lim, C. C. (2007) *The tourism optimisation process: a case of Kangaroo Island in Australia*. Paper presented to The 62nd TOSOK Symposium and Conference, Inchon, Korea, July 2–4.

Mandis Roberts Consultants (1996) *Developing a Tourism Optimisation Model (TOMM). A Model to Monitor and Manage Tourism on Kangaroo Island South Australia*. Mandis Roberts, Surry Hills, New South Wales.

Manuel, M., McElroy, B. and Smith, R. (1996) *Tourism*. Cambridge University Press, Cambridge.

South Australia Tourism Commission (2003) *Kangaroo Island Tourism Profile*. SAC, Adelaide.

Thomson, F. L. and Thomson, N. J. (1994) Tourism, tax receipts and local government: the case of Kangaroo Island. *Journal of Tourism Studies*, 5 (1), 57–66.

Websites

www.kangarooisland.sa.gov.au
www.tourism.sa.gov.au/
www.southaustralia.com/
www.tourkangarooisland.com.au/
www.tomm.info

Surfers Paradise, known as the Gold Coast's holiday capital.
© istockphoto.com/Jenny Bonner

The Revisioning of Tired Destinations: Australia's Surfers Paradise

INTRODUCTION

Across the world, destinations that were created for mass tourism after the Second World War are beginning to feel their age. In many destinations, both the infrastructure and the physical fabric are beginning to reach the end of their useful life and markets are declining. This has prompted a response to rejuvenate and re-position destinations by reformulating the product and diversifying markets. In this case study, the Gold Coast in Queensland, Australia has undergone a significant and innovative 'visioning' exercise to determine its future direction. On completion of this case you will:

1. Recognise the issues related to 'stagnating' destinations.
2. Understand the reasons why 'stagnating' destinations engage in 'visioning' and strategic planning.
3. Recognise the particular characteristics of the Gold Coast as a destination.
4. Be familiar with the innovative approach used to 'vision' the future of the Gold Coast.
5. Understand the outcomes of the Gold Coast visioning (GCV) process.

TOURISM IN CONTEXT

DEMAND

RESOURCES

CLIMATE

TRANSPORT

FUTURES

KEY ISSUES

There are five key issues in this case:

1. The Gold Coast has become a low yield, high-volume tourism destination dependent upon mass-market tourism and, as a result, has decided to re-position itself.
2. The Gold Coast is one of a number of 'stagnating' destinations worldwide that has decided to 'vision' its future as a destination by an extensive planning and consultation exercise.
3. The 'visioning' exercise involved an innovative 'whole of destination' approach, including consultation with the increasing number of residents moving into the area.
4. The visioning exercise is firmly rooted in a sustainable tourism approach.
5. The visioning exercise has had significant outcomes in terms of the organisation and perception of tourism in the destination.

THE GOLD COAST

In Australia, Queensland's Gold Coast is a long strip of coastline stretching from Southport in the north to Coolangata on the New South Wales border, backed by stunning mountain and rainforest scenery, much of which is designated as national park. The coastline is heavily developed, particularly around the core of the destination at Surfer's Paradise – where significant high-rise developments continue to be constructed. The Gold Coast is recognised as Australia's major tourist area, with the largest concentration of bed spaces in the country. Not only is it a significant domestic destination, but it also attracts substantial numbers of international visitors, particularly from Asia. Of course this means that the Gold Coast is vulnerable to fluctuations in the Asian outbound market, initially caused by the currency crisis in the 1990s, but more recently by the downturn in the Japanese economy.

As a destination, the Gold Coast is dependent upon an attractive mix of both natural and man-made attractions. The natural attractions include the area's subtropical climate, the long clean beaches, the Pacific surf and the hinterland of national parks, rainforest and mountains. The man-made attractions include three of Australia's largest theme parks – Seaworld, Movieworld and Dreamworld, as well as a major water park. Along the coast itself there are many smaller attractions and innovative products such as the Aquaduck tours that utilise amphibious craft for a combination of land and water tours; mini-golf, surf schools and nature-based hinterland trips.

VISIONING STRATEGIES FOR STAGNATING DESTINATIONS

The visioning of the Gold Coast is recognition of the need for strategic planning at the destination level. In a turbulent environment for tourism, particularly

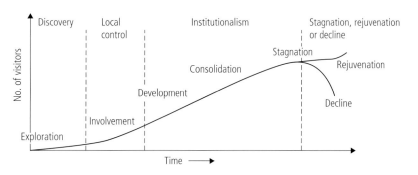

FIGURE 30.1   The tourist area life cycle
Source: Butler (1980)

post-9/11, it is important for destinations to take control of their own future by embarking on such planning exercises. For 'tired' destinations this is particularly important, as the next stage of their evolution is 'decline'. The best framework to consider for this approach is the Tourism Area Life Cycle (TALC) (Figure 30.1). Many destinations have reached the stagnation stage of the cycle and it is these destinations that are exemplified by the Gold Coast. Indeed, across the world destinations such as Waikiki (Hawaii), Pattaya Beach (Thailand), Acapulco (Mexico), while many cold water resorts in Europe and on the eastern seaboard of the USA have embarked upon such exercises. Perhaps the first to do so was Atlantic City in the USA.

For the Gold Coast, and other destinations, the real dangers of the stagnation phase are:

- The dominance of increasingly low-yield, mass-market, short-stay tourists who choose the destination on the basis of price. This leads to a low-yield, high-volume destination (sometimes termed 'profitless volume destinations').
- The danger of tourism exceeding carrying capacity limits in terms of both the local community and the environment of the destination.
- The fact that the destination becomes low yield means that re-investment and refurbishment is difficult and the 'quality' of the destination declines – including the public sector infrastructure as well as private sector facilities.
- The products on offer become increasingly out of step with the demands of the market.
- Market share is eroded by newer destinations that can compete for tourists more effectively as they are more fashionable.

These threats mean that there are significant benefits to a strategic planning exercise. Of course, in any tourist destination there are many conflicting interests, stakeholders, 'destination creators' and groups that can be brought together by a strategic planning exercise. These varied interests can be harnessed to work together for the collective good of the destination. In the strategy planning literature this is known as developing a 'strategic conversation'. Not only do these many stakeholders (such as residents, business, government and charities) begin to work together and collaborate, but they also work out their own roles in the exercise and often key performance indicators (KPIs) are decided upon. These might include a KPI to

TOURISM IN CONTEXT

DEMAND

RESOURCES

CLIMATE

TRANSPORT

FUTURES

increase a particular market spend by a certain percentage; or to reduce the environmental impact of tourism in a particular way – such as reducing litter. An obvious benefit of the strategic approach is the long-term perspective of development that it brings. Effectively, day-to-day actions and decisions (the notorious short-term perspective of tourism) can be placed within the context of a longer-term vision.

The strength of such an approach is that it demands a 'whole of destination' outlook. This means that every element of the destination – including the community – is considered, and in so doing it can act as a 'circuit breaker' to jolt groups into action. It also ensures that the important linkages in the destinations are considered and particular sectors (such as accommodation) are not favoured and develop out of step with visitor attractions or transportation. Visioning is the newest development of strategic planning and adopts a more flexible approach than previous strategic planning approaches, but at the same time it crafts and promotes a clarity of vision for the destination which is then communicated across all stakeholders.

THE GOLD COAST VISIONING EXERCISE (GCV)

The GCV exercise was essentially concerned to map out the future for the Gold Coast as a tourism destination, but also took into account the growing residential population of the area. The Gold Coast/Brisbane corridor is the fastest growing part of Australia in terms of population, partly as a result of the phenomenon known as 'sea change' where retiring baby boomers move to coastal areas with high-amenity values.

The objectives of the GCV were:

1. To provide a systematic and comprehensive overview of the current status of Gold Coast Tourism.
2. To develop scenarios for future global, national and local trends and assess their impact upon the Gold Coast.
3. Combine these scenarios with sustainable tourism principles to deliver a shared vision for the future of the Gold Coast.
4. To utilise this shared vision to generate a set of core values for the Gold Coast that could be used to assess future developments.
5. To arrive at a consensus on preferred tourism development options consistent with the vision.

Effectively this represents a shift from a 'destination marketing' to a 'destination management approach', bringing together all the elements involved in tourism.

The approach of the GCV is shown in Figure 30.2. The elements of the approach were:

1. Scoping studies to discern the key issues, including impacts, sustainability and resident attitudes.
2. An audit to elicit the characteristics of tourism on the Gold Coast.
3. A survey of tourism industry stakeholders on the status of Gold Coast tourism.
4. Futures and visioning workshops held on the Gold Coast to synthesise the findings of the surveys, work out their implications and reach a consensus.

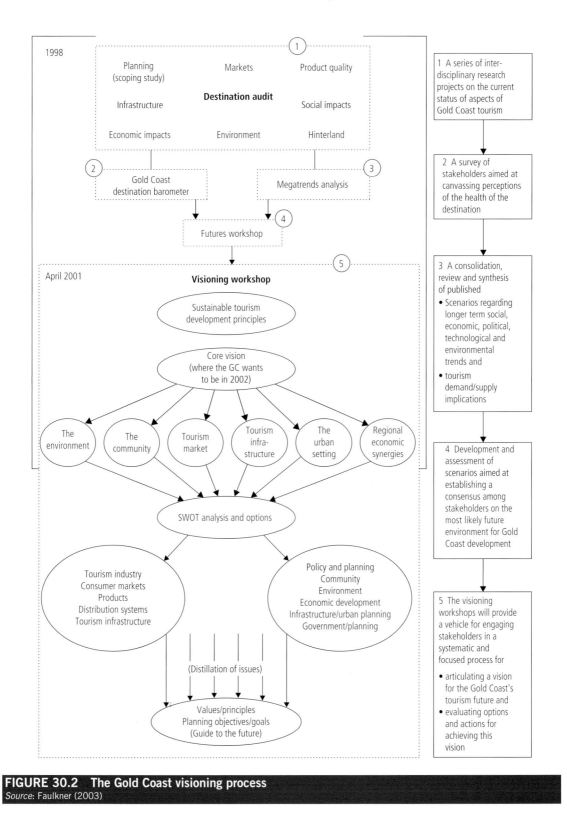

FIGURE 30.2 The Gold Coast visioning process
Source: Faulkner (2003)

TOURISM IN CONTEXT

DEMAND

RESOURCES

CLIMATE

TRANSPORT

FUTURES

To summarise the outcomes of the approach, the Gold Coast has published its preferred future (Faulkner, 2002: iii):

'The Gold Coast will become one of the great leisure and lifestyle destinations of the world. The region will be renowned for sustainable management of its natural and built environment, its sense of self-confidence, the vibrancy and depth of its serviced economy, the continuing well being of its community, and the unique sense of place of a thriving and dynamic resort city.

The destination will be safe, clean, well serviced and uniquely Gold Coast in style. The region will have leading edge organisational, management and marketing structures that will be underpinned by new partnerships between business, community and government. It will have developed a brand and market awareness which positions the Gold Coast as a market leader in targeted domestic and international markets. The Gold Coast will set the pace as the lifestyle and leisure capital of the Pacific Rim'.

The GCV has delivered its promise. The Gold Coast has been prompted into thinking about its future direction as a destination and is acutely aware of the dangers of drifting into decline. The GCV has articulated a set of core tourism values and principles that now underpin the preferred future for the destination in the medium to long term. It has jolted the Gold Coast out of an ad hoc and uncoordinated approach to tourism into a more professional and systematic approach. The GCV has also prompted a rethink of the administration of tourism on the Gold Coast, with a new tourism unit set up within the Gold Coast City Council and a change in leadership of the Gold Coast Tourism Bureau. Whilst the GCV may not be entirely responsible for these changes, the destination is now in a position to utilise tourism research and strategy more effectively and has a shared vision for its future.

The Gold Coast has undergone a significant and innovative 'visioning' exercise to determine its tourism future.

REFLECTIONS ON THE CASE

There is no doubt that a number of destinations across the globe are suffering from the same syndrome as the Gold Coast. Yet, destinations at stagnation are not a fashionable part of tourism; industry leaders tend to focus on growth and expansion, brushing more problematic issues under the carpet. Yet, for destinations reaching the latter stages of the life cycle, there are recognised solutions to preventing decline – solutions that are a combination of business strategy, public sector leadership, marketing and planning. In the case of the Gold Coast, a highly innovative visioning process has prompted a rethink of tourism in Australia's premier tourism destination.

This case is based upon the work of the late Professor Bill Faulkner who championed the GCV process.

DISCUSSION POINTS

1. Take a destination with which you are familiar. Plot a TALC for that destination and annotate the curve with key events and the stages of the cycle. How easy was it to find the relevant information and to identify the stages of the cycle?
2. Locate three other stagnating destinations and using the Internet and print sources examine their plans for rejuvenation. Are there any common elements?
3. The Gold Coast is well known as a coastal destination, but is fortunate in having stunning hinterland scenery. Using the Internet and print sources, put together two-day trip itineraries from the Surfers Paradise that take in the key attractions of the Gold Coast.
4. The Gold Coast is one of the fastest growing population areas of Australia. This complicates plans for tourism, as the local community must be consulted in any future plans. As a local tourism planner, what strategies would you use to ensure that you had succeeded in obtaining representative views of the residents about future tourism plans?
5. Visioning exercises depend upon the willingness of the local community and tourism stakeholders to become involved. Design the programme for a one-day seminar for these groups to 'sell' the visioning approach to them.

TOURISM IN CONTEXT

DEMAND

RESOURCES

CLIMATE

TRANSPORT

FUTURES

TOURISM IN CONTEXT

DEMAND

RESOURCES

CLIMATE

TRANSPORT

FUTURES

KEY SOURCES

Faulkner, W. (2002) *Our Gold Coast: The Preferred Tourism Future*. CRCST, Gold Coast.

Faulkner, W. (2003) Rejuvenating a maturing tourist destination: the case of the Gold Coast, in E. Fredline, C. Jago and C. P. Cooper (eds), *Progressing Tourism Research*. Channelview, Clevedon, pp. 34–86.

Heath, E. and Wall, G. (1992) *Marketing Tourism Destinations*. Wiley, New York.

Ritchie, J. R. B. (1999) Crafting a value-driven vision for a national tourism treasure. *Tourism Management*, 20 (3), 273–282.

WEBSITES

www.verygc.com/

In December 1998, UNESCO included the Summer Palace in Beijing on its World Heritage List.
© istockphoto.com/David Pedre

Outbound Tourism from China

INTRODUCTION

China is set to become one of the world's leading generators of international tourism, changing travel patterns and the face of tourism around the world. On completion of this case you will:

1. Be aware of the factors giving rise to the growth in China's outbound tourism.
2. Understand the pattern and scale of China's outbound tourism.
3. Recognise the influence of the Chinese travel trade and the 'approved destination' scheme on Chinese outbound tourism.
4. Be aware of the characteristics of China's outbound tourism market.
5. Recognise the future trends in the market.

TOURISM IN
CONTEXT

DEMAND

RESOURCES

CLIMATE

TRANSPORT

FUTURES

KEY ISSUES

There are four key issues in this case:

1. China is an excellent example of the growth and development of a new outbound market for tourism that will dominate the pattern of world international tourism by 2020, changing the balance of tourism flows and transport networks.
2. The development and growth of China's outbound tourism has been shaped by government regulation of travel and by the introduction of the 'approved destination status' (ADS) in the late 1980s, an example of how government policy shapes tourism demand.
3. The Chinese outbound market has certain key characteristics which will need to be understood by the receiving destinations as they design products, attractions and infrastructure to cater for this new market.
4. The products that are being developed for this market are changing in response to the preferences and demands of the Chinese, who increasingly aspire to more flexible, personalised trips that allow them to get to know a destination in depth, rather than group tours *en masse*.

DEVELOPMENT OF THE OUTBOUND MARKET

The tourism market in the People's Republic of China (PRC) began to show significant growth from 1978 onwards, following the demise of Mao, the ending of the Cultural Revolution, and the relaxation of the strict controls imposed by the totalitarian Communist regime. However this was mainly for domestic trips. International travel continued to be tightly regulated by the government and was largely confined to Hong Kong and Macau. Although China was now eager to learn from the West, foreign travel was for the purpose of corporate business or study rather than leisure tourism. In 1987 travel to neighbouring countries sympathetic to the Communist regime, such as North Korea, Russia, Mongolia, Myanmar (Burma) and Vietnam was allowed, and in 1988 ADS was extended to Thailand. Domestic travel continued to expand rapidly in the 1990s as the Chinese economy began to boom and as the five day working week and holidays were institutionalised. In the new millennium, China began to be integrated in the global economy with accession to the World Trade Organization, and with growing affluence, a strong currency, government support and an expanding travel trade, the latent demand for outbound travel began to be realised. In 2003 individual travel permits were introduced for Hong Kong and Macau (now Special Administrative Regions of the PRC) as rules continued to be relaxed. By 2006, outbound international travel from China reached a total of 34 million trips representing 10 per cent year-on-year growth. Already China is the largest generator of international travel in

Asia, and it is forecast to be a leading generator of international tourism in the world by 2020 with 100 million outbound trips. VFR tourism will continue to play an important role, mainly to countries with large ethnic Chinese populations in South-east Asia and the Americas.

The World Tourism Organization report on the Chinese outbound market (UNWTO, 2006) identifies three distinct stages in the evolution of this market:

1. The trial stage (1983–1996) – in this stage, the VFR market, and tours of neighbouring countries sympathetic to the PRC began to set the stage for outbound tourism.
2. The initial stage (1997–2001) – when outbound tourism was officially sanctioned and the number of 'approved destinations' increased.
3. Development (2002 onwards) – a stage characterised by a rapid increase in the number of 'approved destinations' and the volume of outbound trips, relaxation of government policies and a diversification of travellers' needs.

CHARACTERISTICS OF THE MARKET

The Chinese outbound market has a number of characteristics:

- The market is concentrated in the three major urban areas of Beijing/Tianjin, Shanghai/Yangtze Delta and Guangzhou/Pearl River Delta.
- The majority of travellers are independent, with only 20 per cent joining groups.
- Upmarket travellers tend to originate in the three major urban generating areas.
- The majority of trips are to other parts of Asia (particularly Hong Kong and Macau), followed by Europe, the Americas and the Pacific.
- Three key market segments dominate the market – mature couples, families with children and young singles and couples.
- The majority of travellers use the Internet to search for information about travel.
- Demand peaks in the three national holiday weeks – Chinese New Year (January/February), the first week in May and the first week in October.
- The desire to gain 'face' and social prestige is important in the travel decision-making process.

The UNWTO report (2006) identifies three sets of products in the Chinese outbound market:

1. Specialised tours such as eco-tourism or cruising where the market is very fragmented but which attract a small volume but high-spending clientele. This sector is set to grow.
2. A sector focused around incentive travel or holiday touring which attracts a larger volume of medium-spending clientele and is also set to grow.
3. The mass market of city tours and sightseeing, which is high volume but low spend.

TOURISM IN CONTEXT

RESOURCES

CLIMATE

TRANSPORT

FUTURES

TOURISM IN CONTEXT

DEMAND

RESOURCES

CLIMATE

TRANSPORT

FUTURES

KEY FACTORS: APPROVED DESTINATION STATUS AND THE TRAVEL TRADE

The unique nature of the Chinese outbound market has been shaped by two key factors – government policy relating to 'approved' destinations for travel and the facilitating role of the Chinese travel trade who assist their clients through the bureaucratic red tape involved in travel overseas.

APPROVED DESTINATION STATUS

The outbound market remains under strict government regulation, although this has relaxed in recent years. The Chinese government only allows Chinese nationals to travel to destinations with ADS. This is only given to countries that fulfil certain conditions to enable them to receive leisure tour group travellers from China. Destinations that do not have ADS can still receive visitors from China, but not leisure tour groups.

In 1988 Thailand was given ADS status, followed by Singapore, Malaysia and the Philippines. Australia was the first Western country to be given ADS (in 1999), followed by New Zealand and in 2005 by the UK. In 2007 Chinese tourists had achieved something approaching Western freedom to travel, with 132 approved destinations available.

THE TRAVEL TRADE

The Chinese travel trade is a major facilitator for outbound travel, given the logistical demands faced by Chinese nationals who wish to travel overseas. The number of authorised travel agencies increased 10-fold between 1997 and 2007 to approach 800, and whilst in the 1990s they were concentrated in the major centres of Beijing and Shanghai, by 2007 they were growing in other urban centres around China. However, these traditional intermediaries are facing a threat from the Internet as the Chinese begin to book online. In addition, air access to China has developed significantly with the world's major carriers flying to Beijing and Shanghai.

THE FUTURE

As Cooper *et al.* (2005) observe, China is unusual among tourist-generating countries in that out of a population of 1.3,000 million, only a small proportion can afford to travel abroad – around 50 million. This means that only a small rise in the percentage of Chinese who have the income to travel internationally would result in a huge increase of travellers. In the future, the growing Chinese young middle class will purchase travel extensively. The Chinese outbound market will diversify and become more customised with specialised products on offer. Tourists will want to get to know destinations in more depth, and will look for more flexibility in itineraries.

REFLECTIONS ON THE CASE

China is a perfect example of the development of a new market. It also demonstrates the important influence of government policy on tourism demand. Until the 1980s, the Chinese market for international travel was small and constrained by restrictions. With the advent of the 'approved destination' policy, travel began to expand. In parallel with this, economic and social conditions in China changed to encourage travel as the classic patterns of first a strong domestic market followed by international travel developed. The case also demonstrates the importance of understanding this new market as destinations struggle to supply relevant products and infrastructure.

DISCUSSION POINTS

1. Identify the major drivers of growth of international travel from China between 1990 and 2005.
2. In class, discuss how destinations will need to adapt their attractions and accommodation for the Chinese market – you should refer here to factors such as *feng shui* and Chinese superstitions about numbers.
3. How might an inbound tour operator begin to research the Chinese market for their products?
4. Design an itinerary for a group of Chinese mature travellers wishing to undertake a two-week tour of Australia. Make sure that your itinerary caters to the preferences of Chinese tourists overseas, including sightseeing, dining and shopping.

KEY SOURCES

Cooper, C., Scott, N. and Kester, J. (2005) New and emerging markets, in D. Buhalis and C. Costa (eds), *Tourism Business Frontiers*. Elsevier Butterworth-Heinemann, Oxford, pp. 19–29.

Lew, A. (2003) *Tourism in China*. Haworth, New York.

Roll, D. (2006) The China challenge. *The Tourism Society Journal* (127), 20–21.

UNWTO (2006) *The Asia and Pacific Intra-regional Outbound: China*. UNWTO, Madrid.

Zhang, H. Q. and Lam, T. (2005) *Tourism and Hotel Development in China*. Haworth, New York.

TOURISM IN CONTEXT

DEMAND

RESOURCES

CLIMATE

TRANSPORT

FUTURES

The whitewashed lighthouse at the Portuguese Guia Fort sits at the highest point in Macau and is the oldest lighthouse on the Chinese coast.

Tourism in Macau

INTRODUCTION

Macau is emerging as the 'Las Vegas of Asia' as it implements a strategy of economic diversification. This case examines the development of tourism in Macau and the issues created. On completion of this case, you will:

1. Be aware of the scale of tourism investment in Macau.
2. Understand the economic contribution of tourism to Macau.
3. Be aware of Macau's advantageous location adjacent to the major generating market of China.
4. Understand Macau's unique mix of heritage attractions and twenty-first century hotel and casino attractions.
5. Recognise the range of tourist facilities and the organisation of tourism in Macau.

TOURISM IN CONTEXT

DEMAND

RESOURCES

CLIMATE

TRANSPORT

FUTURES

KEY ISSUES

There are three key issues in this case:

1. Macau is implementing a strategy of economic diversification with tourism as the main element of that strategy. As a result, Macau's tourism sector is experiencing phenomenal growth.
2. The growth of tourism in Macau is dependent upon demand from China and products that are based primarily on upmarket hotels and casinos.
3. Macau's tourism growth will need to be carefully managed, not only to ensure quality standards are maintained through staff training, but also to prevent further erosion of the region's unique heritage comprising both Portuguese and Chinese culture.

BACKGROUND

Macau is located on the south east coast of China, 60 kilometres from Hong Kong. As a former colony of Portugal, since the handover in December 1999 it has a unique status as a Special Administrative Region (SAR) of the People's Republic of China under the 'one country, two systems' policy, which also applies to Hong Kong. The SAR arrangements provide for Macau to have its own mini-constitution, the Basic Law.

With over half a million people crowded on the peninsula connecting it to mainland China and two small offshore islands, space is at a premium. Like Monaco, its European counterpart, Macau has reclaimed land from the sea, providing the sites for the international airport and the Cotai Strip of new development which links the islands of Taipa and Coloane. Even so the total area of Macau is only 28.2 square kilometres. The climate is sub-tropical and strongly influenced by the monsoon; winter is cool and relatively dry, whereas the months May through September are hot and rainy.

Macau has a rich history, acting as a gateway to China since the sixteenth century. As a result, the cultural heritage of Portuguese colonial rule is a major part of its appeal for tourists. So much of the past has survived because, while Hong Kong prospered under British rule after its acquisition from China in 1841, Macau declined to become a colonial backwater. The heritage of old Macau contrasts with the 'new Macau' landscape of contemporary state-of-the-art casinos and hotels, showcasing its revival since 1999.

Macau is located close to the Pearl River Delta and the cities of Guangzhou (Canton) and Shenzhen, which is a major growth region of China's economy. Tourism plays a major role in Macau's economy and is seen as a means by which the dependence on the production of cheap textiles can be reduced. Whilst in the past the clothing industry accounted for three quarters of the region's export earnings, in 2005 tourism contributed around one-third of Macau's GDP, evidence of successful diversification. Nevertheless, most of the revenue from tourism is derived from gambling, which is illegal in the rest of China.

ATTRACTIONS

As the Las Vegas of Asia, Macau presents a unique combination of historical culture, oriental charm and contemporary splendour. We can classify Macau's attractions into three kinds: first, those endowed by the Portuguese and Chinese heritage, including the distinctive Macanese cuisine; secondly, those which are purpose-built for gaming and entertainment in the twenty-first century; and thirdly, event attractions.

Heritage Attractions Macau's European colonisers prospered through trading in the region. They left a rich legacy of Christian churches, fortresses, houses, gardens and streetscapes that when combined with the Chinese influences create a unique and attractive blend. This is best seen in the UNESCO World Listed Heritage District comprising 25 historic buildings and 7 gracious squares dating from the Portuguese colonial past. The heritage is also interpreted through Macau's many museums, easily accessible in such a compact destination. They include:

- The Museum of Macau – developed to preserve the cultural traditions and heritage of Macau
- Maritime Museum – celebrating Portugal's seafaring heritage
- Wine Museum
- Grand Prix Museum – inaugurated in 1993 to celebrate the 40th anniversary of this motor-racing event, which was modelled on the Monaco Grand Prix
- The Taipa Houses Museum
- The Museum of The Holy House of Mercy
- Jade Cultural Museum
- Lin Zexu Museum, commemorating Chinese government attempts in the nineteenth century to control the opium trade
- Museum of Nature and Agriculture
- Museum of Art
- Crypt and the Museum of Sacred Art
- St. Dominic's Museum
- The Fire Service Museum
- Dr. Sun Yat Sen Memorial House, commemorating one of the founders of modern China

Entertainment Complexes and Casinos In 2002 the Chinese government ended the gambling industry monopoly held for 40 years by a Hong Kong tycoon and granted licenses to a Las Vegas corporation. As a result, Macau is undergoing a massive multi-billion dollar development in terms of new entertainment complexes and casinos. Many of the casinos and hotels are beginning to resemble Las Vegas with huge themed areas and large bed capacity. However, there are cultural differences – slot machines account for only a small percentage of casino takings in Macau and the consumption of alcohol is on a much lower scale. Macau has over 35 casinos including famous names such as The Venetian complex, Wynn Macau, StarWorld Hotel, The Macau Fisherman's Wharf, Crown Macau, The MGM Grand and Casino Sands. Many of these are located along the Cotai Strip, allowing easy travel back and forth for the heritage attractions, beaches and

TOURISM IN CONTEXT

DEMAND

RESOURCES

CLIMATE

TRANSPORT

FUTURES

TOURISM IN CONTEXT

DEMAND

RESOURCES

CLIMATE

TRANSPORT

FUTURES

outdoor activities of Taipa and Coloane. The Strip is still growing with new properties set to open up until 2010. In total, more than 20 000 hotel rooms are planned along with millions of square feet of convention and conference space, along with facilities for shopping, dining and nightlife. As Macau's weather is hot and humid for most of the year, many of the Cotai Strip hotels will have indoor walkways for comfortable access between hotels. In contrast to the Cotai Strip, the casinos on Taipa Island are in smaller, more old-fashioned settings, with the exception of the Crown Macau.

Macau is emerging as the 'Las Vegas of Asia'. ©istockphoto.com/Kenliang Wong

Event Attractions and Sport Facilities   Macau has also developed a successful range of festivals and event attractions, including the Grand Prix, food festivals, arts festivals and golf events. It offers a wide range of sporting facilities and opportunities including golf, cycling, trekking, karting, bowling, skating, windsurfing, canoeing and other water sports, horse and greyhound racing, and soccer.

ACCOMMODATION

In 2005, Macau had 49 hotels and 31 guesthouses. Accommodation investment is booming in Macau, although this creates a crisis in terms of trained manpower to staff the new hotels. New developments encompassing 22 hotels totalling 18 000 new rooms are due for completion in 2009. This will almost triple the city's current room inventory from 12 000 to 30 000, and by 2010 this is set to exceed 40 000. These developments include major themed hotels such as those found in Las Vegas, some exceeding 3000 rooms. Despite this growth, demand shows no sign of diminishing with occupancy rates averaging well over 70 per cent annually.

CONVENTION AND EXHIBITION FACILITIES

Macau is keen to attract the MICE market and has developed excellent facilities for conventions and trade fairs as well as a business tourism centre to support the sector. There are five major facilities:

1. the largest convention facility development is the Venetian complex featuring both conference and exhibition space on the Cotai Strip
2. the Macau Fisherman's Wharf
3. the Macau Forum
4. the Macau DOME
5. the Macau Tower.

TRANSPORTATION

Macau is very well connected to the rest of China, Hong Kong and the East Asia–Pacific Region and it is this well-networked transport system, including easy arrangements for transit, that have contributed to the growth of tourism in Macau.

Surface transport There are regular ferries, jetfoils and catamarans covering the hour-long trip between Macau and both Hong Kong and Shenzhen. Passengers can transit into or out of the Pearl River Delta region through Hong Kong International Airport without the need to go through customs and immigration and luggage is checked through to Macau. Local transport around Macau is by pedicab/cycle-rickshaw, taxi or bus.

Air transport Macau International Airport commenced operation in 1995. Since then, it has become an important link between the Pearl River Delta and the rest of the world. Phase One of the airport is equipped with a full range of passenger facilities designed to handle 6 million passengers. In 2007, passenger numbers exceeded 5 million. The airport is home to four local airlines:

1. Air Macau
2. Viva Macau
3. East Asia Airlines
4. JetAsia

There is also a helicopter service operating between Macau, Shenzhen and Hong Kong catering mainly for business travellers.

ORGANISATION

The government tourism agency is the Macau Government Tourist Office (MGTO), with five sections covering licensing, marketing and product development, projects and research as well as an events division. The MGTO administers the Tourism Fund, designed to encourage inward investment, and the Macau Business Tourism Centre.

TOURISM IN CONTEXT

DEMAND

RESOURCES

CLIMATE

TRANSPORT

FUTURES

DEMAND

Rapidly earning the reputation of the 'Las Vegas of the Orient', and adjacent to the huge market of China, Macau's tourism numbers have doubled since the handover in 1999. Over 2 billion people live within five hours' flying time of Macau, compared to the equivalent population of 400 million within reach of Las Vegas, USA; more significantly, 300 million live within three hour's travel time by surface transport. However, proximity to mainland China and Hong Kong, allied to excellent transport facilities, does mean that around half of all arrivals are excursionists, while staying visitors on average spend just one night in Macau. Nonetheless, arrivals statistics are impressive with more than 22 million tourists visiting Macau in 2006. The growth has been driven primarily by tourists from mainland China (around half of all arrivals), Hong Kong (around one-third of all arrivals) and Taiwan. Visitors travelling overland account for well over half of all arrivals, followed by sea (35 per cent) and then air (5 per cent). Macau's climate and the nature of its attractions mean that seasonality is low with a slight peak in December.

Such impressive growth is not without environmental and social costs, such as fewer green spaces, more traffic, pollution and the loss of manpower from other sectors to the lucrative gambling industry. On the other hand the problem of organised crime, represented by the *triads* during the last years of Portuguese rule, has diminished.

REFLECTIONS ON THIS CASE

This case is evidence of the strong tourism sector in Asia. Since Portugal handed over Macau to China, the region has recognised the need for economic diversification away from textile and garment manufacture. In response Macau has implemented phenomenal investment in tourism, encouraging private-sector investors to develop upmarket hotels and casinos. Of course such growth needs careful management not only to ensure that the quality of the tourist experience is maintained but also that Macau's unique heritage is not compromised.

DISCUSSION POINTS

1. Using the Internet, make an inventory of the events and festivals taking place in Macau. In class discuss (i) the role that Macau's heritage plays in this inventory; and (ii) whether you think that these events compromise the authenticity of Macau's heritage.
2. Macau is unusual in having very little seasonal variation of demand – why do you think this is the case?

3. Design a two-day itinerary for a group of professional architects interested in Macau's Portuguese-built heritage.
4. Locate the web sites of a major casino in Macau and one in Las Vegas. Draw up a chart showing the main differences as well as the similarities between the two casinos.
5. Macau is very dependent upon demand from excursionists. Draft a plan to increase the number of visitors who stay overnight in the region.

KEY SOURCES

www.macaumuseum.gov.mo.
www.airmacau.com.mo.
http://industry.macautourism.gov.mo/en/page/content.php?parent_id=1&page_id=61.
www.dsec.gov.mo/English/PUB/PDF/E_TUR_PUB_2006_Y.pdf.
www.visitcotaiMacau.com/.
www.macautourism.gov.mo/en/discovering/entertainment.php.
www.gcs.gov.mo/files/spage/CFA8_E.html.
www.macau-airport.gov.mo/transportation_local.phtml.
www.macautouristguide.com/en/transport.html.

TOURISM IN CONTEXT

DEMAND

RESOURCES

CLIMATE

TRANSPORT

FUTURES

Iconic yellow taxis waiting for customers in New York, USA.
© istockphoto.com/Nikada

Tourism in New York City

INTRODUCTION

New York is one of the world's great tourist cities with many iconic attractions. This case examines the functioning of tourism in New York. On completion of this case, you will:

1. Be aware of the scale of tourism in New York.
2. Understand the economic contribution of tourism to the city.
3. Be aware of New York's advantageous location.
4. Understand the range of premier attractions in the city.
5. Recognise the range of tourist facilities and the scale of organization of tourism in New York.

TOURISM IN CONTEXT

DEMAND

RESOURCES

CLIMATE

TRANSPORT

FUTURES

KEY ISSUES

There are three key issues in this case

1. New York is one of the top tourist cities in the world. The true scale and economic contribution of tourism to New York was only fully realised when the attacks of 9/11 significantly reduced the volume and value of tourism to the city.
2. New York has a large range of premier attractions located in a relatively small area, making it ideal as a tourist city.
3. The support facilities, particularly transportation and accommodation, and organization of tourism in New York are impressive and testify to the importance of tourism in the city.

NEW YORK

The terrorist attacks of 9/11 highlighted the importance of New York City (NYC) as one of the world's top ten tourist destinations. Tourism is of major significance to the city's economy, generating almost 25,000 million and supporting 368 000 jobs. Although it is not the national capital – or even the capital of the state of New York (which is Albany) – New York is the country's primary city in many other respects. It is for example, the USA's leading financial centre and conference venue, and it is also a major centre for fashion and the arts. Until the 1960s it was the unchallenged 'gateway to America', and the Statue of Liberty in New York Harbor was for most immigrants and visitors their first sight of the New World. Nowadays few visitors arrive by sea, but New York remains the leading point of entry for tourists from Europe. New York plays an international role as the seat of the United Nations Assembly, while events in Wall Street have an even greater impact on the world economy.

New York stands on one of the world's finest harbours, created by the confluence of the Hudson and East Rivers, which also divide the city into a number of peninsulas and islands, linked by bridges, tunnels and ferries. NYC, as distinct from the rest of the metropolitan area in New Jersey and New York State, has an area of almost 800 square kilometres and a population of 8.2 million. It consists of five boroughs, namely:

- Manhattan, which is one of the most densely populated and ethnically mixed areas in the world. High land costs have resulted in the distinctive landscape of skyscrapers, particularly in the 'midtown' commercial area south of Central Park. Although Manhattan accounts for only 7 per cent of New York's land area, it is the main focus of tourist activity.
- Brooklyn and Queens contain some well-defined ethnic neighbourhoods.
- The Bronx is mainly known for urban decay, but also contains Yankee Stadium – 'the home of baseball' and the New York Botanical Gardens.
- Staten Island is a relatively quiet residential area.

New York's appeal is its cultural diversity and dynamism as 'the city that never sleeps'. The downside is the excessive crowding and hustle in a city that has fewer

TOURISM IN CONTEXT

DEMAND

RESOURCES

CLIMATE

TRANSPORT

FUTURES

green open spaces than London or Paris. Summers are notoriously hot and humid, with episodes of high air pollution, while winters are cold and Central Park is often blanketed in snow. More than most cities, New York has suffered from a negative image of urban decay, sleaze and violent crime. In fact it is by no means the most dangerous city in the USA, and a policy of zero tolerance by the civic authorities has greatly reduced the incidence of crime on the subway and in the streets, making most of New York safe for tourists.

ATTRACTIONS

The fact that New York has so many attractions within a tightly packed area means that there are 'multipass' admission offers – such as the Culture Pass and the City Pass – allowing multiple visits to certain attractions. The following is a selection from the variety New York can offer the tourist:

- Historic monuments such as the Statue of Liberty and Castle Clinton.
- Major cultural attractions in the fields of music, art, science and heritage, including the Metropolitan Opera House in the Lincoln Center and Carnegie Hall, the Guggenheim Museum, the Metropolitan Museum of Art, the Museum of Modern Art, the American Museum of Natural History, the Intrepid Sea–Air–Space Museum, the Museum of Jewish Heritage and the Ellis Island Immigration Museum, (the former holding station where over 12 million people were processed for admission to the USA between 1890 and 1954). Some of the most important of New York's many museums are located along Fifth Avenue's 'Museum Mile'.
- The 'downtown' financial district centred on Wall Street attracts leisure tourists as well as business travellers. Attractions include the American Stock Exchange, the New York Stock Exchange and the Museum of American Financial History.
- Sports venues include the Yankee Stadium, Shea Stadium, Flushing Meadows – home of the US Tennis Open – and the Madison Square Garden.
- Recreational areas include:
  - Central Park, a beautifully landscaped area covering 340 hectares in the heart of Manhattan. The park provides a wide range of activities and includes a Wildlife Center (formerly Central Park Zoo).
  - Coney Island was in the early part of the twentieth century, the popular beach and amusement park area for New Yorkers. Nowadays it is mainly visited for the New York Aquarium.
  - The Bronx Zoo (officially the Bronx Wildlife Conservation Society).
- Architectural landmarks such as:
  - The Empire State Building, perhaps the best-known 1930s skyscraper.
  - The Chrysler Building – distinguished by its Art Deco spire.
  - The Rockefeller Center – which includes Radio City Music Hall and the NBC Studio Tour.
  - The United Nations Assembly Building.
    Until 9/11 the twin towers of the World Trade Center dominated the skyline of Lower Manhattan. Plans for redevelopment of the site include pools, waterfalls and gardens as well as a museum commemorating the event with exhibition spaces largely underground.

TOURISM IN CONTEXT

DEMAND

RESOURCES

CLIMATE

TRANSPORT

FUTURES

- City districts with a strong identity, some of which are ethnic enclaves, for example:
  - Chinatown.
  - Little Italy.
  - Harlem – in the 1920s this was a middle class Black American community, famous for its contribution to the development of jazz. After a long period of decline it is now undergoing regeneration.
  - Spanish Harlem – the *barrio* occupied by Puerto Ricans and other Spanish-speaking immigrants.
  - Greenwich Village and Soho on the other hand, are historic neighbourhoods, defined by their associations with artists, writers and craft industries.
  - The theatre district is located around Times Square, between 42nd and 50th Streets and the midtown section of Broadway, and has 38 theatres.
  - South Street Seaport – a section of New York's waterfront that has undergone extensive restoration, featuring historic ships, a maritime museum, shops and restaurants.
- Shopping attractions – shopping weekends to New York's Fifth Avenue stores such as Macy's, Bloomingdales, Saks Fifth Avenue, and Tiffany's, are becoming popular with the European market, encouraged by competitive air fares.
- Dining – with 18 700 restaurants, New York offers cuisine from all over the world, and also a large number of themed restaurants.
- A range of event attractions, the best known being the St. Patrick's Day parades.

TRANSPORT

The main international air gateways to New York are:

- La Guardia (LGA) 13 kilometres to the east of midtown Manhattan, used mainly for domestic flights but with some services to Canada and Mexico.
- John F Kennedy (JFK) 20 kilometres southeast of midtown Manhattan.
- Newark International (EWR) 26 kilometres to the southwest in New Jersey.

Domestic and charter carriers also use:

- MacArthur Airport.
- Stewart International Airport (only international for livestock!).
- Teterboro Airport.
- Westchester County Airport.

The Metropolitan Transportation Authority (MTA) oversees the extensive transport network within the city. Bus companies such as Gray Line and New York Apple Tours provide 'hop-on, hop-off' sightseeing circuits, and companies such as Circle Line or New York Waterway offer sightseeing river cruises. Public transport includes rapid transit overland services as well as the underground railway system – the famous subway. The Staten Island Ferry is a favourite with visitors, with its views of the Statue of Liberty and the Manhattan skyline. The city has a number of major transport terminals such as Penn Central Station and the Port Authority bus station. Visitors can purchase passes that allow multiple rides on the public transport systems, although many opt to use the yellow taxi cabs. New York has a number of companies offering tailor-made walking tours and personal greeters can be organized to show visitors around the city.

ACCOMMODATION

In 2007, NYC had a hotel capacity of some 72 250 rooms, mainly concentrated in Manhattan. Hotels range from budget to luxury in price, from boutique (small up-market hotels of character) to themed hotels (on a particular period for example), and from suites to self-catering apartments. Accommodation is at a premium, particularly in Manhattan, where occupancy rates generally reach 85 per cent and hotel tariffs are higher than average for the USA.

ORGANIZATION

The main tourist organization for NYC is NYC & Company (formed in 1999 and formerly the New York Convention and Visitors Bureau). This is the city's official marketing agency and has been in existence since 1935 in various forms. It is a private, non-profit making organization with a large membership of tourism businesses. It sees the business and convention market as vital to the city's economy. The New York State government has also played an important role, with its "I love New York" campaign of the 1980s. This was remarkably successful in turning around NYC's negative image and generating a greater volume of visitors. The City has also been a pioneer in facilitating the use of locations for film and TV productions, guaranteeing worldwide recognition with 40 000 location shoots annually.

DEMAND

The events of 9/11 only momentarily decreased the numbers of visitors to New York. Out of the estimated 43.8 million visitors in 2006, almost 20 per cent were international and over half were day visitors. New York is the number one destination for foreign visitors to the USA, ahead of Los Angeles, Miami and Orlando. In fact NYC receives over 20 per cent of the USA's international visitors. In terms of staying tourists, the UK is the main contributor, followed by Canada and Germany. Of course much of this is VFR travel, given the very diverse ethnic mix of New York.

REFLECTIONS ON THIS CASE

New York is one of the world's top tourism cities and this is reflected in the scope of this case. Simply scanning the attractions, the accommodation, transport links and scale of demand to New York demonstrates this.

TOURISM IN CONTEXT

DEMAND

RESOURCES

CLIMATE

TRANSPORT

FUTURES

TOURISM IN CONTEXT

DEMAND

RESOURCES

CLIMATE

TRANSPORT

FUTURES

However, it also demonstrates how vulnerable tourism destinations are to terrorist attacks as witnessed by 9/11, and the need for destinations to have in place crisis and risk-management plans to cope with future events.

DISCUSSION POINTS

1. Debate the proposals for the redevelopment of the World Trade Center site and assign key roles representing the various stakeholders to members of the class.
2. Explain the growth in popularity of New York as a short-break destination for tourists from Britain and other European countries since the 1980s.
3. You have been asked by the editor of your college magazine to write a report on two of New York's visitor attractions. Your report should include information on access, the nature of the product, the target market, product interpretation and visitor management, on-site catering and merchandising (the sale of materials to promote the attraction).
4. Evaluate the strengths and weaknesses of New York as a venue for a major international sporting event.
5. Discuss the influence of two of the following – films, TV, theatrical productions, popular literature and music – in raising awareness of New York as a destination, using specific city locations as examples.

KEY SOURCES

Fennell, D. (ed.) (2006) *North America*. Channelview, Clevedon.

WEBSITES

www.nycvisit.com
www.national911memorial.org/

Traditional Inuit sealskin boots hung on a washing line.
© istockphoto.com/Oversnap

Nunavut: The Involvement of Indigenous Communities in Tourism in the Canadian Arctic

INTRODUCTION

This case examines the issues surrounding the involvement of indigenous communities in the Canadian Arctic. On completion of the case you will:

1. Be aware of the geographical and cultural features of Nunavut.
2. Recognise that technology has made Nunavut more accessible for tourism than in the past.
3. Understand how the Inuit communities can benefit from tourism.
4. Recognise the tourism resource base of Nunavut and the constraints that this places upon development.
5. Understand how tourism can act as a medium for the Inuit to engage with the wider world.

TOURISM IN CONTEXT

DEMAND

RESOURCES

CLIMATE

TRANSPORT

FUTURES

KEY ISSUES

There are five key issues in this case:

1. Nunavut is a newly designated Canadian territory in the Arctic. Its role in the history of exploration and the heritage and culture of the Inuit make it attractive to visitors.
2. Nunavut has benefited from improvements in transport technology and cold weather clothing and equipment, enabling the opening up of vast territories to visitors in a way that was not possible in the 1950s.
3. Tourism brings with it a range of economic and social benefits for the Inuit people, providing access to the wider world and yet sustaining their culture.
4. Tourism development can utilise Nunavut's natural and cultural resource base but the inhospitable climate and the remoteness of most of the territory also place constraints on the level and type of tourist development.
5. There are a variety of initiatives in Nunavut that have allowed the Inuit communities to engage in tourism.

NUNAVUT

In 1999 the Canadian government created a new territory – Nunavut – out of the Northwest Territories and settled land claims to some 350000 square kilometres with the indigenous population. These are the Inuit – 'the people', but better known to the outside world as Eskimos (the name given to them centuries ago by the Cree Indians, meaning 'eaters of raw meat').

Nunavut, which means 'our land' in the Inuktitut language, is a vast and challenging wilderness that includes most of Canada's Arctic archipelago, and the tundra region known as the 'Barren Lands' lying between Hudson Bay and the Arctic Ocean. It covers an area of 1.9 million square kilometres – as large as Alaska and California combined – and yet contains less than 8000 households, widely dispersed in 28 isolated communities (see Figure 34.1). The Inuit make up 85 per cent of the population, the rest being mainly incomers, such as professional and technical workers, from southern Canada. As the majority, the Inuit will gain political control of the territory and its potential wealth in mineral resources. Tourism also offers prospects for development, and is a sector in which Inuit guides and outfitters, with their unrivalled knowledge of the country and skills in improvisation, are already playing an important role. Inuit communities are involved in the management of the national parks that have been designated for the territory.

The Arctic regions are nowadays perceived as unspoiled wilderness areas, and visits there are part of the growing eco-tourism movement. This contrasts with the earlier view of the Arctic as a 'white hell', a grim test of endurance for expeditions seeking the North West Passage to Asia or a route to the North Pole. Explorers such as Peary and Amundsen, who were prepared to learn survival skills from the Inuit and adapt to the environment, were invariably more successful than those who carried their cultural baggage around with them, like the ill-fated Franklin

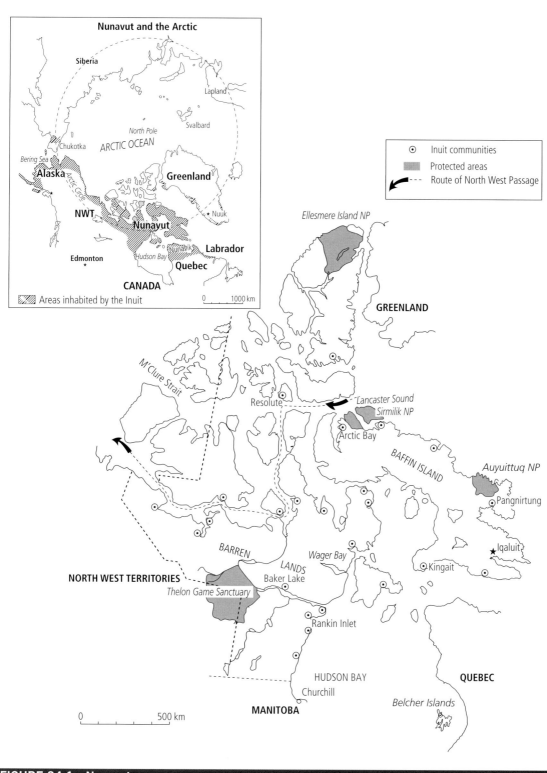

FIGURE 34.1 Nunavut

TOURISM IN CONTEXT

DEMAND

RESOURCES

CLIMATE

TRANSPORT

FUTURES

TOURISM IN CONTEXT

DEMAND

RESOURCES

CLIMATE

TRANSPORT

FUTURES

expedition. Tourists can now retrace these journeys in comfort and in a matter of a few days rather than the months or years it took the explorers, thanks to:

- The accessibility brought about by aviation, especially Twin Otter charter aircraft that are capable of landing on either ice or gravel airstrips.
- Advances in cold weather technology applied to clothing, equipment and shelter.
- The ending of the Cold War, which opened up areas of the Arctic formerly closed by Russia or the Western powers for strategic reasons. For example, it is now possible, with the use of icebreakers, for shipping to navigate the North West Passage from the Atlantic as far as Provediniya on the Russian side of the Bering Strait in a single summer season.

Tourism should also help to revive the culture of the Inuit as well as their economic well-being, and in recognition of this, the Canadian government announced a C$2 million funding scheme to support Nunavut tourism. In the 1950s the age-old way of life of the Inuit was still based on the hunting of caribou and sea mammals for subsistence, although they traded Arctic fox furs with the Hudson Bay Company in exchange for guns, tobacco and tea. Changes in fashion and the subsequent collapse in fur prices resulted in the Inuit becoming much more dependent on the social welfare programmes introduced by the Canadian government. Permanent settlements of identikit wooden buildings replaced the skin tents used in summer and the winter snow houses or igloos. Dog teams have been largely replaced by skidoos (snowmobiles) that in the words of one young Inuk are 'fast, don't eat meat, and don't stink' (quoted by Davis, 1998). Nevertheless the traditional image persists in the outside world.

While the material improvements have made life less hazardous for the Inuit, they have suffered from a high degree of social dislocation due to the rapidity of change from a nomadic Stone Age culture with a communal ethos, to one dominated by Western technology and value systems. The resulting social problems include a great deal of alcohol and drug abuse, and a suicide rate six times the Canadian average. A low level of educational attainment leaves Inuit communities vulnerable to manipulation by outside commercial interests. The birth rate is much higher than in southern Canada, with the result that 40 per cent of the population is less than 15 years of age. This poses a demographic 'time bomb' as more young people come on to the labour market with unrealistic expectations of what the new territory can provide. All this has implications for Nunavut's economic development, including its fledgling tourism industry.

TOURISM DEVELOPMENT

Nunavut's rigorous climate, vast distances and forbidding terrain discourage independent travel. With seas, lakes and rivers frozen for eight months or more, and with no roads outside the main settlements, most tourist transport is by air. Tourism development faces the following problems:

- **High development costs** Building hotels on permafrost is expensive, as special provision has to be made for utilities and waste disposal. Businesses are also 60 per cent more expensive to operate than in southern Canada, due primarily to high transport costs. Since Nunavut has no agriculture or manufacturing industry, almost everything has to be brought in by supply ship during the brief Arctic summer, or airlifted at even greater expense.

- **Limited accommodation**   In 2001 there were only about 1400 bed spaces in the entire territory, mainly in lodge-style accommodation. Even the capital, Iqaluit had insufficient hotel capacity to house guests at the inauguration ceremonies for the new territory.
- **Limited air transport**   Although several regional airlines operate scheduled services between the main communities in Nunavut and cities in southern Canada, interconnections between communities often involve a flight back to Iqaluit. This makes travel time-consuming and expensive. Airport delays are also frequent due to unpredictable weather throughout the year.
- **Seasonality**   Despite attempts to promote snow-based activities such as sledging, snowmobiling and cross-country skiing during the late winter and early spring, most tourism takes place during the very short summer season.
- **Cultural attitudes**   The environmental sensibilities of Western tourists, particularly animal lovers, are at odds with the attitudes of Inuit communities with their hunting traditions. In a society where nothing is wasted, what appear to be unsightly piles of garbage contain butchered carcasses and machine parts. The Inuit see hunting as an escape route from welfare dependency and a renewal of their close relationship with the land. This is generally accepted by the Canadian government, which has allocated hunting quotas to Inuit communities. What is more controversial is the fact that polar bear hunting tags are then sold to wealthy American tourists seeking trophies.

We can summarise Nunavut's resource base for tourism as:

- A vast wilderness of tundra and glacial mountains, threaded by pristine lakes, rivers and fjords.
- The wildlife of the tundra and the marine life – whales, narwhal and walrus – of the Arctic seas.
- The traditional culture of the Inuit, perfectly adapted to one of the world's harshest environments.
- The heritage of polar exploration, particularly the quest for the North West Passage and the race for the North Pole.

BAFFIN ISLAND

Baffin Island offers the largest share of Nunavut's attractions and amenities, including the territory's capital – Iqaluit. The town is set to grow as a regional hub for air services, with connecting flights to Nuuk and Kangerlussuaq (Sondre Stromfjord) in Greenland. Outfitters based in Iqaluit and other communities such as Pangnirtung and Arctic Bay, provide access to the following tourism resources:

- The spectacular scenery of the eastern part of Baffin Island, with its serrated mountains, extensive glaciers and a rugged coastline deeply indented by fjords. This culminates in the Auyuittuq National Park, which attracts growing numbers of adventure-seeking tourists.

TOURISM IN CONTEXT

DEMAND

RESOURCES

CLIMATE

TRANSPORT

FUTURES

TOURISM IN CONTEXT

DEMAND

RESOURCES

CLIMATE

TRANSPORT

FUTURES

- Other opportunities for adventure tourism include fishing for Arctic char in the island's lakes and rivers, and sea kayaking (the kayak was an Inuit invention). Wildlife tours focus on the coastal waters of Lancaster Sound, the summer habitat of vast numbers of migratory birds and whales.
- Inuit communities, notably Kingait (Cape Dorset) and Pangnirtung, are centres for handicrafts such as soapstone carving and printmaking using local materials and traditional skills. These are marketed throughout Canada by a native-run cooperative, thus benefiting the local economy. The designs are popular with tourists, because they are inspired by Arctic wildlife and Inuit nostalgia for the past.

THE BARREN LANDS

The Barren Lands, accessed from communities such as Rankin Inlet and Baker Lake, offer a different type of tourism experience. Here the scenery is low key compared to eastern Baffin Island, but the effects of past glaciation are evident in a tundra landscape seamed with gravel-strewn eskers and pitted with countless lakes. Although the autumn migration of vast caribou herds is rarely seen nowadays, wildlife resources are abundant in the Thelon Game Sanctuary and around Wager Bay, where the Sila Lodge provides facilities for eco-tourism. The many rivers attract canoeists, but with a season restricted to a few weeks of unpredictable weather, the risks are higher than in southern Canada.

THE ELLESMERE ISLAND NATIONAL PARK

The Ellesmere Island National Park, situated in the northernmost part of Canada, only 800 kilometres from the North Pole, represents the extremely cold and dry climate conditions and glacial terrain characteristic of the High Arctic. Here tourists number less than a hundred annually. This is mainly because access is limited to expensive charter flights from the airbase at Resolute, the most northerly community on the scheduled air network, which lies 1000 kilometres to the south. Even a limited number of visitors may make a severe impact on the fragile plant cover, which is extremely slow to regenerate, and on the animal life – including musk oxen and Arctic hare – that show little fear of humans in this remote location.

NUNAVUT AND THE WIDER WORLD

Nunavut is forging links through sport and cultural events with the people of other Arctic lands, such as the Sami of Lapland. One notable example is Inuit participation in the Riddu Riddu summer music festival held at Mandalen in northern Norway. Nunavut is now more closely associated with other Inuit communities living in the Northwest Territories, Nunavik (northern Quebec) and Labrador, and outside Canada – in Greenland, Alaska and Chukotka in north-eastern Siberia. The Inuit language and traditions are declining in some areas, and all these communities face similar problems, namely:

- A high birth rate.
- Economic dependence on a few primary products.

- The effect of global warming in reducing the ice cover of the Arctic seas.
- The impact of pollutants, carried by winds and ocean currents from industrialised regions to the south, on Arctic ecosystems. This has grave consequences for the traditional food supplies and health of the Inuit people.

Nunavut is opposed to the ban on commercial seal hunting, imposed by the Canadian government in 1989, seeing a market for sealskin products in the Far East. Its leaders are nevertheless showing the way forward in environmental campaigns to limit airport expansion, and to persuade the Canadian government to implement the Stockholm Convention on the control of industrial chemicals and pesticides, and the Kyoto Protocol on the control of greenhouse gases.

REFLECTIONS ON THIS CASE

Although previously difficult to access, and despite the hostile Arctic environment, the newly created Canadian territory of Nunavut is developing a fledgling tourism industry. The industry is benefiting Inuit communities in the territory, not only in terms of their economy and culture, but also as a medium of wider engagement with the world. Nunavut is a good example of community involvement in tourism.

DISCUSSION POINTS

1. Describe particular initiatives that have encouraged Inuit involvement with the tourism sector.
2. Explain why Westerners have for long been fascinated by the Inuit way of life. Suggest a code of conduct for present day tourists visiting Inuit communities.
3. Discuss the future prospects for tourism in Nunavut stemming from developments in transport, communications (including information technology), building technology and education.
4. A group of American students propose to retrace the route taken by the explorer Robert McClure in his search for the North West Passage, using Victorian technology, and man-hauled sledges instead of dog teams, for the sake of 'historical authenticity and the environment'. Discuss the feasibility of such an expedition.
5. Design a 'mini-guide' giving advice and information for a group of college students planning an expedition using canoes or kayaks on the lakes and rivers of the Barren Lands.

TOURISM IN CONTEXT

DEMAND

RESOURCES

CLIMATE

TRANSPORT

FUTURES

KEY SOURCES

Berton, P. (1988) *The Arctic Grail*. McClelland and Stewart, Toronto.

Butler, R. and Hinch, T. (1996) *Tourism and Indigenous Peoples*. International Thomson Business Press, London.

Davis, W. (1998) The Arctic. *CondéNast Traveler*, January, 110–121, 197–200.

Hall, C. M. and Johnston, M. (1995) *Polar Tourism*. Wiley, Chichester.

Mason, P. (1997) Tourism codes of conduct in the Arctic and Sub-Arctic region. *Journal of Sustainable Tourism*, 5 (2), 151–165.

Mason, P., Johnston, M. and Twynam, D. (2000) The world wide fund for nature Arctic tourism project. *Journal of Sustainable Tourism*, 8 (4), 305–323.

Notzke, C. (1999) Indigenous tourism development in the Arctic. *Annals of Tourism Research*, 26 (1), 55–76.

Roslin, A. (2007) The 1000-mile diet. *Canadian Geographic*, 127 (6), 76–88.

Selwood, J. and Heidenreich, S. (2000) Tourism in Nunavut: problems and potential, in M. Robinson *et al.* (eds), *Reflections on International Tourism Management, Marketing and the Political Economy of Travel and Tourism*. Sheffield Hallam University, Sheffield, pp. 415–426.

Twynam, G. D. and Johnston, M. E. (2002) The use of sustainable tourism practices. *Annals of Tourism Research*, 29 (4), 1165–1168.

Wight, P. A. and McVetty, D. (2000) Tourism planning in the Arctic: Banks Island. *Tourism Recreation Research*, 25 (2), 15–26.

WEBSITE

www.nunatour.nt.ca/new/site/default.asp

Tiki torches burn at a luau in Hawaii.
© istockphoto.com/RonTech2000

CASE 35

Tourism in Hawaii

INTRODUCTION

Hawaii is one of the iconic tourism destinations in the world with an image based on Hollywood films and TV programmes. This case examines tourism in Hawaii and the consequent impacts. On completion of this case you will:

1. Understand that Hawaii is a chain of volcanic islands in the Pacific Ocean.
2. Be aware of the historical development of tourism on Hawaii.
3. Recognise the scale of Hawaii's attractions and support facilities for tourism.
4. Understand the key dimensions of the market for tourism in Hawaii.
5. Be aware of some of the impacts of tourism on the islands.

TOURISM IN CONTEXT

DEMAND

RESOURCES

CLIMATE

TRANSPORT

FUTURES

KEY ISSUES

There are five issues in this case:

1. Hawaii is an iconic tourism destination with an image based upon Hollywood portrayals of idyllic Pacific islanders. However, in fact Hawaii is the major tourism destination in the Pacific.
2. Hawaii has a long history of tourism development and, in the twenty-first century the environmental and cultural impacts of tourism are being questioned and influencing future developments.
3. Hawaii's market is complex with both domestic and international visitors.
4. Hawaii's' tourist attractions are based upon its natural and cultural resources.
5. Tourism in Hawaii has a number of negative impacts that are the subject of planning and management.

HAWAII

Many millions of people the world over, who have never visited the islands, have a clear perception of Hawaii. The image of a 'tropical South-Pacific paradise', exotic but safe, was largely created by the American media – particularly the Hollywood film industry in the 1930s. This image has spawned a multi-billion dollar industry and attracted over 6 million visitors a year to the islands at the beginning of the twenty-first century. Hawaii's location in mid-Pacific sets it apart as a destination from the rest of the United States, but its popularity is mainly due to the American connection.

Hawaii consists of a chain of volcanic islands that originated as a geological *hot spot* in the ocean floor of the North Pacific – in fact the state takes its name from the largest of these islands. Hawaii is geographically isolated – 4000 kilometres from the North American mainland but an even greater distance from Asia and the rest of Polynesia. The islands were first settled by Polynesians from Tahiti and the Marquesas Islands between 500 and 800 AD. However, it was not until 1795, shortly after Captain Cook's arrival, that the various tribes were united by Kamehameha the Great, founder of the Hawaiian monarchy. In the course of the nineteenth century, Hawaii came increasingly under American influence through the activities of whalers, missionaries and traders, some of whom became plantation owners after acquiring tribal lands. Labour was imported from China, Japan and other countries to work the plantations, eventually resulting in the multi-racial society that now characterises the islands. These developments had a number of environmental and social impacts:

- Most of the native plants and animals, that had previously been protected by isolation, were displaced by introduced species, and are now found only in remote mountain areas.
- The native Hawaiians became a marginalised minority in their own country, with their traditional culture in danger of disappearing.

TOURISM DEVELOPMENT

Although the first tourist facility on the islands – the Royal Hawaiian Hotel in Honolulu – opened as early as 1872, this catered mainly for business travel. Leisure tourism did not really develop until after Hawaii became a territory of the United States in 1898. In 1901 the Manoa Hotel opened, the first of many resort hotels along Waikiki Beach, but catering strictly for a moneyed clientele. In 1903 the Hawaiian Promotion Committee was formed, but in the early part of the twentieth century the islands were expensive to reach, involving a voyage lasting from four to six days, by luxury liner out of San Francisco or Long Beach. It was not until the 1950s that a rapid expansion of tourism took place as a result of:

- Economic prosperity on the US mainland following the Second World War, during which large numbers of American servicemen had been stationed on the islands.
- The introduction of cheaper and more frequent air services, using jet aircraft, which ended the comparative isolation of the islands.
- The use of Hawaii as a location for film and TV productions.
- The achievement of statehood in 1959, which integrated Hawaii more fully into the mainstream of American life.

Tourism stemmed out-migration from the islands and provided an alternative source of employment to a declining agricultural sector based on sugar and pineapple production. By the 1970s, inclusive air tours had brought Hawaii within reach of Americans on modest incomes and the age of mass tourism had arrived. Between 1950 and 1980 the number of visitors grew from 46000 to 4 million, a rate of increase almost without parallel in any other destination. After reaching a peak in 1990 with almost 7 million arrivals, tourism stagnated during the next decade, largely as a result of the first Gulf War and the Asian currency crisis. Since then the major resorts have repositioned themselves to meet changing demands, and in 2006 arrivals stood at 7.5 million.

Most tourism development has been concentrated on Oahu, the third largest of the islands in area, but the most important in other respects, as it contains 75 per cent of the population, the bulk of the tourist accommodation, and the capital Honolulu. Although the majority of tourists staying in Oahu visit one or more of the 'neighbour islands', such visits tend to be brief. There is little doubt that mass tourism has had an undesirable impact on Oahu, particularly at Waikiki where development has been largely unplanned. The state government has therefore encouraged projects on the other islands, and these are generally of a higher standard. On Maui for example, most of the development consists of condominiums, with some apartments owned on a time-share basis, catering mainly for wealthy Americans. However, these projects have been criticised for contributing even less to the community than the large high-rise hotels that characterise Waikiki. The Japanese have invested heavily in Hawaii, not just in hotel developments, but in golf courses, travel agencies and real estate.

Although Hawaii is not lacking in cultural and other attractions, the bulk of the demand is for beach tourism, and is generated from the following countries:

- **The United States and Canada** The United States mainland accounts for three quarters of all visitors to Hawaii. Thanks to cheap domestic air

TOURISM IN CONTEXT

DEMAND

RESOURCES

CLIMATE

TRANSPORT

FUTURES

TOURISM IN CONTEXT

DEMAND

RESOURCES

CLIMATE

TRANSPORT

FUTURES

fares and competitive tour pricing, visitors from cities in the Middle Atlantic and Midwestern states can reach the islands almost as easily as those from California.

- **Japan**   The Japanese on average spend much more than the Americans; however, this market has declined since the late 1990s. Young Japanese are particularly attracted to the islands as a honeymoon destination. Honolulu is a major hub on the network of trans-Pacific air services, bringing Tokyo as close to Hawaii as many cities in the USA.
- **Australia and New Zealand**   These are important markets, due to increased accessibility.
- **Western Europe**   The region generates less demand due to the greater distance and higher cost of air travel, with relatively few tourists visiting islands other than Oahu. All travel between the islands and to the mainland is by air, except for cruises based on Honolulu, and there is virtually no public transport on the islands.

TOURISM RESOURCES

Hawaii's appeal as a tourist destination is due to a combination of factors – a favourable climate, beautiful coastal and mountain scenery, the opportunities for surfing and a wide range of outdoor activities – and not least the Polynesian culture. We will now look at some of these resources in more detail.

CLIMATE

The Hawaiian islands lie in the path of the prevailing north-east trade winds, which strongly influence the climate, moderating the heat and humidity of these tropical latitudes. However, from time to time, the trades are interrupted by *kona* winds blowing from the south or south-west that bring spells of more humid weather and have an important effect on surf levels off the beaches. As the islands are mountainous, there are also striking differences in climate and vegetation between the leeward and windward slopes. Most of the resort developments are on the more sheltered south and west coasts of the islands that enjoy a dry climate with abundant sunshine.

SURFING BEACHES

Hawaii can claim to be the home of surfing, and offers some of the most powerful waves in the world. These often originate as a result of winter storms in the Aleutian Islands, 4000 kilometres to the north. There is no intervening landmass to diffuse the ocean swells, and no continental shelf to reduce their impact before they reach the beaches. The northern coast of Maui and the better known North Shore of Oahu are the favoured locations for experienced surfers seeking the big waves in the winter months. At Pipeline surfers *ride the tube*, challenging waves shaped into hollow cylinders by a combination of a powerful swell and a shallow reef. Summer is the best time for surfing at Waikiki, where white American settlers adopted the sport from the native Hawaiians and introduced it to California and Australia in the 1920s. Since the Second World War, light fibreglass boards, undergoing constant improvements in design, have replaced the heavy long-boards made from native hardwoods, while the film, music and clothing industries and a professional competition circuit have spawned an international surf culture. A recent development is *power surfing*, using jet skis as tow-in craft to tackle the really big waves – needless to say this is decried by purists.

HAWAIIAN CULTURE

Islanders of part-native Hawaiian descent form the largest ethnic group on Hawaii, accounting for 40 per cent of the population. There is some resentment of the *haole* (white American) domination of the economy, but race relations have generally been better than in the mainland United States. Islanders from all racial groups now take pride in the native Hawaiian heritage, but this has changed considerably since Captain Cook's time. The question of authenticity is a matter for discussion, given the way cultural traditions are presented as part of the tourist image. These include:

- The *lei* or garland of welcome presented to visitors at the airport on arrival, symbolising *Aloha*, the islanders' tradition of hospitality
- The *luau* or banquet staged in the hotels, featuring a pig baked in an earth oven, recalling the harvest festivals
- Hawaiian music and dance, of which the *hula* is the best known. This originally served a religious purpose, recounting the history and legends of the people through facial expressions, hip movements and hand gestures. However, Hawaiian music has adopted elements from other cultures, such as the ukulele (introduced by Portuguese immigrants), and was largely re-invented by the American entertainment industry in the 1930s.

Hawaii can claim to be the home of surfing

TOURISM IN CONTEXT

DEMAND

RESOURCES

CLIMATE

TRANSPORT

FUTURES

TOURISM IN CONTEXT

DEMAND

RESOURCES

CLIMATE

TRANSPORT

FUTURES

THE MARINE ENVIRONMENT

The seas around the Hawaiian Islands provide opportunities for a range of activities including:

- Diving, based on the coral reefs along the leeward coasts of the islands. Since the 1980s it has also become possible to explore the underwater world in safety and comfort using submersible craft
- Yachting and windsurfing, particularly off Maui
- Whale-watching, especially off Maui where it is a major business. However, this very popularity may threaten the survival of the humpback whale as a species.

THE NATURAL HERITAGE

The U.S. National Park Service protects outstanding examples of the natural heritage of the islands, the best known being the Volcanoes National Park on the 'Big Island' of Hawaii. Hiking tours and ecotourism are developing in the interior of the islands, providing an alternative to the high-consumption tourist lifestyle, based on the beach and the shopping mall that is typical of the resorts. Although certain features are common to all the islands, such as surfing beaches, waterfalls and volcanic scenery, each of the major islands has a distinct character:

- **Oahu** Aptly known as the *Gathering Place*, Oahu is the most visited of the islands. The features that make Honolulu different from other large American cities are:
  - The world-famous beach at Waikiki, and the landmark of volcanic origin known as Diamond Head
  - The Bishop Museum – one of the world's finest collection of Pacific arts and crafts
  - The Iolani Palace, with its reminders of the Hawaiian monarchy.
    The naval base at Pearl Harbor, of Second World War fame, is situated near Honolulu. Another major attraction is the Polynesian Cultural Centre at Lae, which combines education with entertainment as a living showcase for the folklore of the seven Polynesian nations of the Pacific.
- **Maui** The green *Valley Isle*, contains a number of exclusive resorts such as Kapalua and Kaunapaali – which is now integrated with the former whaling port of Lahaina. Major attractions include the Haleakala Crater, one of the world's largest, and the Seven Pools of Hana.
- **Kauai** The *Garden Isle* is particularly renowned for its lush scenery, exemplified by:
  - The Fern Grotto at Wailua.
  - The Waimea Canyon.
  - The beaches of Hanalei – world famous as the location for 'Bali Hai' in the film 'South Pacific'.
    Much of the island is only accessible by helicopter, boat or hiking trail. Kauai was badly affected by the Iniki hurricane disaster of 1992, which caused the island authorities to revise their tourism policy to favour small locally owned enterprises and native Hawaiian communities.

- **Hawaii**   the *Big Island* offers the greatest contrasts in climate, due to the high volcanic peaks of Mauna Loa and Mauna Kea. Kilauea is one of the world's most active volcanoes, and its frequent eruptions have created a lunar landscape of fire pits, craters and lava caves in the south eastern part of the island, and the characteristic beaches of black and green sand. Elsewhere cattle ranches, coffee plantations, and rainforests add variety to the landscape.
- **Molokai, Lanai** and **Niihau**   The other inhabited islands have as yet been little influenced by tourism. The main attraction of Molokai – *'The Friendly Isle'* – is the rugged coastal scenery of the Kaleapapa National Park, site of a former leper colony. Lanai until recently depended on its pineapple plantations but has now diversified into upmarket tourism.

THE IMPACTS OF TOURISM

Tourism has provided economic benefits to Hawaii, but at a cost to the environment and the island lifestyle. The dominance of the tourism sector is particularly opposed by native Hawaiian activists, who see it as threatening their agricultural lands, sacred sites, water supplies and fishing grounds, as well as trivialising their cultural traditions. Golf courses not only make enormous demands on water resources but are also a major source of pollution, due to the constant applications of fertiliser and weed killer that are needed. The owners of large hotels have been accused of denying locals access to public beaches. Tourism has also been blamed for a rising crime rate, family breakdown and rising land prices that deny local people access to the housing market. Nevertheless since the 1980s, efforts have been made to introduce conservation measures and curb inappropriate tourism developments. At the same time the larger resorts such as Waikiki have begun to reposition themselves away from high volume, low yield mass tourism, with environmental improvements and investment in the accommodation stock. The biggest long-term threat may not be from the growth of tourism as such, but from population growth, caused by immigration from the mainland of the United States.

REFLECTIONS ON THIS CASE

Despite its image as an idyllic Pacific paradise, Hawaii is the major tourism destination in the Pacific with a large and professional tourism sector. Tourism development has a long history in Hawaii and in the twenty-first century the islands are paying heed to the impacts of tourism and developing sustainable tourism products and repositioning some of the older resorts.

DISCUSSION POINTS

1. Most people have stereotyped images of foreign countries, peoples and faraway places, which are referred to in the tourism industry as 'icons',

TOURISM IN CONTEXT

DEMAND

RESOURCES

CLIMATE

TRANSPORT

FUTURES

TOURISM IN CONTEXT

DEMAND

RESOURCES

CLIMATE

TRANSPORT

FUTURES

and these are often portrayed in travel brochures and posters. Identify those features of the culture and landscapes of Hawaii that might qualify as icons. To what extent do these images give a misleading impression to potential visitors and differ from the reality of life for Hawaiians?

2. You have been asked to give a presentation on surfing in Hawaii to your class, taking into account the *demand* for surfing worldwide as well as the *supply* of resources and facilities for the sport.

3. Investigate the part played by feature films, television and popular literature in publicising Hawaii as a holiday destination, using some of the locations portrayed as examples.

4. Native Hawaiians claim that their traditions have been debased for tourist consumption, while some tourists are disappointed by what they see as commercialisation and 'staged authenticity' in the presentation of Hawaiian culture. Discuss whether these views are justified by the evidence.

5. Despite their geographical location in the middle of the world's largest ocean, the Hawaiian Islands are well served by a number of airlines. With reference to the ABC World Airways Guide, compare the frequency of flights from London, Sydney, New York and Tokyo to Honolulu with those to another Pacific island destination such as Tahiti.

KEY SOURCES

Cooper, C. and Hall, C. M. (eds) (2005) *Oceania*. Channelview, Clevedon.

Farrell, B. H. (1982) *Hawaii, the Legend that Sells*. University Press of Hawaii, Honolulu.

Lynch, R. (1997) Tourism in independent Hawaii. *Contours*, 7 (11/12), 24–26.

Mak, J. and Moncur, J. E. T. (1995) Sustainable tourism development: managing Hawaii's "Unique" tourist resource: Hanauma Bay. *Journal of Travel Research*, 33 (4), 51–57.

Sheldon, P. J. and Abenoja, T. (2001) Resident attitudes in a mature destination: the case of Waikiki. *Tourism Management*, 22 (5), 435–443.

Tamirisa, N. T., Loke, M. K., Leung, P. and Tucker, K. A. (1997) Energy and tourism in Hawaii. *Annals of Tourism Research*, 24 (2), 390–401.

Tarlow, P. E. (2000) Creating safe and secure communities in economically challenging times. *Tourism Economics*, 6 (2), 139–149.

Wyllie, R. W. (1998) Not in our backyard: opposition to tourism development in a Hawaiian community. *Tourism Recreation Research*, 23 (1), 55–64.

Wyllie, R. W. (1998) Hama revisited: development and controversy in a Hawaiian tourism community. *Tourism Management*, 19 (2), 171–178.

WEBSITES

www.gohawaii.com/

General view of Rio from a favela or shanty town.
© istockphoto.com/Brasil2

The Regeneration of Rio de Janeiro

INTRODUCTION

Rio de Janeiro is one of many world-class resorts that are looking to revision themselves for the twenty first century. This case examines tourism in Rio and the revisioning process. On completion of the case you will:

1. Understand the reasons for Rio's reputation as one of the world's great tourism cities.
2. Be aware of Rio's trajectory on the destination area life cycle.
3. Recognise the range of attractions and facilities for tourism in Rio.
4. Understand the social and environmental problems that have emerged for this destination in the last 30 years.
5. Be aware of Rio's process of revisioning and the steps taken to reposition the city in the international tourism market.

KEY ISSUES

There are four key issues in this case:

1. Rio is one of the world's great tourism cities and has completed virtually all of the stages of the destination area life cycle.
2. Rio's development as the leading resort in Brazil over many years has brought with it a range of social and environmental problems that have threatened the sustainability of Rio's growth and markets for the future.
3. Like many other resorts in the world, Rio has embarked upon an ambitious revisioning plan to reposition itself for the visitors of the twenty first century.
4. Rio's revisioning integrates tourism with other economic and social sectors of the city and to date has been a success.

RIO

Rio de Janeiro (or Rio) is one of the world's great tourist cities for the following reasons:

- The spectacular beauty of its setting, between one of the world's finest harbours – Guanabara Bay – and a number of granite peaks, including Sugar Loaf and Corcovado – which is crowned by the famous statue of Christ the Redeemer.
- Some 80 kilometres of fine sandy beaches, of which the best known are Copacabana and fashionable Ipanema. These are ideal for people-watching (but not for bathing due to the heavy Atlantic surf). Some beaches are characterised by a particular activity – for example Copacabana for football and volleyball, Arpoador for surfing.
- The uninhibited dance rhythms and extravagant costume parades of the Carnival, one of the greatest shows on Earth.

To complement these resources the city has a good transport infrastructure, including two major airports, and world-class hotels that are concentrated in the Copacabana area. Yet, despite these resources, in the last quarter of the twentieth century Rio reached the later stages of the tourism area life cycle and began to suffer from a number of problems. These are related to the fall in tourist demand for Rio, the changing nature of that demand and competition from other, newer resorts. In addition, many of the city's problems stem from the fact that not only is Rio no longer the capital of Brazil, and the loss of political influence this entails, but also São Paulo has overtaken Rio as a commercial centre. At the same time, the city still acts as a magnet for a massive influx of poor rural immigrants, while the rugged topography makes planning for growth difficult.

In response to these problems Rio embarked upon a major regeneration initiative. This fits in well with the Brazilian government's aims of:

- Creating a modern and efficient state.
- Reducing social and regional inequalities.
- Modernising the economy.
- Enhancing competitiveness in world markets.

THE DEVELOPMENT OF TOURISM IN RIO

In the nineteenth century, Rio not only attracted the Brazilian elite, but also wealthy visitors from Europe and the USA, but it was not until the late 1950s that tourists arrived in large numbers, attracted by the beaches and the climate.

GROWTH OF TOURISM, 1960S AND 1970S

Growth in both tourist numbers and facilities was rapid between 1960 and 1975, with international visitors complementing the domestic market. In the early 1970s, the Galeão International Airport opened, providing the impetus to attract the major hotel chains.

THE EMERGENCE OF PROBLEMS, 1980S AND EARLY 1990S

By the 1980s problems were emerging, based on the city's lack of planning and uncoordinated approach to tourism. Between 1985 and 1993 international arrivals declined substantially from 621 000 to 378 000, and average hotel occupancies fell to 50%. Visitors were increasingly concerned about security and not getting value for money. By this stage of Rio's tourism development the specific problems included:

- Lack of integration between the public and private sectors.
- Lack of professionalism in the tourism industry.
- Lack of tourist information at key attractions.
- A scarcity of employees speaking English or a language other than Portuguese.
- Minimal diversification of the product away from beach tourism.
- An expanding population competing with tourists for services and infrastructure.
- Beach pollution.
- Price inflation due to the unstable Brazilian currency.
- Crime against tourists.

THE REGENERATION STRATEGY, 1990S

It was at this time that the authorities decided that a concerted regeneration strategy was needed, both for the city itself and also for tourism.

TOURISM IN CONTEXT

DEMAND

RESOURCES

CLIMATE

TRANSPORT

FUTURES

TOURISM IN CONTEXT

DEMAND

RESOURCES

CLIMATE

TRANSPORT

FUTURES

THE REGENERATION OF RIO

In 1993, the mayor of Rio with the support of the private sector drew up the city's first strategic plan. This was followed in 1997 by a strategic plan specifically for tourism in co-operation with Embratur, Brazil's tourism development agency. The plan was designed to run until 2006 with rolling reviews of the plan's five major programmes. The main objectives of the plan were to:

- Increase receipts from tourism.
- Maintain Rio's leading competitive position in domestic tourism.
- Make Rio competitive in the international market.
- Reposition the image of Rio.

We can summarise the five programmes and their key objectives as follows.

PROGRAMME 1: NEW PRODUCT DEVELOPMENT TO ATTRACT NEW AND EXISTING MARKETS

- Diversification of entertainment facilities.
- Development of new products, such as eco-tourism. Here Rio is fortunate in having the Tijuca Reserve – a surviving example of coastal rainforest within the city limits.
- Development of products relating to the city's culture and history. Rio is well known for its samba schools and contribution to world music, but it also boasts a rich artistic heritage, dating back to the long colonial period and the reign of Dom Pedro II, who brought stability to Brazil in the nineteenth century.
- Development of sport tourism: Rio boasts the Maracaná Stadium, one of the world's largest, and Brazil is internationally celebrated for its achievements in football and motor racing.

PROGRAMME 2: UPGRADING OF CURRENT TOURISM PRODUCTS TO BOTH ENHANCE QUALITY AND REPOSITION THE RESORT

- Conservation of existing features such as the famous Sugar Loaf.
- Improvement of access and signposting to the city's attractions.
- Conservation of streetscapes and other features to enhance the quality of the visitor experience.
- Encouragement of private-sector involvement in upgrading products.

PROGRAMME 3: DEVELOPMENT OF A DATABASE FOR TOURISM AND THE ENHANCEMENT OF TOURIST INFORMATION IN THE CITY

- Development of a statistical database for tourism.
- Development of tourist information centres.

PROGRAMME 4: IMPLEMENTATION OF A DISCIPLINED MARKETING APPROACH FOR RIO

- Creation of a new image of a culturally vibrant city 'Incomparable Rio', and the promotion of this new image to the travel trade, the media and the public.
- Development of a public relations campaign targeted at the local population and the media.

PROGRAMME 5: DEVELOPMENT OF A SKILLED AND PROFESSIONAL WORKFORCE FOR THE TOURISM SECTOR

- Development of a tourism education system in Rio.
- Establishment of a quality management system for tourism in Rio.

DISCUSSION

The regeneration strategy for Rio is a good example of a disciplined response to a problem in a tourist destination. The strategy has had a range of positive outcomes. For example:

- The city is now in a better position to bid for major sporting events.
- International visitors have reached over 2 million a year, whilst domestic visitors are estimated at 5 million.
- The various stakeholders at the destination are working together with a more unified purpose. Rio's coordinating agencies – the Rio Convention Bureau and the City's tourism agency – Riotur – have taken a leading role in the regeneration of the city.

However, although much has been done to improve security for tourists and improve the image of the city overall, tourism has so far done little to benefit the more than one million people who live in the 500 or so *favelas*. These are the shanty towns, without basic infrastructure, on the hillsides overlooking the affluent areas, where gang rule prevails. Roçinha, the largest of these slums has been the scene of a private initiative to train local guides, who can show visitors the 'hidden side of Rio'. An award-winning film based on another *favela*, called Cidade de Deus (City of God) had greater impact, persuading the Brazilian government in 2003 to allocate much needed funding to these deprived areas.

REFLECTIONS ON THE CASE

Rio is one of the world' great cities but in the last 25 years has reached the stagnation stage of the destination area life cycle. To maintain its position

TOURISM IN CONTEXT

DEMAND

RESOURCES

CLIMATE

TRANSPORT

FUTURES

TOURISM IN
CONTEXT

DEMAND

RESOURCES

CLIMATE

TRANSPORT

FUTURES

as one of the leading resorts of the world, Rio has embarked upon an ambitious programme of revisioning and regeneration which integrates tourism with other economic and social sectors of the city. This is proving to be successful and is having a number of positive outcomes.

DISCUSSION POINTS

1. Evaluate the importance of Rio de Janeiro as an international venue for major sports events.
2. Debate the pros and cons of favela tours, from the viewpoint of the tour organisers, local people representing the visited communities, the city authorities and the tourists themselves. Assign roles to members of the class.
3. Describe the social and environmental problems that threaten Rio's prospects as a sustainable tourist destination. What is being done to address these problems?
4. Investigate the features that make Rio's Carnival one of the world's great event attractions, and assess its economic and social impact on local communities.
5. Discuss in class whether there are any common 'lessons for success' from this case and the Isle of Man case (case 16).

KEY SOURCES

Santana, G. (2001) *Tourism in South America*. Haworth, New York.
This study is mainly adapted from Railson Costa do Souza, 1998.

WEBSITES

www/embratur.gov.br/
www/rioconventionbureau.com.br
www/rio.rj.gov.br

A lodge for eco tourists, staying in the Amazonian rainforest. Cuyabeno National Park, Ecuador.

CASE 37

Ecotourism in the Ecuadorian Amazon

INTRODUCTION

The fate of the world's largest rainforest and its native inhabitants is a matter of global concern. This case study focuses on ecotourism in Ecuador's share of the Amazon Basin, as an alternative to less sustainable forms of development. On completion of this case you will:

1. Appreciate the biodiversity of Ecuador's rainforests and their potential for ecotourism.
2. Understand the challenges facing Indian communities in the Amazon and the role of community-based ecotourism (CBE) as an economic alternative to the petroleum and logging industries.
3. Recognise that community-based tourism accounts for only a small share of Ecuador's tourism market.
4. Be aware of the range of ecotourism projects in the Ecuadorian Amazon and the types of accommodation and transport used by ecotourists.

TOURISM IN CONTEXT

DEMAND

RESOURCES

CLIMATE

TRANSPORT

FUTURES

KEY ISSUES

There are five key issues in this case:

1. The need for ecotourists and non-governmental organisations to work together to convince governments of the need to conserve the rainforest resource.
2. The dilemma facing a developing country like Ecuador, which finds it difficult to promote sustainable development in the face of pressing economic problems.
3. The fact that well-managed ecotourism can deliver economic and social benefits to indigenous communities.
4. The many challenges facing indigenous communities in developing self-sufficiency and self-reliance through ecotourism.
5. The need for responsible behaviour on the part of tourists and tour operators visiting such communities.

THE SCOPE OF ECOTOURISM

Ecotourism is the sector of the international tourism industry that has shown the fastest growth since the mid-1990s. The value of this sector to the economy of a developing country like Ecuador is significant, but difficult to measure with any precision. According to the Travel Industry Association of America, 83 per cent of US tourists are prepared to spend more with environmentally responsible companies (Szuchman, 2001). Tour operators in South America are only too ready to add the eco-label to their products to attract tourists concerned about environmental issues, but in practice few hotels meet recognised eco-certification standards. There is no generally accepted definition of ecotourism, but it is more than just nature-based travel with definitions including an element of education, and most destinations are far from being uninhabited wilderness. Wherever there are local communities, the indigenous people should gain long-term economic benefits from such tourism rather than being excluded, as has too often been the case in the national parks and game reserves of Africa, for example. Ecotourism should accept the resource as it is, with the understanding that this may limit the number of visits over a given period, and promote ethical responsibilities and behaviour in the actions of all those involved.

If we apply ecotourism to Leiper's model of a tourism system, the tourist-generating area – for example, the UK – has a deficit of wildlife resources and accounts for much of the demand, whereas Ecuador has an abundant supply, including many unique species of plants and animals. In the generating area the ecotourist will be motivated by attitudes of 'responsible consumption' towards nature-based products and will be educated to an above-average level. Many individual tourists will be far from wealthy (although they may be perceived as such by the host community), and for them it is likely to be the 'holiday of a lifetime', involving months of preparation – the anticipation phase of the trip – as well as recollection of the experience to other potential tourists long after their return to their country of origin. In the destination area, nature will be the main attraction, while the ancillary services (accommodation, catering and guiding) should be well managed and 'environmentally friendly'. Participation in a learning experience is the primary objective of the trip, while shopping, night-time entertainment and recreation facilities are of less concern than is the case for other types of tourism. In the transit zone, where the tourists' journeys take place, the ecotourist would ideally seek locally owned transport operators and non-polluting modes of transport. This might be an option for internal travel, from, say, the tourist's base on arrival in the destination country to the national park or other protected areas that are to be visited. However, ecotourism destinations like the Ecuadorian Amazon are almost by definition remote places, and reaching them from generating areas such as Britain requires a journey halfway across the world by air. Since aircraft are a prime source of carbon emissions possibly contributing to 'global warming', this is the weakest link in the argument that ecotourism is the 'greenest' form of tourism.

ECOTOURISM IN ECUADOR

Some 17 per cent of Ecuador is officially protected with national park or nature reserve status. Although it is one of the smallest countries of South America, Ecuador boasts a great variety of life zones and scenic attractions in its section of the Andes, including the volcanic peaks of Cotopaxi, Chimborazo and Sangay, all within a short distance of the capital, Quito. The Pacific coastline now features on the international surfing circuit, but has been largely undeveloped for beach tourism. Cultural tourism, based on the Indian and Spanish colonial heritage of the Sierra, Ecuador's Andean region, has been overshadowed by better-known attractions in neighbouring Peru. Economic crises in the mid-1990s helped to raise the profile of tourism, and it is now second only to exports of petroleum and bananas as an earner of foreign exchange with international arrivals approaching 900 000. Ecotourism, followed by adventure tourism in the form of river-running, trekking and horse riding, are the major growth sectors.

Nevertheless, Ecuador lacks an effective programme of tourism promotion involving both the private and public sectors. Although there is a Ministry of Tourism and a national tourist organisation (CETUR), government support for the industry has been inconsistent. CETUR is funded by taxation and tourism businesses, but many of these are not officially registered as they form part of the country's large informal economy. The transport infrastructure is inadequate, and moreover the money raised from airport departure taxes is diverted to other projects rather than funding much-needed improvements to terminal facilities at Quito and Guayaquil. However, ecotourism is taken seriously and a new sustainable tourism development plan was launched in 2007, focusing on the Amazon, the Galápagos, the Andes and the Pacific coast.

Ecotourists are attracted primarily to the Galápagos Islands, the subject of a previous case study, rather than the mainland of Ecuador. Other significant resources include the mangrove swamps of the Pacific coast (now much diminished due to the growth of the lucrative shrimp-farming industry), the *páramos* (moorlands) and cloud forests of the High Andes, and the rainforests in the north-west and east of the country. In north-west Ecuador the Cotocachi-Cayapas Reserve, lying

TOURISM IN CONTEXT

DEMAND

RESOURCES

CLIMATE

TRANSPORT

FUTURES

TOURISM IN CONTEXT

DEMAND

RESOURCES

CLIMATE

TRANSPORT

FUTURES

between the Andes and the Pacific coastal lowlands, has been the focus of an international project for a 'rainforest corridor' extending to the Chocó region in western Colombia.

A much more extensive area of primary forest lies to the east of the Andes in the region known to Ecuadorians as El Oriente, which forms part of the vast Amazon Basin. Although Ecuador's share of Amazonia is small compared to that of Brazil, it is richer in biodiversity than any other part of the world, including Costa Rica, which is much better known as an ecotourism destination. The forests, rivers and freshwater lagoons of the region provide a variety of habitats for wildlife. In primary rainforest the larger trees form a dense leaf canopy at a height of 30–45 metres, preventing sunlight from reaching the forest floor, which is relatively free of undergrowth. In between there is an understorey of smaller trees and a layer of shrubs, festooned with lianas and epiphytes (air plants such as orchids). In the Cuyabeno Reserve there are over 400 species of birds, dolphins (at a distance of 4000 kilometres from the Atlantic Ocean), not to mention the abundance of fish species. However, this biodiversity is not only a tourism resource; there is also the trade in animals and birds destined largely for private collections, and the issue of 'bio-piracy', where American companies have sought to secure patents on medicinal plants as yet unknown to science. Since the late 1960s the rainforest of the Oriente has diminished considerably in extent, for the following reasons:

1. The discovery of oil and the associated development, which has caused widespread disturbance to wildlife and the contamination of water resources. Even the Yasuni National Park, which is designated by UNESCO as a World Biosphere Reserve, is under threat from the international oil companies.
2. The commercial logging of tropical hardwoods, much of it illegal. Since these trees rarely occur in pure stands and are widely scattered throughout the forest, indiscriminate felling is almost inevitable.
3. The influx of large numbers of settlers from the Sierra and the Pacific coastal lowlands who have cleared land for agriculture.
4. Even so the six provinces that comprise the Oriente only account for 6 per cent of the population of Ecuador, and this region has a frontier character. Although the oil industry has provided a transport infrastructure in the northern Oriente that can be used by tourism, most localities can only be accessed by motorcanoe along navigable rivers such as the Napo, or by light aircraft.

THE RISE OF COMMUNITY-BASED ECOTOURISM

The rainforest of the Oriente is home to nine indigenous groups who are facing severe pressures. Most of these groups now number less than a thousand individuals. Their age-old way of life was based on hunting, fishing and gathering, with some subsistence agriculture on small clearings in the forest. In the course of the twentieth century some elements of the traditional culture were discarded, largely as the result of missionary influence. The most warlike of these Indians – the Huaorani (formerly known as Aucas) – were responsible for the killing of American missionaries in 1956, while artefacts of the Shuar (Jivaros), such as blowguns and *tsantsas* (the shrunken heads of defeated enemies), are found in many museum

TOURISM IN CONTEXT

DEMAND

RESOURCES

CLIMATE

TRANSPORT

FUTURES

collections. The lowland Quechua, who speak the same language as the Indians of the Sierra, are by far the largest group and have been in the forefront of CBE projects. From the late 1960s the indigenous people increasingly faced the loss of their hunting grounds through the encroachment of the oil and logging industries, and the movement of settlers into the region. The growth of ecotourism persuaded the government to set aside areas as national parks or nature reserves, but this was done without consulting local communities. Moreover some Quito-based tour operators presented the native people as a curiosity or exploited them as cheap labour.

As a consequence, the indigenous peoples of the Oriente are increasingly turning to CBE as one of a number of strategies towards self-reliance. Political organisation plays an important role in this process. Considering their small numbers relative to the Indian population of the Sierra, groups from the Oriente have been active in the Pachacutik movement which seeks greater representation in the National Congress in Quito, and the recognition in the Ecuadorian Constitution of the special rights of indigenous communities to retain their languages and traditions. With the help of NGOs (non-governmental organisations), they have fought to legalise the communal ownership of their ancestral lands. Finally, indigenous organisations have emphasised their conservation role as 'guardians of the forest', as INEFAN (the government agency responsible for nature reserves) is under-resourced.

Community-based enterprises take a number of forms:

1. In their purest form they are owned and managed by the community, with their members employed on a rotation basis so that income from tourism is spread evenly. There are problems with this approach; if the building of an airstrip or tourist accommodation does not produce income or jobs in the short term the community may lose interest in the project.
2. A more flexible form of CBE involves particular families taking on responsibility for management, yet providing work for others according to the pattern of tourism demand.
3. A third type involves joint ventures between an indigenous group and an outside partner, usually a tour operator based in Quito. The tour operator provides the tourists, transportation and a bilingual guide, and offers training and marketing expertise, while the community takes care of the day-to-day arrangements for its guests. In the case of the Kapawi Eco-Lodge, which is situated in a reserve near the Peruvian border, the tour operator obtained a long-term lease for the development on land belonging to the Achuar tribe. It is intended that they will take over full responsibility for managing the project in 2011.

The majority of ecotourists to the Ecuadorian Amazon stay in hotels of varying standard in the gateway towns of Puyo, Tena and Misahualli and use these as bases for their tours, which may involve a lengthy trip by river transport. Others stay in lodges close to the reserves, which are usually in more remote locations and managed by large national or international tour companies. One of the perceived advantages of CBE is that the host community has made a conscious choice in favour of tourism, so that the visitor feels like a welcome guest rather than an intruder. The indigenous guide not only has an unrivalled knowledge of the forest and its wildlife, but due to differences in temperament shows little of the machismo that characterises Latin American male attitudes. To keep negative social impacts to a minimum, no more than 12 visitors are allowed on any one

TOURISM IN CONTEXT

DEMAND

RESOURCES

CLIMATE

TRANSPORT

FUTURES

tour, while visits may be limited to one group per month. The tourist accommodation is likewise sited some distance from the village, and is built in the traditional style using local materials, usually as open-sided *cabañas* with a thatched roof, elevated on stilts to take advantages of any breezes. Tour programmes are flexible and unhurried, giving visitors the opportunity to interact with village life and for cultural exchange between hosts and guests. In some areas the forest trails have been improved for hiking tours, with boardwalks, rope bridges and even observation towers, while river journeys are undertaken in dugout canoes.

The disadvantage of most CBE enterprises for conventional tourism is their lack of sophistication, as it has been a steep learning curve for indigenous people to adjust to the requirements and expectations of Western tourists. Some of these are unrealistic; tourists looking for 'authenticity' will be disappointed by the fact that their hosts aspire to live in modern houses with tin roofs and wear Western-style clothing, while others may disapprove of the continuing importance of hunting. As yet there are few English-speaking guides, so tourists need to be adequately prepared for their visit. Lodging and catering facilities are fairly basic, except in a few joint enterprises such as the Kapawi Eco-Lodge. Although some food is produced locally, most supplies have to be brought in from the nearest town, which may involve a lengthy journey by motor-canoe. Access to an assured tourist market is a major problem, as most communities lack modern means of communication. Here visitors can play an important role by 'spreading the word' to potential tourists on returning to their country of origin.

Community-based ecotourism has brought benefits to indigenous groups, allowing them to retain aspects of their traditional lifestyle and embrace change on their own terms. A limited amount of employment has been provided in the community for guides, canoeists and cooks, while other households gain income from the sale of handicrafts such as basketwork, hammocks (an Amerindian invention), pottery and woodcarvings, and these also help to revive traditional skills. Involvement in CBE encourages protection of the forest and its resources, and generates pride in the native culture. At the same time it improves communication with the wider world. Some money is now available for access to modern healthcare in Quito, but more exposure to the market economy results in greater dependence on imported consumer goods. Taking a short-term view, there is an 'opportunity cost' for those involved in CBE, since by doing so they forego more stable and better paid jobs with the oil companies. Logging and oil can provide more immediate income than tour groups, and community leaders find it difficult to resist the blandishments of the oil companies. Community enterprises also face competition from cut-price tour operators, who are less concerned about ethics and environmental issues. In a wider sense the development versus conservation dilemma is faced by the whole of Ecuador with its faltering economy.

REFLECTIONS ON THE CASE

The ultimate aim of ecotourism is to help indigenous peoples retain their traditional lifestyle, since they know best how to achieve sustainable management of the rainforest. In CBE as practised in the Ecuadorian Amazon, the forest Indians have assumed control over the numbers and activities of tourists in their territories. Ecotourism not only generates income for communities living in remote areas with few other resources, but also encourages them to value their culture. However, there is constant pressure from the oil industry and other drivers of change, and these communities need outside help from NGOs and supportive tour operators to improve their product and maintain their way of life. From the viewpoint of the ecotourists themselves, for many CBE could be a disappointing experience. They may well prefer to spend most of their time viewing animals, and stay in a lodge with modern conveniences and familiar foods, than 'interact' with indigenous people.

DISCUSSION POINTS/ASSIGNMENTS

1. As indigenous communities cannot rely solely on ecotourism for a livelihood, suggest a number of activities related to an ecotourism programme that could generate additional income.
2. Discuss the opinion that the reality of ecotourism in the Ecuadorian Amazon falls some way short of the ideal.
3. Draw up a code of conduct for tourists visiting an Indian community in the Amazon.
4. Like other forms of tourism, ecotourism responds to changes in fashion, and indigenous communities have to compete with established tour operators for a share of the market. Suggest ways in which indigenous communities can stay ahead of the competition by specialising in a niche market.
5. A retired school teacher living in Manchester is planning 'the trip of a lifetime' to the Ecuadorian Amazon. Put together all the components of the tourism experience, including:
   - the 'anticipation phase', including advice on preparing for the trip
   - the journey to the destination, including all stopovers and transfers
   - a detailed itinerary for the visit, which involves staying in Indian communities
   - advice on networking, so that our client can effectively spread the word about CBE.

KEY SOURCES

Braman, S. and Fundación Acción Amazonia (2001) Practical strategies for pro-poor tourism: tropic ecological adventures – Ecuador. *PPT Working Paper 6*.

Colvin, J. (1994) Capirona: a model of indigenous tourism. *Journal of Sustainable Tourism*, 2 (3), 174–177.

Dahles, H. and Keune, L. (2002) *Tourism Development and Local Participation in Latin America*. Cognizant, New York.

TOURISM IN CONTEXT

DEMAND

RESOURCES

CLIMATE

TRANSPORT

FUTURES

Jeffreys, A. (1998) Tourism in northwest Ecuador. *Geography Review* (January), 26–29.

Leiper, N. (1990) *Tourism Systems: An Interdisciplinary Perspective*. Massey University, Auckland.

Mann, M. (ed.) (2002) *The Good Alternative Travel Guide*. Earthscan/Tourism Concern, London.

Szuchman, P. (2001) Eco-credibility. *Condé Nast Traveler*, August, 46.

Wesche, R. and Drumm, A. (1998) *Defending our Rainforest: A Guide to Community-based Ecotourism in the Ecuadorian Amazon*. Acción Amazonia, Quito.

Wood, M. E. (1998) *Meeting the Global Challenge of Community Participation in Ecotourism: Case Studies and Lessons from Ecuador*. The Nature Conservancy, Arlington.

Woodfield, J. (ed.) (1994) *Ecosystems and Human Activity*. Collins Educational, London.

WEBSITES

www.gn.apc.org/tourismconcern
www.planeta.com
www.vivecuador.com/

TOURISM IN CONTEXT

DEMAND

RESOURCES

CLIMATE

TRANSPORT

FUTURES

Several thousands of King Penguins breeding in a large penguin colony in Antarctica.
© istockphoto.com/Alexander Hafemann

Antarctica: Tourism or Conservation?

INTRODUCTION

Antarctica is the world's largest wilderness, but differs from other destinations for nature lovers and adventure-seekers in not having any indigenous communities to be affected by tourism. In the 1970s 'the white continent' was tourism's last frontier; now there is a Lonely Planet guidebook to the Antarctic and the number of tourists arriving during the summer months of November through March exceeds the resident population of scientists and support personnel at the research stations. Nature-loving tourists are attracted by the unique wildlife, awe-inspiring glacial scenery, and the heritage of polar explorers such as Amundsen, Scott and Shackleton; yet, aside from space, Antarctica is probably the most hostile environment known to mankind. On completion of this case you will:

1. Understand that ecotourism may be the only type of tourist activity compatible with the polar environment.
2. Recognise that there are significant differences between Antarctica and other wilderness areas visited by ecotourists.
3. Understand that the great majority of tourists arrive on cruise ships and spend only a short time ashore.
4. Be aware that the greatest challenge is from the growth of adventure tourism and the resulting demand for tourist facilities in Antarctica.
5. Understand the special political status of Antarctica and how this could be threatened by external pressures.

TOURISM IN
CONTEXT

DEMAND

RESOURCES

CLIMATE

TRANSPORT

FUTURES

KEY ISSUES

There are four key issues in this case:

1. Antarctica can support only a limited range of tourist activities, and even these can have a negative impact on wildlife.
2. Tourism is highly concentrated in a very small part of Antarctica, so visitor sites are under pressure.
3. The infrastructure and facilities for tourism in Antarctica are extremely limited, and any expansion would contravene the Antarctic Treaty that protects its unique environment.
4. The environmental guidelines for tourists depend on the willingness of stakeholders to comply, as no one country can enforce rules or effectively monitor tourist activity.

BACKGROUND

Although they feature in Antarctic cruise itineraries and guidebooks, we should first distinguish the sub-Antarctic islands of the Southern Ocean, which are situated in middle latitudes, from the continent of Antarctica. These islands lie close to the Antarctic Convergence, where the cold surface water spreading outwards from the continent meets warmer water from the north. The climate is bleak and cloudy, but the temperatures are mild compared to Antarctica. The islands' resources were exploited in the nineteenth century by whalers, sealers and even would-be colonisers, who introduced alien species that devastated the native plants and birds. Unlike Antarctica, the islands are under the sovereignty of a number of countries, namely Australia, Britain, France, New Zealand, Norway, and South Africa. Visits to these islands, which include South Georgia, Macquarie Island (an Australian World Heritage Site), the Auckland and Campbell Islands, and Kerguelen, are restricted for conservation reasons.

Over 98 per cent of the continent of Antarctica's 14 million square kilometres of land surface (larger than Australia or Europe) is permanently covered by an ice sheet which is over 2000 metres thick. The coast is fringed by floating ice shelves, which spawn huge tabular icebergs. Because of its high altitude, the interior of Antarctica is extremely cold and very dry, while the coast is swept by pitiless winds. The ice-free areas can only support a few fragile mosses and lichens. As a tourist destination Antarctica differs from the Arctic in the following ways:

- It is much less accessible. Antarctica is separated from the nearest populated lands in the Southern Hemisphere by vast expanses of stormy ocean in the latitudes known as the 'Roaring Forties', the 'Furious Fifties' and the 'Screaming Sixties', and is moreover ringed by a barrier of pack ice for most of the year. It is therefore unlikely that Antarctica was visited by man before its discovery by American, British and Russian explorers in the early nineteenth century.

Permanent scientific bases have only been established since the 1940s. No international air routes cross the southern polar regions. Travel from the major tourist-generating countries is expensive and time-consuming, involving up to two days of air travel, plus a sea voyage lasting from two to ten days from the nearest ports in South America, South Africa, Australia and New Zealand.

- The Antarctic south of latitude 60 degrees is politically 'no-man's land'. Under the terms of the 1959 Antarctic Treaty, the territorial claims made by seven of the signatory governments, namely Argentina, Australia, Britain, Chile, France, New Zealand and Norway, are in abeyance. Antarctica serves as a vast laboratory for international co-operation in scientific research, currently involving 26 different countries, most of which operate research stations year-round. There is a concentration of these – some doubling as military bases – on King George Island in the South Shetlands. It was in Antarctica that the hole in the ozone layer was identified in the 1980s, and it is here that global pollution trends are monitored. Environmental protection is given priority, and there is a moratorium on mineral exploitation. However in 2007, Britain laid claim to 1 million square kilometres of sea bed adjoining the Antarctic Peninsula, a claim which is disputed by Chile and Argentina. Australia has made a similar claim to the continental shelf adjoining its territory in East Antarctica.
- Although the adjoining seas teem with marine life, the interior of Antarctica is virtually sterile, in contrast to the Arctic tundra. The coast provides a summer habitat for penguins, which in fact are more at home in the sea than on dry land. The Emperor penguin is the only species of bird to overwinter in Antarctica.

The continent of Antarctica is now thought to be two geologically distinct landmasses beneath the icecap, separated by the Transantarctic Mountains. West Antarctica includes the most accessible part of the continent – the Antarctic Peninsula – which is only 1000 kilometres from Cape Horn in South America. East Antarctica includes the 'Far Side' of the continent which is remote even from Australia and New Zealand. Extensive mountain ranges and many sub-glacial lakes lie buried deep below the surface of the ice sheet. Investigation of the largest of these – Lake Vostok – poses a dilemma, because of the risk of contamination to a pristine environment.

Tourism, as distinct from government-sponsored expeditions (which never carried paying passengers), began in the late 1950s with the first charter flights from Chile and New Zealand; the first Lindblad cruise followed in 1966. However, it was not until an Antarctic Treaty conference in 1977 that tourism received official attention. It has grown rapidly in recent years, with over 30 000 tourist arrivals in the 2006–07 summer season, compared to only 6000 in 1992–93. This growth is largely due to the following factors:

- Increased competition between tour operators offering cruises to Antarctica.
- Since the collapse of the Soviet Union, Russia's scientific institutes have been eager to lease their ice-breaker ships at bargain rates to Western tour operators. This has opened up previously inaccessible areas, such as the Ross Sea, to cruising, and made it possible to circumnavigate Antarctica in a single season.
- Advances in cold-weather technology have also made it possible to promote the interior of Antarctica as well as the coastal fringe for adventure tourism.

TOURISM IN CONTEXT

DEMAND

RESOURCES

CLIMATE

TRANSPORT

FUTURES

TOURISM IN CONTEXT

DEMAND

RESOURCES

CLIMATE

TRANSPORT

FUTURES

We can distinguish between the following types of tourism, based on transport arrangements:

- Land-based – with air support, where tourists stay in tented accommodation or at a research station
- Over-flights
- Sea-based – where the ship provides the accommodation and all other facilities. Visits from cruise ships account for the great majority of tourist arrivals in the Antarctic.

LAND-BASED TOURISM

Compared to the Arctic regions of North America, there is a lack of ground facilities for commercial aircraft. Although the research stations are served by an elaborate infrastructure of aircraft, supply ships, specialised vehicles (such as 'sno-cats' and snowmobiles) and fuel depots, this is very costly to maintain. Most governments are therefore reluctant to support tourism ventures because of the health and safety issues involved, and the possible disruption to scientific programmes. However, between 1984 and 1993 Chile actively promoted air-inclusive tours to its military base on King George Island in the South Shetlands, and more recently Russia has attempted a similar venture. Russia needs the hard currency, while Chile and Argentina have used tourism to bolster their long-standing (and conflicting) territorial claims to this sector of Antarctica. A few specialist tour operators fly wealthy adventure-seeking clients to the interior of the continent for mountain climbing in the Vinson Massif, kite-skiing and even sky diving at the South Pole! 'Blue-ice' landing strips are used, where the snow is packed hard, and skidoos provide ground transportation. Despite the intense solar radiation in summer and the high risk of sunburn, temperatures here can fall to $-40\,°C$, compared to the comparatively balmy $0–4\,°C$ tourists normally experience in the Antarctic Peninsula.

OVER-FLIGHTS

In the 1970s, over-flying Antarctica was popular in New Zealand, until an Air New Zealand Boeing 747 crashed on Mount Erebus, killing all onboard. In 1994 a Melbourne-based company resumed flight-seeing tours from Australian cities, and by 2001 over 10 000 passengers had viewed the spectacular icefalls and glaciers of the Transantarctic Mountains from the air.

SEA-BASED TOURISM

This includes a few expeditions by private yacht, but cruising is far more significant, with most of the ships carrying between 40 and 150 passengers. The west coast of the Antarctic Peninsula and the South Shetland Islands are the most-visited areas, since they have a milder climate than the rest of Antarctica, and are relatively close to the ports of departure – Punta Arenas in Chile, Ushuaia in Argentina and Port Stanley – and cruise itineraries can include the Falklands, South Georgia and the fiords of southern Chile. These cruises do not penetrate south of the Antarctic Circle, and itineraries are subject to weather and ice conditions. Zodiac landing craft carry ashore groups of tourists, accompanied by a naturalist-guide, to visit penguin rookeries, where they experience the stench of guano and the noise before sighting the birds. Other attractions include:

- Deception Island – a volcanic caldera with a geothermal spring
- Historic sites associated with the former whaling industry
- Port Lockroy – a former British Antarctic Survey (BAS) base which is now a heritage attraction visited by over a hundred cruise ships each season
- Visits to research stations, where tourists are usually welcome, providing a break in routine for scientists and support workers, and (in the case of the stations run by less wealthy countries) some much-needed revenue.

Ecotourism boats landing for expedition. ©istockphoto.com/Dawn Nichols

A smaller number of cruises, using ice-breaker ships and departing from Fremantle and Hobart in Australia, and Christchurch and Bluff in New Zealand, undertake the long voyage to the Ross Sea, which is geographically much closer to the South Pole than the Antarctic Peninsula. The cruising season is shorter, lasting from late December to late February. Tourists can view colonies of Emperor penguins and other attractions such as:

- Cape Evans – with its relics of Scott's ill-fated expedition to the South Pole
- the US McMurdo Base (the largest research station in Antarctica)
- the Mount Erebus volcano
- the Ross Ice Barrier, the edge of the immense Ross Ice Shelf.

The ice-free 'Dry Valleys' of the interior – said to be the nearest thing on Earth to the landscape of Mars – can be reached by onboard helicopters.

TOURISM IN CONTEXT

DEMAND

RESOURCES

CLIMATE

TRANSPORT

FUTURES

TOURISM IN
CONTEXT

DEMAND

RESOURCES

CLIMATE

TRANSPORT

FUTURES

THE IMPACTS OF TOURISM

Tourism in Antarctica is an outstanding example of co-operation between the various stakeholders, which include:

1. the commercial sector, represented by the International Association of Antarctic Tour Operators (IAATO)
2. the governments that are signatories to the Antarctic Treaty and the 1991 Madrid Protocol on Environmental Protection
3. the tourists themselves.

Cruise operators to Antarctica generally subscribe to strict codes of conduct laid down by IAATO. Passengers during their 2 hours ashore are kept under constant surveillance, for their own safety, and to prevent pollution, disturbance to wildlife and contamination by non-indigenous pathogens. (It is for the last reason that dogs are banned by the Madrid Protocol.) Conservation measures include:

- the separation of poultry products from other food waste, to prevent the spread of avian flu to penguins
- the shipping out of waste of any kind
- tourists are prohibited from approaching wildlife too closely
- the prohibition on taking 'souvenirs' other than photographs
- the disinfection of tourist's boots between shore trips.

Tourists generally respond favourably to these restrictions. They are predominantly from the older age groups, but not all are particularly affluent or widely travelled – for some it may be the trip of a lifetime. The most important market for Antarctic cruises is the USA, followed by the UK and Germany.

Despite the vast extent of Antarctica, tourists follow established routes, are concentrated in a relatively few sites during the short summer season and the time interval between visits by different groups to a site is often only a few hours. Many believe this has an adverse effect on the breeding patterns of seals and penguins, but others argue that the presence of human visitors protects young birds from predators. Emissions from the outboard motors of the zodiacs pollute the water, while not all cruise ships dispose of waste in accordance with environmental guidelines, and there is always the risk of a major oil spill. The sinking of the *MS Explorer* – the veteran of many Antarctic cruises – in November 2007 was a wake-up call for cruise operators to use ice-strengthened ships, and led to demands that the International Maritime Organisation (IMO) should impose stricter controls on Antarctic cruise tourism. Nevertheless, land-based tourism represents a much greater threat to the environment, if we consider the impact already made by the permanent scientific research stations. Tourism accounts for less than 1 per cent of all person days logged in Antarctica compared to more than 99 per cent for personnel at the research stations, who arguably do much more damage. Ironically, it was the negative publicity generated by returning cruise passengers about the garbage at one American base that forced the authorities to clean up their act.

REFLECTIONS ON THE CASE

It is not just the growth in the numbers of tourists that threatens the environment, but the changing nature of the demand. The typical Antarctic cruise passenger is predominantly from the older age groups and is content with a passive role as an eco-tourist, seeing Antarctica from a distance and responding positively to the restrictions imposed by tour operators. They are also good ambassadors for Antarctica; without publicity in the media, it would be difficult to gain popular support for the idea that the 'white continent' should remain purely a preserve for scientific research. The future is likely to see a growth in adventure tourism, attracting younger visitors who may show less concern for the environment and their own safety. With no one country able to enforce planning controls, this could lead inexorably to a demand for more ground facilities, as in other destinations. A future energy crisis could pose an even greater problem, as it would set off a 'free for all' among competing nations for mineral rights in Antarctica, effectively putting an end to the Antarctic Treaty.

DISCUSSION POINTS

1. Many scientists believe that tourists have no reason to be in Antarctica, while those in the travel industry maintain that is the right of humankind to see and experience the world's wild places. In class debate these opposing viewpoints, and role-play the various stakeholders involved in Antarctic conservation and tourism.
2. The melting of the ice shelves of the Antarctic Peninsula is often described by the media as evidence of global warming and an imminent worldwide rise in sea level. By using data from the British Antarctic Survey and other scientific organisations, assess the evidence for climate change in Antarctica and the effect on plant growth and animal behaviour.
3. The Lindblad cruise ship, *MS Explorer*, thought to be unsinkable, was holed by an iceberg on the night of 23 November 2007, at latitude 62°24′ south and longitude 57°17′ west. Investigate the particular circumstances of the sinking and the rescue mission to save the passengers and crew, and discuss the lessons that we can learn from this incident for the future of cruising in the Antarctic.
4. Scuba diving is generally regarded as a warm weather activity, but it is also practised in Antarctic waters as part of the growth in adventure tourism. Describe the conditions divers experience in Antarctica and the rewards, such as discovering new species of marine life. Draw up a code of conduct for divers and dive operators in Antarctica.
5. Discuss the extent to which the professionalism of the naturalist-guides is essential to the success of the Antarctic cruise experience.

TOURISM IN CONTEXT

DEMAND

RESOURCES

CLIMATE

TRANSPORT

FUTURES

KEY SOURCES

Bauer, T. (2002) Antarctic tourism: where are the limits? *Tourism 2002* Tourism Society, 18–20.

Davis, P. B. (1998) Beyond headlines: a model for Antarctic tourism. *Annals of Tourism Research*, 23 (3), 546–553.

Dove, J. (1997) Antarctica: tourism's last frontier. *Geography Review* 8(3), 14–18.

Hall, C. M. and Johnston, M. (1995) *Polar Tourism*. Wiley, Chichester.

Thomas, T. (1994) Ecotourism in Antarctica: the role of the naturalist-guide in promoting places of natural interest. *Journal of Sustainable Tourism*, 2 (4), 204–209.

WEBSITES

www.antarctica.ac.uk
www.quarkexpeditions.com

TOURISM IN CONTEXT

DEMAND

RESOURCES

CLIMATE

TRANSPORT

FUTURES

PART 4

Useful Sources

Sources to Support Work on the Case Studies

This section of the book is designed to support your work on the case studies. Whilst we have provided a set of relevant sources at the end of each case study, there is also a range of other material that you will find useful when tackling the cases. These include abstracting services, handbooks and dictionaries of tourism and the academic tourism journals. We have not provided a listing of trade publications (such as *Travel Trade Gazette*) for two reasons; first, there will be different trade journals and newspapers available to you depending upon which part of the world you live in, and secondly, in our view, the material tends to date rapidly.

The World Wide Web is now a major source of information about tourism and destinations. Of course, the web is disorganised and lacks any form of information quality control, but the official tourism sites in particular provide instant access to countries, cities and resorts. Other sites are now available that provide destination accounts, photographs and statistics. Because we feel that this is such a valuable source for everyone working on the cases in this book, we have provided a list of the website addresses of national tourist organisations of the major tourism countries in the world. In addition, the companion website to the book provides a comprehensive listing of travel and tourism websites, including search engines. However, we would not recommend that you use only Internet sources in your approach to these cases, but use the web to supplement print sources.

TOURISM IN CONTEXT

DEMAND

RESOURCES

CLIMATE

TRANSPORT

FUTURES

This list of sources is organised to cover the following types of reference material:

- general texts on tourism and the geography of travel and tourism
- reports, dictionaries, yearbooks and encyclopaedias
- abstracting services
- statistical sources
- tourism journals
- website addresses of national tourism organisations.

BOOKS ON TOURISM AND THE GEOGRAPHY OF TRAVEL AND TOURISM

Aramberri, J. and Butler, R. (2004) *Tourism Development*. Channel View.

Ashworth, G. (1984) *Recreation and Tourism*. Bell & Hyman.

Ateljevic, I., Pritchard, A. and Morgan, N. (2007) *The Critical Turn in Tourism Studies*. Elsevier.

Ball, S., Horner, S. and Nield, K. (2007) *Contemporary Hospitality and Tourism Management Issues in China and India*. Elsevier.

Beech, J. and Chadwick, S. (2005) *The Business of Managing Tourism*. Pearsons.

Bierman, D. (2003) *Restoring Destinations in Crisis*. Allen and Unwin.

Buckley, R. (2008) *Environmental Impacts of Ecotourism*. CABI.

Bull, A. (1998) *The Economics of Travel and Tourism*. Longman.

Burkhart, A. J. and Medlik, S. (1991) *Tourism, Past, Present and Future*. Heinemann.

Burns, P. M. and Holden, A. (1995) *Tourism: A New Perspective*. Prentice Hall.

Burns, P. M. and Novelli, M. (2007) *Tourism and Politics*. Elsevier.

Burton, R. (1995) *Travel Geography*. Addison Wesley Longman.

Butler, R. W. and Pearce, D. G. (1993) *Tourism Research*. Routledge.

Callaghan, P. (1989) *Travel and Tourism*. Business Educational.

Church, A. and Coles, T. (2006) *Tourism, Power and Space*. Routledge.

Coltman, M. (1989) *Introduction to Travel and Tourism*. Van Nostrand Reinhold.

Conlin, M. V. and Baum, T. (1995) *Island Tourism*. Wiley.

Cooper, C. and Hall, C. M. (2008) *Contemporary Tourism*. Elsevier.

Cooper, C. P., Fletcher, J., Fyall, A., Gilbert, D. and Wanhill, S. (2008) *Tourism Principles and Practice*. Pearson.

Crotts, J. C. and Van Raaij, W. F. (1993) *Economic Psychology of Travel and Tourism*. Haworth Press.

Daher, R. (2006) *Tourism in the Middle East*. Channel View.

Daye, M., Chambers, D. and Roberts, S. (2008) *New Perspectives in Caribbean Tourism*. Routledge.

De Kadt, E. (1979) *Tourism: Passport to Development*. Oxford University Press.

Deuschl, D. (2006) *Travel and Tourism Public Relations*. Elsevier.

Dowling, R. (2006) *Cruise Ship Tourism*. CABI.

Drakakis-Smith, G. and Lockhart, D. (1997) *Island Tourism: Trends and Prospects*. Pinter.

Dredge, D. (2006) *Tourism Planning and Policy*. Wiley.

Dumazedier, J. (1967) *Towards a Society of Leisure*. Free Press.

Fennell, D. (2006) *North America*. Channel View.

Fennell, D. A. (2007) *Ecotourism*, 3rd edn. Routledge.

Frechtling, D. (2001) *Forecasting Tourism Demand*. Elsevier Butterworth-Heinemann.

Frost, W. and Hall, C. M. (2008) *Tourism and National Parks: International Perspectives on Development, Histories and Change*. Routledge.

Fyall, A. and Garrod, B. (2004) *Tourism Marketing*. Channel View.

Gee, C. Y., Choy, D. J. L. and Makens, J. C. (1997) *The Travel Industry*. Van Nostrand Reinhold.

Getz, D. (2005) *Event Management & Event Tourism*. Cognizant Communication.

Gibson, C. and Connell, J. (2005) *Music and Tourism*. Channel View.

Glyptis, S. (1993) *Leisure and the Environment*. Wiley.

Goeldner, C. R. and Ritchie, J. R. B. (2008) *Tourism: Principles, Practices, Philosophies*, 11th edn. Wiley.

Guichard-Anguis, S. and Moon, O. (2008) *Japanese Tourism and Travel Culture*. Routledge.

Gunn, C. A. (1997) *Vacationscape: Designing Tourist Regions*. Van Nostrand Reinhold.

Gunn, C. and Var, T. (2002) *Tourism Planning*. Routledge.

Hall, C. M. (1994) *Tourism and Politics*. Wiley.

Hall, C. M. and Jenkins, J. M. (1994) *Tourism and Public Policy*. Routledge.

Hall, C. M. and Lew, A. (2009) *Understanding and Managing Tourism Impacts: An Integrated Approach*. Routledge.

Hall, C. M. and Page, S. (2002) *The Geography of Tourism and Recreation*. Routledge.

Hall, C. M. and Williams, A. (2008) *Tourism and Innovation*. Routledge.

Hara, T. (2008) *Quantitative Tourism Industry Analysis*. Elsevier.

Harrison, D. (1994) *Tourism and the Less Developed Countries*. Wiley.

Harrison, D. (2002) *Tourism in the Less Developed World*. CABI.

Hayllar, B., Griffin, T. and Edwards, D. (2008) *City Spaces-Tourist Places*. Elsevier.

Henderson, J. C. (2007) *Tourism Crises*. Elsevier.

Holden, A. (2008) *Environment and Tourism*, 2nd edn. Routledge.

Holloway, J. C. and Taylor, N. (2006) *The Business of Tourism*, 7th edn. Pearson.

Horner, S. and Swarbrooke, J. (2003) *International Cases in Tourism Management*. Elsevier Butterworth-Heinemann.

Howell, D. W. (1993) *Passport: An Introduction to the Travel and Tourism Industry*. South Western.

Hsu, C. H. C. (2008) *Tourism Marketing*. Wiley.

Hudman, L. E. (1980) *Tourism: A Shrinking World*. Wiley.

Hudman, L. E. and Jackson, R. H. (1999) *The Geography of Travel and Tourism*. Delmar.

Inskeep, E. (1991) *Tourism Planning: An Integrated Planning and Development Approach*. Van Nostrand Reinhold.

Ioannides, D. and Debbage, K. G. (1998) *The Economic Geography of the Tourist Industry*. Routledge.

Jeffries, D. (2001) *Governments and Tourism*. Elsevier Butterworth-Heinemann.

Jennings, G. (2001) *Tourism Research*. Wiley.

Kelly, J. R. (1990) *Leisure*. Prentice Hall.

TOURISM IN CONTEXT

DEMAND

RESOURCES

CLIMATE

TRANSPORT

FUTURES

Kolb, B. (2006) *Tourism Marketing for Cities and Towns*. Elsevier.

Kozak, M. and Andreu, L. (2006) *Progress in Tourism Marketing*. Elsevier.

Kozak, M. and Decrop, A. (2008) *Handbook of Consumer Research in Tourism: Theory & Research*. Routledge.

Laws, E., Prideaux, B. and Chon, K. (2006) *Crisis Management in Tourism*. CABI.

Leiper, N. (1990) *The Tourism System*. Massey University Press.

Lennon, J. J. (2003) *Tourism Statistics*. Allen and Unwin.

Lennon, J. and Foley, M. (2002) *Dark Tourism*. Continuum.

Leslie, D. (2008) *Tourism Enterprises and Sustainable Development: International Perspectives on Responses to the Sustainability Agenda*. Routledge.

Lew, A., Hall, C. M. and Williams, A. M. (2004) *A Companion to Tourism*. Wiley.

Likorish, L. and Jenkins, C. L. (1997) *An Introduction to Tourism*. Butterworth-Heinemann.

Lundberg, D. E. (1975) *The Tourist Business*. Van Nostrand Reinhold.

Lundberg, D. E., Stavenga, M. H. and Krishanmoorthy, M. (1995) *Tourism Economics*. Wiley.

Maitland, R. and Newman, P. (2008) *World Tourism Cities: Developing Tourism Off the Beaten Track*. Routledge.

Mason, P. (2008) *Tourism Impacts, Planning and Management*. Elsevier.

McCabe, S. (2007) *Marketing Communications in Tourism and Hospitality*. Elsevier.

Medlik, S. (1995) *Managing Tourism*. Butterworth-Heinemann.

Mercer, D. (1980) *In Pursuit of Leisure*. Sorret.

Middleton, V. T. C. and Hawkins, R. (1998) *Sustainable Tourism: A Marketing Perspective*. Elsevier Butterworth-Heinemann.

Middleton, V. T. C. and Lickorish, L. J. (2007) *British Tourism*. Elsevier.

Mill, R. C. (1990) *Tourism: The International Business*. Prentice Hall.

Mill, R. C. and Morrison, A. (1992) *The Tourism System: An Introductory Text*. Prentice Hall.

Morpeth, N. D. (2007) *Religious Tourism and Pilgrimage Management an International Perspective*. CABI.

Mowforth, M., Charlton, C. and Munt, I. (2007) *Tourism and Responsibility*. Routledge.

Mowforth, M. and Munt, I. (2008) *Tourism and Sustainability*. Routledge.

Muller, D. K. and Jannson, B. (2006) *Tourism in Peripheries*. CABI.

Murphy, P. E. (1991) *Tourism: A Community Approach*. Methuen.

Newsome, D., Moore, S. and Dowling, R. (2001) *Natural Area Tourism*. Channel View.

Orams, M. (1999) *Marine Tourism*. Routledge.

Page, S. (2007) *Tourism Management*. Elsevier.

Page, S. (2008) *Tourism Management: Managing for Change*. Elsevier Butterworth-Heinemann.

Page, S. J. and Connell, J. (2006) *Tourism: A Modern Synthesis*. Thomson Learning.

Pearce, D. (1989) *Tourist Development*. Longman.

Pearce, D. (1992) *Tourist Organizations*. Longman.

Pearce, D. (1995) *Tourism Today: A Geographical Analysis*. Longman.

Pearce, D. and Butler, R. (1993) *Tourism Research: Critiques and Challenges*. Routledge.

Pearce, D. and Butler, R. (1995) *Change in Tourism: People, Places, Processes*. Routledge.

Pearce, D. G. and Butler, R. W. (2001) *Contemporary Issues in Tourism Development*. Routledge.

Poon, A. (1993) *Tourism, Technology and Competitive Strategies*. CAB.

Prideaux, B., Timothy, D. and Chon, K. (2007) *Cultural and Heritage Tourism in Asia and the Pacific*. Routledge.

Pritchard, A., Ateljevic, I., Morgan, N. and Harris, C. (2007) *Tourism and Gender: Embodiment, Sensuality and Experience*. CABI.

Reid, R. D. and Bojanic, D. C. (2005) *Hospitality Marketing Management*, 4th edn. Wiley.

Reisinger, Y. and Dimanche, F. (2008) *International Tourism*. Elsevier.

Ritchie, J. R. B. and Crouch, G. I. (2003) *The Competitive Destination*. CABI.

Ritchie, J. R. B. and Goeldner, C. R. (1994) *Travel, Tourism and Hospitality Research: A Handbook for Managers and Researchers*. Wiley.

Robinson, H. (1976) *A Geography of Tourism*. Macdonald & Evans.

Ross, G. F. (1996) *The Psychology of Tourism*. Hospitality Press.

Ryan, C. (2002) *The Tourist Experience*. Continuum.

Ryan, C. (2003) *Recreational Tourism*. Channel View.

Ryan, C. (2007) *Battlefield Tourism*. Elsevier.

Ryan, C. and Huimin, G. (2008) *Tourism in China: Destination, Cultures and Communities*. Routledge.

Scott, N., Baggio, R. and Cooper, C. (2008) *Network Analysis and Tourism*. Channel View.

Sharpley, R. (1994) *Tourism, Tourists and Society*. Elm.

Sharpley, R. and Telfer, D. (2002) *Tourism and Development*. Channel View.

Shaw, G. and Williams, A. (1994) *Critical Issues in Tourism*. Blackwell.

Sinclair, T. and Stabler, M. (1991) *The Tourism Industry: An International Analysis*. CAB.

Sinclair, T., Stabler, M. and Papatheodorou, A. (2009) *The Economics of Tourism*. Routledge.

Smith, M. (2003) *Issues in Cultural Tourism Studies*. Routledge.

Smith, M. and Robinson, M. (2006) *Tourism in a Changing World*. Channel View.

Smith, S. L. J. (1983) *Recreation Geography*. Longman.

Smith, S. L. J. (1996) *Tourism Analysis: A Handbook*. Addison Wesley Longman.

Smith, V. and Brent, M. (2003) *Hosts and Guests Revisited*. Cognizant.

Smith, V. L. (1989) *Hosts and Guests*. University of Pennsylvania Press.

Smith, V. L. and Eadington, W. R. (1995) *Tourism Alternatives: Potential Problems in the Development of Tourism*. University of Pennsylvania Press.

Stronza, A. (2008) *Ecotourism and Conservation in the Americas*. CABI.

Su, X. and Teo, P. (2008) *The Politics of Heritage Tourism in China: A View from Lijiang*. Routledge.

Swarbrooke, J. (2001) *The Development and Management of Visitor Attractions*. Elsevier Butterworth-Heinemann.

Swarbrooke, J. and Horner, S. (2007) *Consumer Behaviour in Tourism*. Elsevier.

Telfer, D. J. and Sharpley, R. (2007) *Tourism and Development in the Developing World*. Routledge.

TOURISM IN CONTEXT

DEMAND

RESOURCES

CLIMATE

TRANSPORT

FUTURES

Theobald, W. F. (1994) *Global Tourism: The Next Decade*. Butterworth-Heinemann.

Thomas, R. and Augustyn, M. (2007) *Tourism in New Europe*. Elsevier.

Timothy, D. J. and Boyd, S. W. (2003) *Heritage Tourism*. Prentice Hall.

Timothy, D. J. and Nyaupane, G. (2008) *Cultural Heritage and Tourism in the Developing World*. Routledge.

Towner, J. (1994) *An Historical Geography of Recreation and Tourism*. Belhaven.

Tribe, J. (1995) *The Economics of Leisure and Tourism: Environments, Markets and Impacts*. Butterworth-Heinemann.

Tribe, J. and Airey, D. (2007) *Developments in Tourism Research*. Elsevier.

Turner, L. and Ash, J. (1975) *The Golden Hordes: International Tourism and the Pleasure Periphery*. Constable.

Van Egmond, T. (2007) *Understanding Western Tourists in Developing Countries*. CABI.

Veal, A. J. (2007) *Research Methods for Leisure and Tourism: A Practical Guide*. Pearson.

Vellas, F. and Becherel, L. (1995) *International Tourism*. Macmillan.

Wahab, S. (1993) *Tourism Management*. Tourism International Press.

Weaver, D. (2001) *The Encyclopaedia of Ecotourism*. CABI.

Weaver, D. (2008) *Ecotourism*, 2nd edn. Wiley.

Weaver, D. and Lawton, L. (2006) *Tourism Management*, 3rd edn. Wiley.

Weed, M. (2007) *Olympic Tourism*. Elsevier.

Wilks, J., Pendergast, D. and Leggat, P. (2006) *Tourism in Turbulent Times*. Elsevier.

Williams, S. (2004) *Tourism, Critical Concepts in the Social Sciences*. Routledge.

Williams, S. (2009) *Tourism Geography*. Routledge.

Witt, S., Brooke, M. Z. and Buckley, P. J. (1995) *The Management of International Tourism*. Unwin Hyman.

Woodside, A. and Martin, D. (2008) *Tourism Management: Analysis, Behaviour and Strategy*. CABI.

World Tourism Organization (2001) *Tourism in the Least Developed Countries*. WTO.

World Tourism Organization (2002a) *Tourism and Poverty Alleviation*. WTO.

World Tourism Organization (2002b) *Enhancing the Economic Benefits of Tourism through Poverty Alleviation*. WTO.

World Tourism Organization (2002c) *Making Tourism More Sustainable*. WTO.

World Tourism Organization (2002d) *Sport and Tourism*. WTO.

World Tourism Organization (2003) *Worldwide Cruise Ship Activity*. WTO.

World Tourism Organization (2005a) *Tourism's Potential as a Sustainable Development Strategy*. WTO.

World Tourism Organization (2005b) *City Tourism and Culture*. WTO.

World Tourism Organization (2007a) *A Practical Guide to Destination Management*. WTO.

World Tourism Organization (2007b) *Policies, Strategies and Tools for the Sustainable Development of Tourism*. WTO.

World Tourism Organization (2008a) *Climate Change and Tourism. Responding to Global Challenges*. WTO.

World Tourism Organization (2008b) *The Impact of Rising Oil Prices on Tourism*. WTO.

TOURISM IN CONTEXT

DEMAND

RESOURCES

CLIMATE

TRANSPORT

FUTURES

REPORTS, DICTIONARIES, YEARBOOKS AND ENCYCLOPAEDIAS

TOURISM IN CONTEXT

DEMAND

RESOURCES

CLIMATE

TRANSPORT

FUTURES

In addition to books, journals and trade press coverage of tourism destinations and cases, there are a number of useful sources to be found in consultant's reports (including those online such as www.euromonitor.com), tourism dictionaries, yearbooks and encyclopaedias. Some of the key sources include:

Beaver, A. (2002) *A Dictionary of Travel and Tourism Terminology*. Oxford University Press.

Cooper, C. and Lockwood, A. (1989) *Progress in Tourism, Recreation and Hospitality Management*, Vols. 1–6. Belhaven and Wiley.

Economic Intelligence Unit publications.

Euromonitor publications.

Europa Publications (annual) The Europa World Yearbook. Europa Publications.

INSIGHTS, English Tourist Board.

Jones, I. and Mason, P. (2008) *Routledge Dictionary of Leisure and Tourism*. Routledge.

Jafari, J. (2000) *The Encyclopedia of Tourism*. Routledge.

Khan, M., Olsen, M. and Var, T. (1993) *Encyclopedia of Hospitality and Tourism*. Van Nostrand Reinhold.

Luck, M. (2008) *The Encyclopedia of Tourism and Recreation in Marine Environments*. CABI.

Medlik, S. (2002) *Dictionary of Transport, Travel and Hospitality*. Butterworth-Heinemann.

Paxton, J. (annual) *The Statesman's Yearbook*. Macmillan.

Ritchie, J.R.B. and Hawkins, D. (1991–1993) *World Travel and Tourism Review*. Vols. 1–3. CAB.

Seaton, A., Wood, R., Dieke, P. and Jenkins, C. (eds), (1994) *Tourism: The State of the Art – The Strathclyde Symposium*. Wiley.

Witt, S. F. and Mountinho, L. (1995) *Tourism Marketing and Management Handbook*, Student edn. Prentice Hall.

World Tourism Organization (2001) *Thesaurus on Tourism and Leisure Activities*. WTO.

World Travel and Tourism Council Special Country Reports, WTTC.

ABSTRACTING SERVICES

Using electronic searching and abstracting services is a very effective way of searching the available literature and a great way to begin a case. The key services include:

Articles in Tourism (monthly) Universities of Bournemouth, Oxford Brookes and Surrey.

International Tourism and Hospitality Data Base CD-ROM. The Guide to Industry and Academic Resources. Wiley.

Leisure, Recreation and Tourism Abstracts (quarterly) CAB.

The Travel and Tourism Index. Brigham Young University Hawaii Campus.

Tour CD – Leisure Recreation and Tourism on CD-ROM.

STATISTICAL SOURCES

There is still a limited range of sources that draw together tourism statistics and trends. Nonetheless, the UNWTO's increasingly user-friendly reports are well-worth consulting for both global and regional trends – but beware the distinctions between travellers, tourists and day visitors in the tables. The key sources are:

Organization for Economic Co-operation and Development (annual) *Tourism Policy and International Tourism in OECD Member Countries*. OECD.
Pacific Asia Travel Association (PATA) (annual) *Annual Statistical Report*. PATA.
Pacific Asia Travel Association (PATA) (2008) *Asia Pacific Tourism Forecasts 2008–2010*. PATA
World Tourism Organization (annual) *Compendium of Tourism Statistics*. WTO.
World Tourism Organization (annual) *Tourism Highlights*. WTO.
World Tourism Organization (annual) *Yearbook of Tourism Statistics*. WTO.
World Tourism Organization (monthly) *World Tourism Barometer*. WTO.
World Tourism Organization (1994) *Recommendations on Tourism Statistics*. WTO.
World Tourism Organization (1999a) *Observations of International Tourism Volume 1* WTO.
World Tourism Organization (1999b) *Observations of International Tourism Volume II* WTO.
World Tourism Organization (2004) *International Tourism. The Great Turning Point*. WTO.
World Tourism Organization (2006) *Tourism Market Trends*, 6 volumes. WTO.

JOURNALS

The growth in tourism journals has brought with it a rich source of case study and statistical material. In addition, the geographical and leisure journals are increasingly publishing tourism-related papers. Journals with content relevant to the geography of travel and tourism include:

Annals of Leisure Research
Annals of Tourism Research
ASEAN Journal of Hospitality and Tourism
Asia Pacific Journal of Tourism Research
Australian Journal of Hospitality Management
China Tourism Research
Current Issues in Tourism
e-Review of Tourism Research (www.ertr.tamu.edu)
Event Management
Festival Management and Event Tourism
Geography Review
Hospitality and Tourism Educator
International Journal of Contemporary Hospitality Management
International Journal of Hospitality and Tourism Administration

International Journal of Hospitality Management
International Journal of Service Industry Management
International Journal of Tourism Research
Journal of Air Transport Geography
Journal of Air Transport Management
Journal of Convention and Exhibition Management
Journal of Ecotourism
Journal of Heritage Tourism
Journal of Hospitality, Leisure, Sport and Tourism
Journal of Hospitality and Leisure Marketing
Journal of Hospitality and Tourism Research
Journal of Hospitality Marketing & Management
Journal of Information Technology & Tourism
Journal of International Volunteer Tourism and Social Development
Journal of Leisure Research
Journal of Quality Assurance In Tourism & Hospitality
Journal of Sport Tourism
Journal of Sustainable Tourism
Journal of Teaching in Travel and Tourism
Journal of Tourism and Cultural Change
Journal of Tourism Consumption and Practice
Journal of Tourism History
Journal of Tourism Studies
Journal of Travel and Tourism Marketing
Journal of Travel Research
Journal of Travel and Tourism Research
Journal of Vacation Marketing
Leisure Futures, Henley Centre for Forecasting
Leisure Management
Leisure Sciences
Leisure Studies
Managing Leisure
Pacific Tourism Review
Progress in Tourism and Hospitality Research
Scandinavian Journal of Hospitality and Tourism
Service Industries Journal
The Tourist Review
Tourism Analysis
Tourism and Hospitality Research
Tourism Culture and Communication
Tourism Economics
Tourism Geographies
Tourism in Focus
Tourism Management
Tourism Recreation Research
Tourist Studies
Travel and Tourism Analyst
World Leisure and Recreation Association Journal

TOURISM IN CONTEXT

DEMAND

RESOURCES

CLIMATE

TRANSPORT

FUTURES

WEBSITE ADDRESSES OF NATIONAL TOURISM ORGANISATIONS

The World Wide Web is now a rich source of material for anyone researching tourism cases. Destinations, organisations, companies and individuals provide millions of web pages containing material and information that was previously only available by contacting the organisation concerned. Of course this source of information needs to be used with care, as there is no quality control of much of the material that is available on the web. The companion website for this book provides an annotated list of useful travel and tourism websites. It is the aim of this section of the compendium to provide the reader with a list of the official tourism sites of governments and tourist boards for each country in the world. This is a good source of initial information about a country, and, as well as providing excellent destination information, many sites have web pages for professionals and students, providing statistics and useful material about planning, marketing and policy for tourism in the country concerned. Nonetheless, even within Europe, the quality of the websites is variable – the official site for Hungary, for example, is excellent, providing comprehensive tourism information for the professional as well as the traveller, whilst the site for Poland, in our view, is inadequate.

At the time of writing (mid-2008) these addresses were correct, but you must remember that they may change and you will need to use a search engine to find the new address. The companion website to this book provides hints about searching the World Wide Web.

Country	Website
Algeria	www.mta.gov.dz
Andorra	www.turisme.ad
Angola	www.angola.org
Anguilla	www.net.ai
Antigua and Barbuda	www.interknowledge.com/antigua-barbuda
Argentina	www.sectur.gov.ar
Aruba	www.interknowledge.com/aruba
Australia	www.australia.com
Austria	www.austria-tourism.at
Bahamas	www.interknowledge.com/bahamas
Bangladesh	www.bangladesh.com
Barbados	www.barbados.org
Belgium	www.visitbelgium.com
Belize	www.travelbelize.org
Bermuda	www.bermudatourism.com
Bhutan	www.tourisminbhutan.com
Bolivia	www.bolivia.com/noticias/tourismo.asp

Bonaire	www.interknowledge.com/bonaire/index.html
Brazil	www.embratur.gov.br
Bulgaria	www.mi.government.bg/eng/tur/pol/orgs.html
Cambodia	www.tourismcambodia.com
Cameroon	www.compufix.demon.co.uk/camweb
Canada	www.visitcanada.com
Cayman Islands	www.caymanislands.ky
Chile	www.turismochile.cl
China	www.chinatour.com
Colombia	www.presidencia.gov.co
Costa Rica	www.tourism-costarica.com
Croatia	www.vlada.hr
Cuba	www.cubaweb.cu
Curaçao	www.interknowledge.com/curacao
Cyprus	www.cyprustourism.org
Czech Republic	www.czechtourism.com
Denmark	www.visitdenmark.com
Ecuador	www.ecuador.us
Egypt	www.egypttourism.org
Estonia	www.tourism.ee
Ethiopia	www.ethiopia.ottawa.on.ca/tourism.htm
Falkland Islands	www.tourism.org.fk
Federated States of Micronesia	www.fsmgov.org
Fiji	www.BulaFiji.com
Finland	www.finland-tourism.com
France	www.maison-de-la-france.fr
French Guiana	www.guyanetourisme.com
Gabon	www.tourisme-gabon.com
Gambia	www.gambiatourism.info
Georgia	www.parliament.ge/TOURISM
Germany	www.germany-tourism.de
Gibraltar	www.gibraltar.gi/tourism
Greece	www.greektourism.gr
Greenland	www.greenland-guide.dk
Grenada	www.interknowledge.com/grenada
Guadeloupe	www.antilles-info-tourisme.com/guadeloupe

TOURISM IN CONTEXT

DEMAND

RESOURCES

CLIMATE

TRANSPORT

FUTURES

TOURISM IN CONTEXT

DEMAND

RESOURCES

CLIMATE

TRANSPORT

FUTURES

Guam	www.visitguam.org
Guatemala	www.visitguatemala.com
Guyana	www.turq.com/guyana.html
Hawaii	www.hawaii.gov/tourism
Honduras	www.turq.com/honduras.html
Hong Kong	www.hkta.org
Hungary	www.hungarytourism.hu
Iceland	www.icetourist.is
India	www.tourindia.com
Indonesia	www.tourismindonesia.com
Iran	www.itto.org
Ireland	www.ireland.travel.ie
Isle of Man	www.isle-of-man.com
Israel	www.infotour.co.il
Italy	www.enit.it
Jamaica	www.visitjamaica.com
Japan	www.jnto.go.jp
Jersey	www.jtourism.com
Jordan	www.jordanembassyus.org
Kenya	www.bwanazulia.com/kenya
Korea (South)/(Republic of Korea)	www.knto.or.kr
Laos	www.mekongcenter.com
Lebanon	www.Lebanon-tourism.gov.lb
Liechtenstein	www.news.li/touri/index.htm
Luxembourg	www.etat.lu/tourism
Macau	www.macautourism.gov.mo/login.html
Macedonia	www.tarm.org.mk
Malaysia	www.tourism.gov.my
Maldives	www.visitmaldives.com/intro.html
Malta	www.tourism.org.mt
Martinique	www.martinique.org
Mauritius	www.mauritius.net
Mexico	www.mexico-travel.com
Micronesia	www.visit-fsm.org
Monaco	www.monaco.mc/monaco/guide_en.html
Mongolia	www.mongoliatourism.gov.mn

Morocco	www.tourisme-marocain.com
Myanmar	www.myanmartourism.com
Namibia	www.namibiatourism.co.uk
Nepal	www.visitnepal.com
Netherlands	www.visitholland.com
New Zealand	www.purenz.com
Nicaragua	www.intur.gob.ni
Nigeria	www.nigeria-tourism.net
Northern Ireland	www.nitb.com
Norway	www.tourist.no
Palau	www.visit-palau.com
Palestine	www.pna.org
Panama	www.panamainfo.com
Papua New Guinea	www.pngtourism.org.pg
Peru	www.peruonline.net
Philippines	www.tourism.gov.ph
Poland	www.polandtour.org
Portugal	www.portugal.org
Puerto Rico	www.gotopuertorico.com
Romania	www.turism.ro
Russian Federation	www.interknowledge.com/russia/index.html
Saba	www.turq.com/saba
Saint-Pierre and Miquelon	www.saint-pierre-et-miquelon.com
Scotland	www.travelscotland.co.uk
Senegal	www.earth2000.com
Serbia	www.serbia.sr.gov.yu
Seychelles	www.seychelles.com
Singapore	www.visitsingapore.com
Slovakia	www.scar.sk
Slovenia	www.slovenia-tourism.si
South Africa	www.environment.gov.za
Spain	www.tourspain.es
Sri Lanka	www.lanka.net/ctb
St Barthelemy	www.st-barths.com
St Eustatius (Netherlands Antilles)	www.turq.com/statia
St Kitts & Nevis	www.interknowledge.com/stkitts-nevis

TOURISM IN CONTEXT

DEMAND

RESOURCES

CLIMATE

TRANSPORT

FUTURES

TOURISM IN
CONTEXT

DEMAND

RESOURCES

CLIMATE

TRANSPORT

FUTURES

St Lucia	www.st-lucia.com
St Maarten	www.st-maarten.com
St Martin	www.interknowledge.com/st-martin
St Vincent & The Grenadines	www.turq.com/stvincent
Sudan	www.sudan.net
Sweden	www.visit-sweden.com
Switzerland	www.switzerlandtourism.ch
Syria	www.syriatourism.org
Taiwan	www.tbroc.gov.tw
Tanzania	www.tanzania-web.com
Thailand	www.tourismthailand.org
Tibet	www.tibet-tour.com
Trinidad and Tobago	www.visittnt.com
Tunisia	www.tourismtunisia.com
Turkey	www.turkey.org
Turks & Caicos	www.interknowledge.com/turks-caicos
Uganda	www.uganda.co.ug/tour.htm
United Kingdom	www.visitbritain.com
Uruguay	www.turismo.gub.uy
US Virgin Islands	www.usvi.net
USA	www.tinet.ita.doc.gov
Vanuatu	www.vanuatu.net.vu
Venezuela	www.venezlon.demon.co.uk
Vietnam	www.vn-tourism.com/index.htm
Wales	www.visitwales.com
Western Samoa	www.visitsamoa.com
Yemen	www.yementourism.com
Zambia	www.africa-insites.com/zambia
Zanzibar	www.zanzibar.net/zautalii/index.html
Zimbabwe	www.zimbabwetourism.co.zw/defaulta.htm

Index